Mastering Sprint Macro Programming

Eddy Conway

Philip C. Seyer

Scott, Foresman and Company
Glenview, Illinois   London

A Philip Seyer Association Book

Trademark List (Sprint Macro Programming)
Sprint, Paradox, and Quattro are trademarks of Borland International.
dBase and Framework are trademarks of Ashton-Tate.
XyWrite is a trademark of XyQuest.
Vax and VMS are trademarks of Digital Equipment Corporation.
WordPerfect is a trademark of WordPerfect Corporation.
Tops is a trademark of the Tops Corporation.
MacIntosh is a trademark of Apple Computer.
DOS is a trademark of the Microsoft Corporation.
CMS is a trademark of International Business Machines.
"ff.exe" is a program developed by Peter Norton.
CompuServe is a trademark of CompuServe Corporation.
Hayes Smartcom and Smartmodem are trademarks of Hayes Microcomputer, Inc.

1 2 3 4 5 6 MVN 94 93 92 91 90 89

ISBN 0-673-38953-7

Library of Congress Cataloging-in-Publication Data

Conway, Eddy.
    Mastering Sprint macro programming / Eddy Conway, Philip C. Seyer.
      p. cm.
    ISBN 0-673-38953-7
    1. Sprint (Computer Program) 2. Macroprogramming. 3. Word
processing. I. Seyer, Philip C., 1941- . II. Title.
    Z52.5.S67C66   1990
    682.5'536–dc20   89-70090
                                  CIP

Notice of Liability

The information in this book is distributed on an "As is" basis, without warranty. Neither the author nor Scott, Foresman and Company shall have any liability to the customer or any other person or entity with respect to any liabiity, loss, or damage cause or alleged to be caused directly or indirectly by the programs contained herein. This includes, but it is not limited to, interruption of service, loss of business or anticipatory profits, or consequential damages from the use of the programs.

Scott, Foresman professional books are available for bulk sales at quantity discounts. For more information, please contact Marketing Manager, Professional Books Group, Scott, Foresman and Company, 1900 E. Lake Avenue, Glenview, IL 60025.

PROGRAM LISTINGS ON DISKETTE

Save yourself the time and trouble of typing and proofreading the program listings in this book. Order the Mastering Sprint Macro Programming diskette. Only $20.00 including shipping.

```
Seyer Associates          Please send me the
1079 Mohr D14             Mastering Sprint Macro
Concord, CA  94518        Programming diskette
```

____
NAME

____
ADDRESS

___________________________________   ___________   ___________
CITY   STATE   ZIP

Enclosed is my check for $20.00. (Calif. residences add sales tax.)

Table of Contents

CHAPTER 3   Learning from Sprint's Source Code   33

CHAPTER 4   Building Your Own Interface   55

CHAPTER 5   Cursor Control, Q Registers, and Hypertext   72

CHAPTER 6　Creating Hypertext Command Buttons　　**99**

CHAPTER 7　Programming Style and Hypertext Reference Buttons　　**114**

Introduction

You can program Sprint from top to bottom, and this book will show you how! With Spring you can

- Modify any command.
- Achieve almost any printing format.
- Rearrange and customize menus.
- Rotate foles through windows and change their positions in a queue.
- Call procedures automatically.
- Write programs that analyze data, dial phone numbers, run external programs, and even recognize hypertext links.

Sprint programs can ask for input, process it, and send output to a wide variety of places: to the screen, to internal buffers, to external files, to programs, and even to I/O ports.

Sprint achieves this through a special macro language similar to C. The Sprint macro language lets you issue low-level commands, effective down to the bit of a single word, and high-level commands, effective on several files at once. Sprint itself is largely a set of programs written in the macro language. When compiled, Sprint operates through an editor and a formatter. The formatter is a more transparent program that pages text for the screen and printer.

The Purpose of This Book
The purpose of this book is to help you master the fundamentals of programming Sprint with its macro language. Besides learning how to

customize Sprint, you will come away with some useful programs you can immediately put to work to increase your productivity.

Entering Skills

As you enter into the world of Sprint macro programming, it helps to have some computer language experience. We recommend that you have experience with at least one other language. Most of the language elements of Sprint are drawn from the C lexicon, and some familiarity with it will be a definite asset.

The Interface to Use

As you may know, Sprint has several interfaces. When reading this book and doing the exercises, be sure to use the Borland Advanced User Interface. Many of our examples rely on macros contained in this interface.

What We Include in This book

In our explanation of the Sprint language, we include

- Shortcuts to avoid unnecessary coding.
- Modifying existing code.
- Discussion of constants, variables, operators, statements, and complex expressions.
- Examples of short, independent routines.
- Listings of longer programs with calls to subroutines.

The sample code is fast, and we have commented it meticulously for your reading pleasure.

Besides sample code, you will find several programs that begin a hypertext system, a system that enables you to create and navigate easily among a network of files and programs. Our discussion pushes toward the horizon of text management, providing search and editing functions that range beyond any one document or program.

Chapter 1 shows you how to run macros with the Sprint Glossary. We begin with the Glossary because knowing how to use it can save you a lot of time. Using the Glossary you can immediately create some simple macros without even having to write code.

Chapter 2 introduces you to what we call coded macros. You'll learn how to compile and use the *MatchPair* macro supplied by Borland.

In Chapter 3 you will learn how to unpack and make use of the source code to Sprint. You'll learn about the basic elements of the Sprint language. The chapter also reveals a little-known method for compiling and testing macros.

Chapter 4 offers some ideas on how you can use Sprint ot build your own unique interface, one that will best suit your purposes.

After you finish Chapter 5, you will be an expert at managing the cursor and you will have a hypertext macro you can use to jump from one file to another by pressing a hotkey.

Chapter 6 builds on the hypertext theme by showing you how you can hotkey into external programs from Sprint.

Chapter 7 continues to build on the concept of hypertext and also clarifies several programming concepts. We discuss decision making, branching I/O operations, and debugging techniques. The chapter concludes with a unique program that will enable you to build your own hypertext help system.

Several appendices follow Chapter 7. They will help you understand Sprint in more depth after you have digested the material in Chapters 1 through 7.

We hope you will enjoy your journey as you explore the exciting world of Sprint macro programming.

Eddy Conway, Belmont, California
Philip Seyer, Concord, California

Chapter 1

Running Macros in the Sprint Glossary

INTRODUCTION

In this chapter we'll get you off to a running start with macros in Sprint. In our view, Sprint supports three kinds of macros:

1. **Coded macros:** simple to highly complex macros you code with Sprint's full-featured macro programming language. Most of this book focuses on coded macros.
2. **Block select text macros:** macros you define by block selecting text and then choosing the Define command from the Glossary menu.
3. **Keyboard recorded macros:** macros you create by recording your keystrokes, using the Glossary menu.

Coded macros are one of Sprint's best-kept secrets—they're potentially much more powerful than macros supported in other word processors. Why? Because with Sprint's macro language you can truly customize Sprint. As you'll see later, you can

- Scoop up text directly from the screen.
- Prompt the user for various values.
- Launch external programs under Sprint program control.
- Drop into the operating system.
- Issue commands directly to the hardware.
- Peek into any memory location.
- Jump into files just by pointing to their names.
- Build your own menu and help systems.
- Jump to predefined locations.
- Build programming tools.
- Carry out math operations.

...and even create your own database system!

Appreciating Sprint

The power of Sprint lies in doing all that dynamically, *under program control*. Sprint macros are not just preprogrammed routines. Sprint can go into loops or branch to different tasks based on user input or on the contents of selected parts of a file. That's why you can program Sprint to play musical tunes, make telephone calls, or instantly load Paradox or Quattro, without running out of memory!

What We'll Do in This Chapter

We'll explain the Glossary utility, which allows you to store macros—coded macros as well as keyboard recorded macros and block select text macros. You'll learn how to set up a stationery form and pop it and the current date into a file with just a few keystrokes. You'll also learn the basic structure of macros as they appear in the glossary.

Most programming texts don't deal with a macro library such as Sprint's Glossary, or with keyboard recording. We discuss the glossary in detail for several reasons. The treatment of the glossary in the original documentation is a bit spare. We also want to conserve programming effort. Several services already are available through the glossary, in efficient macro routines. A look into the glossary provides exposure to some Sprint coding, an explanation of how code is compiled and read, and a resource for larger utilities you might wish to develop later.

The Sprint Glossary is the stepping off point for the free-form coding we'll do later.

Clarifying Some Terms

Sprint defines the term *glossary* as a "utility that allows you to assign commonly used keystrokes to abbreviations you can recall or assign to a single key." Actually, the glossary in Sprint also embraces what some word processors call a library, which is a listing of routines you can use. It is a compendium of keyboard shortcuts, a library you can edit, expand, or cut.

Sprint's default glossary has a variety of coded macros. Here is a list of them:

- *Blockcursor*—Block cursor.
- *Dtn*—Current date in the format mm/dd/yy.
- *Dtx*—Current date in the format month, day, year.
- *Finddouble*—Find each occurrence of repeated words.
- *Footer*—Footer with centered, italic page number.
- *Line*—Divider line.
- *Memohead*—Memorandum header.
- *Page*—Page number.
- *Pdtn*—Print date in the format mm/dd/yy.
- *Pdtx*—Print date in the format month, day, year.
- *Ptime*—Print time, 24 hour format.
- *Ptime*—Print time, 12 hour format.
- *Spellbad*—Write all words not in the dictionary to disk.
- *Time12*—Current time, 12 hour format.
- *Time24*—Current time, 24 hour format.
- *Ulcursor*—Underline cursor.
- *Wc*—Word count.

Note: The glossary is a handy tool for managing a number of short macros. As we mentioned earlier, we won't get into Sprint's full-blown macro programming language yet. We thought you'd enjoy starting with something quick and clean. For now, just note that you can add three different kinds of macros to the glossary: coded macros, block select text macros, and keyboard recorded macros.

USING THE GLOSSARY MENU

The Extensive Glossary Utility

You can get to the glossary tools by working through the menus. We frequently use the Utilities menu. To get to it, just press **Alt-U**, (hold down **Alt** and tap **U**). To get to the Glossary menu, (located under the Utilities menu) press **Alt-U G** (hold down **Alt** and tap **U** followed by **G**). We'll be going to the Glossary menu often in this chapter. We'll remind you how to get there a few times. After that we'll just tell you to go to the Glossary menu. Figure 1.1 shows the Glossary menu.

SPG Files

A file named Standard.spg holds the macro code for the items in the glossary library. The .spg extension tells Sprint that the file is a glossary file. Standard.spg is the default Glossary file. Sprint won't use

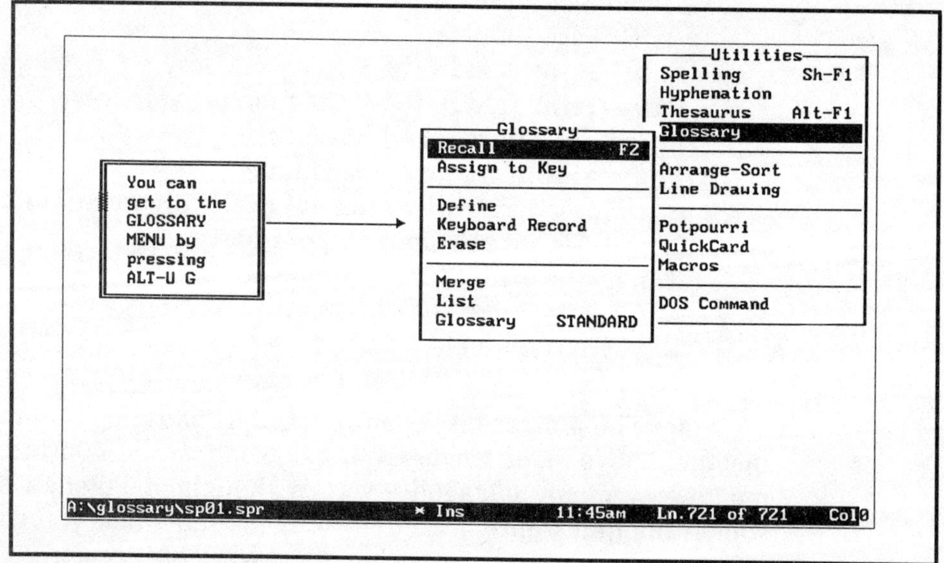

Figure 1.1
The Glossary menu.

a file as a glossary unless it has an .spg extension. If you write another glossary file, as we will in this chapter, its filename can have a different root, such as Test. But it must have the .spg extension.

Precautions

Before continuing, be sure to make a backup copy of Standard.spg. We suggest you copy it to a file called Standard.sav. Then you can always restore the original glossary by renaming Standard.sav to Standard.spg.

We also hope you avoid changing Standard.spg directly. One mistake we made when working with glossaries was using the default glossary, Standard.spg, for our little experiments, spoiling our original file. Don't do it. Before you make any customized glossary entries, you could make a test file called Test.spg. Here's how:

1. Press **Ctrl-F3** and open a new file called Test.spg.
2. Go to the top of the new, empty file and delete the ruler. Ruler lines are poison to macros or glossary items.
3. Press **Ctrl-K R** to begin the process of reading an external file into the current file. At the prompt enter **Standard.spg**. Now press **Ctrl-F2** to save the file. You now have a test glossary file that has some working items in it. Next let's tell Sprint about this new glossary file.
4. From the glossary menu choose the Glossary command (press **Alt-U G G**). Then change the name of the default glossary from Standard.spg to C:\Sprint\Test.spg. (Use the full path name to be sure Sprint looks in the Sprint subdirectory.)
5. Now, with the Glossary menu still up, press **L** to choose the List option. That will read the new Test glossary into memory. Notice that Sprint displays the message "Building Glossary List" on the status line.
6. You will now be in a file called Test.spr. Sprint creates the Test.spr file on demand. It's a file that lists the glossary entries. So you don't get confused with too many test files, we suggest you close this file immediately without saving it (press **Ctrl-F4 N**). You can always re-create the file if you need it by choosing the List option on the Glossary menu.

Now you can play with all the code that comes with the standard glossary. If the current glossary isn't already on your screen, just press

Ctrl-F3, and at the prompt enter **C:\Sprint\Test.spg**. You will see something like Figure 1.2 on screen. Notice in this figure that spaces are shown as tiny dots.

EXAMINING A CODED MACRO

Usually, it is better not to edit .spg files directly. And you need not be concerned with the details of the binary codes in .spg files. But as a programmer and power user, you may find the information useful and interesting. If not, feel free to jump ahead to the section in this chapter on the glossary menu recall option.

The listing in Figure 1.2 is not as hard to read as it might seem. The first glossary item—which actually is a coded macro—is called as *blockcursor*. The name *blockcursor* seems to be indented one space from the left margin. Actually, there is an ASCII 255 in the file here, sometimes called a null character. A null character looks just like a space in the Sprint editor.

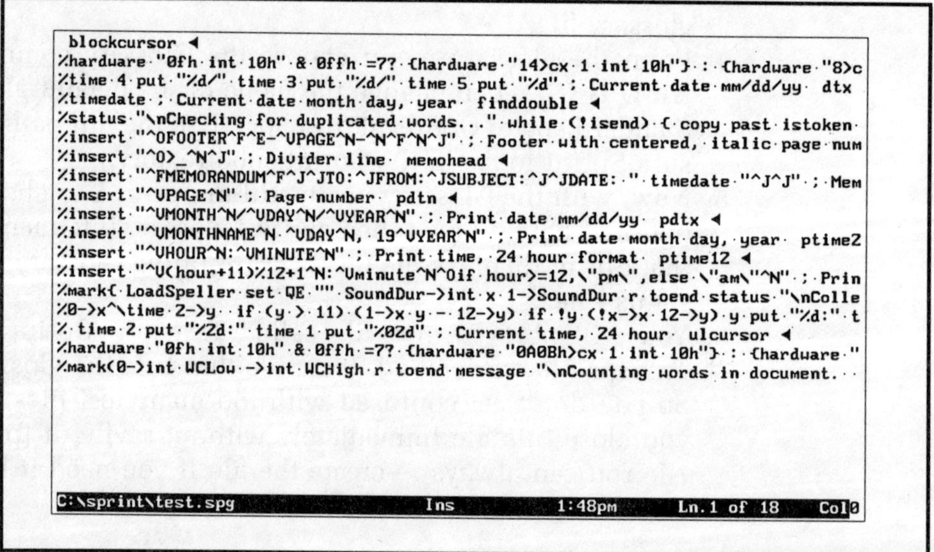

Figure 1.2
Part of newly created TEST.SPG file.

The name of each glossary item is preceded (and followed) by ASCII 255 characters.

The coding begins on the next line after a % sign. The % tells Sprint that the item is a coded macro for the glossary—one created by programming rather than by block selecting or keyboard recording.

You can't see the entire second line on screen without scrolling to the right. To see the end of the line press the **End** key. There you'll see something like this:

```
: {hardware "8>cx 1 int 10h"} ; Block cursor dtn
```

Within a glossary file, the code for a coded macro must appear as a single line. Near the end of the line is a semicolon that signifies a comment: Block cursor. The final characters on the line—an ASCII 255 and dtn—mark the beginning and the name of the next glossary item. dtn is probably an abbreviation for date now.

The date now macro code continues with a % sign on the following line. Near the end of the line is the comment, ";Current date mm/dd/yy." There is a space, an ASCII 255, and then the name of the next macro in the glossary—and so on. *Notice that the label of the next macro always appears at the end of a line. Code must begin on a newline after a name.*

The Blockcursor Macro

Let's go back to the first glossary item. The *blockcursor* macro, in version 1.01, reads

```
blockcursor
%hardware "0fh int 10h" & 0ffh = 7? {hardware "14>cx 1 int 10h"}:
{hardware "8>cx 1 int 10h"} ; Block cursor.
```

Those using version 1.0 of Sprint see a much simpler coded macro; this entry in the glossary was improved in version 1.01. To benefit from that, version 1.0 users could simply copy the code from this text.

This glossary item, the coded macro, goes to the hardware by using a DOS service and checks to see what kind of monitor is installed. Then it changes the cursor to a blinking block. The code reads:

```
%hardware "0fh int 10h" & 0ffh = 7?
```

Check the monitor and if it is monochrome and in text mode,

```
{hardware "14>cx 1 int 10h"}
```

change the cursor from underscore to a 14-line block; and

```
:{hardware "8>cx 1 int 10h"} ; Block cursor
```

otherwise the monitor must be color, so change the cursor from underscore to an 8-line block.

To change the cursor, a program needs to set certain values and then send an interrupt to the Basic Input-Output System. Normally, you do this kind of programming in assembly language or C. That's because you need to set certain internal hardware registers. For example, you need to set AH, the high-byte of the accumulator, to tell the system which service to call. And you need to set CX, the count register, to tell the service what number to use. Then you call BIOS interrupt 10H. If you have a monochrome monitor, Sprint sets CX to 14. For other monitors, Sprint sets CX to 8 instead.

Pretty technical. But you can do it in Sprint. We won't go into more detail here, except to say that in the glossary, Sprint is using service zero of interrupt 10H to check for the kind of monitor installed. Based on the value returned, Sprint sets the CX register and then calls service one of interrupt 10H to change the shape of the cursor.

Sprint uses ? with a colon to form a kind of abbreviated if-then-else statement. We'll discuss this kind of structure in more detail later in Chapter 7. See Appendix C for a list of Sprint symbols and their meanings.

We explained the blockcursor routine to show that glossary entries are actually coded macros and to show that the macro language can send commands directly to the hardware, if necessary.

The Recall Option on the Glossary Menu

Want to change your cursor to a block? Go to the Glossary menu and choose the Recall command. Then press **Enter** to get a list of all the glossary items. Put the selection bar on blockcursor, press **Enter** again, and Sprint launches the coded macro. If you are following along on your screen, the underscore cursor should have turned into a block.

To do all this, Sprint looks in the current .spg file (normally Standard.spg). If you have been following our advice, your .spg file is now Test.spg, so Sprint will look there rather than to Standard.spg.

Remember that Sprint needs a file it can look into for glossary items, and that the file can have a name other than Standard, as long as it ends in .spg. Whatever the glossary file name, Sprint also must have read the file into memory either on start-up, or after start-up through a Recall command or a List command. When you give either command, Sprint presents the names of the items in the current glossary. With the List command, Sprint also creates a file and shows the comments that go along with the names of the items in the glossary.

Your First Coded Macro

Now that you've looked at a coded macro, let's write a short but useful one and put it in Test.spg. This macro will quickly pop you out of Sprint and put you in DOS. (You'll love this if you are addicted to the DOS prompt, as many of our friends are.) Please note that we will explain how this macro works later in Chapter 6. For now we just want you to type it in and use it.

Enter this line in any temporary text file:

```
%0 call "command"
```

To highlight the line, move the cursor to the first letter of the string and press **F3**. Then press **End** to move the cursor to the end of the line. Next, select Define on the Glossary menu by pressing **Alt-U G D**.

Sprint will prompt you for a name for this macro. Type **DOS**. Press **Enter**.

Now assign a hotkey to the macro:

1. Press **Alt-U G A**.
2. Press a hotkey, such as **Shift-Alt-D**.
3. When the list of glossary items pops up, select DOS.

After you use the macro to exit to DOS, be sure to enter **EXIT** *to return to Sprint. The macro is short and sweet, but it does not remind you to enter* **EXIT** *to return to Sprint.*

BUILDING A BLOCK SELECT TEXT MACRO

The Define and Assign to a Key commands on the Glossary menu are handy for assigning a string of text to a hotkey. When you use these options, you actually create a new item for the glossary. Suppose you are writing an instructional manual and the boss says that she wants you to start each chapter with: "When you finish this chapter, you will be able to:". Let's assign this string to **Shift-Alt-A**, because we know these keys are uncommitted. Here are the steps:

1. Type the string and then highlight it. (Move the cursor to the first letter of the string and press **F3**. Then move the cursor to end of the string.)
2. Choose Define on the Glossary menu. (Press **Alt-U G D Enter**.) The Define command picks up whatever character string was highlighted and stores it in memory in what Sprint calls a clipboard.
3. At the prompt, enter a name for the string. Let's call it *Whenyou*. After you type the name and press **Enter**, the menu disappears.
4. Choose Assign to Key on the Glossary menu. (Press **Alt-U G A**.) Sprint will prompt you for the hotkey you will later use to launch the macro. For now press **Shift-Alt-A**.
5. Sprint now displays a menu of all the items in the glossary. Move the selection bar to *Whenyou* and press **Enter**.

Now, *while you are in the current session*, **Shift-Alt-A** will always summon the handle *whenyou* which, in turn, will summon the string: When you finish this chapter, you will be able to:, and it will insert the string in the current file.

Saving Your Glossary Macros

An important aspect of this glossary item, or any macro, is that it stays in memory only until the end of the computing session.

If lightning doesn't strike, and you end your session normally by quitting from the Main menu, Sprint will prompt you to save the changes (the text string) to the glossary. Now you can make the macro permanent in the current .spg file, or you can scuttle it. If you decide to keep it, *then and only then*, Sprint writes the glossary item to the glossary file.

An Exercise

To see this for yourself try this exercise:

1. Take a look now at the Test.spg file. Scan the entire file. Do you see the *whenyou* glossary item?
2. Now exit from Sprint with **Alt-Q**. When Sprint asks you if you want to save the changes to the Test.spg file, enter **Y**.
3. Restart Sprint from DOS. Open the Test.spg file. Do you see the *Whenyou* glossary item now?
4. Go to the Glossary menu. What .spg file is Sprint using?

Answers to Exercise

When you first look into Test.spg you will not find the *Whenyou* item. But suppose you exit to DOS by pressing **Alt-Q** and save the glossary changes to Test.spg file. Then on returning to Sprint you will find that the *whenyou* item appears at the end of the Test.spg file. When you now go to the Glossary menu, you will find that Sprint is again using the default Standard.spg file.

Tip

So that you can continue to experiment, be sure to pick the Glossary option on the Glossary menu and reset the .spg file to c:\sprint\test.spg.

There are only a few more options from the Glossary menu to discuss before we start getting more intense with macro code. Next, let's consider the Erase option shown in Figure 1.3.

The Erase Option

It speaks for itself. Because we sometimes entangle our glossary, we have a special place in our heart for this particular option. By the way, if you need details on what any option does in Sprint, don't forget Sprint's nifty help system. Just highlight the menu option you want to learn about and press **F1**. Figure 1.4 shows an example of a message you typically get from Sprint's help system.

We'll discuss the Keyboard Record option and the Merge command

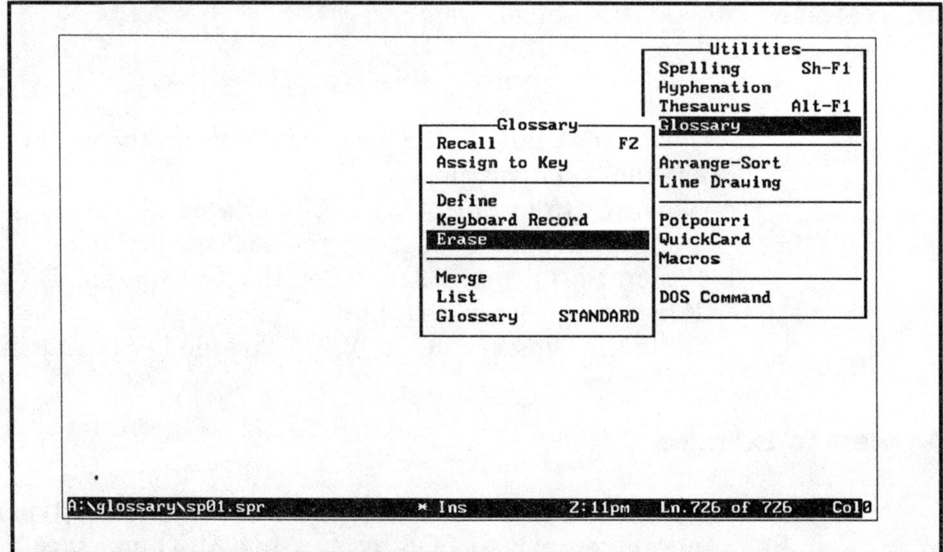

Figure 1.3
The Erase option on the Glossary menu.

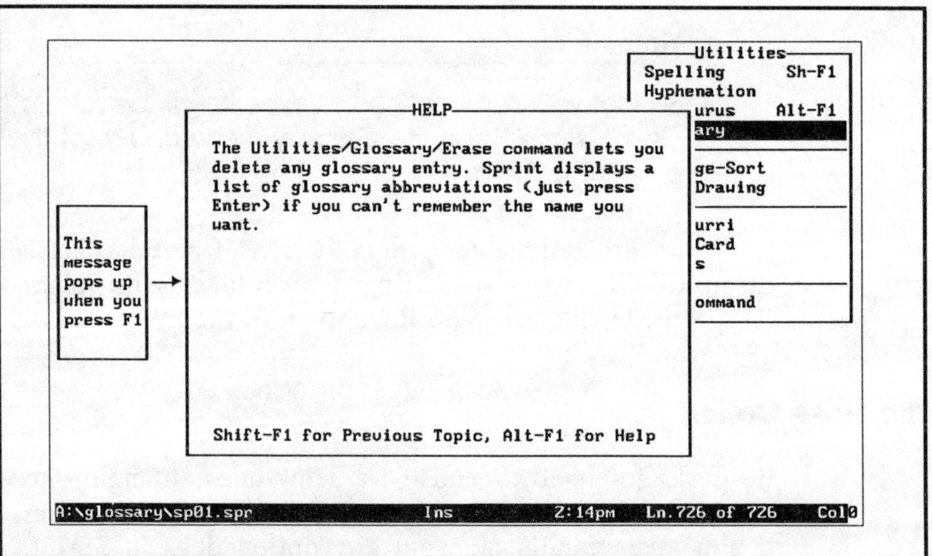

Figure 1.4
Getting help on a specific menu option.

in a moment. For now, we direct your attention again to the last option on the menu, the Glossary option.

The Glossary Option

As you may have noticed, Sprint will remind you if you have made changes to the current glossary file. It will prompt you to save to disk. That prompt requires a careful response. While cutting and pasting glossaries, we once mistakenly saved a partial glossary, and overwrote a perfectly good glossary. We recovered without much work, but it was embarrassing.

Remember that if you switch glossaries, it is not enough to name the new glossary with the Glossary command. Macro code won't immediately come alive.

Tip

To activate the new Glossary, be sure to go to the Glossary menu and select the List or Recall command, as we mentioned earlier.

KEYBOARD RECORDING

When you finish with the test glossary, you can merge working items to the original Standard glossary for safekeeping. But you may want to keep a couple of glossaries around and switch among them, rather than incorporate all your glossary items into one file. Although it's redundant, you can cut-and-paste among them, and you will have a backup file if you mistakenly record over a good glossary. In this next exercise, we suggest you create two extra .spg files.

An Exercise in Keyboard Recording

Let's make a new glossary item by using the Keyboard Record option on the Glossary menu.

1. Go to the Glossary menu and pick the Glossary command. At the prompt, enter **letterhd**. Reply **Y** to the prompt, "Create it?"
2. Turn on keyboard recording. (Press **Alt-U G K**.)
3. Enter the text in Figure 1.5. Don't worry about small mistakes. When done, press **Esc**.
4. Sprint now prompts you for a name. Sprint expects a short name with no spaces. For testing purposes, please enter **letterhd**. (The same name that we used for the current .spg file.)
5. Sprint now prompts you for a description. You can enter a one-line description. For now just enter **Letter head**.

To launch the new glossary item, just press **F2** for the glossary prompt and enter the item name, **letterhd**. Or press **F2** and **Enter**, highlight letterhd, and press **Enter** again. On your screen, the text will appear. You can also assign this glossary item to a hotkey, like any other one.

Saving Changes to the Glossary File

Although this keyboard recorded glossary item now works, it will not appear in the Letterhd.spg file until we save it to a glossary file. Go

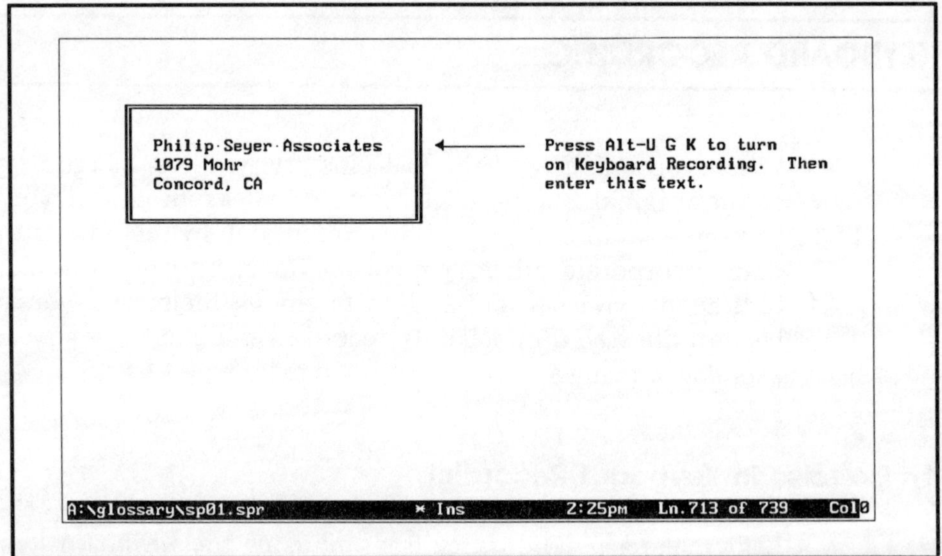

Figure 1.5
Text to enter with Keyboard Recording on.

to the Glossary command on the Glossary menu. Then say yes when Sprint asks you if you want to save your changes. When Sprint asks for the name of the new glossary, just press **Esc** to avoid changing glossaries.

Now your work will be saved in the Lettrhd.spg file. But we made some mistakes in trying to write this macro from the keyboard, which frequently happens when keyboard recording. In this example, we forgot to include the suite number and the telephone number. So we're going to show you how it is possible to edit a keyboard recorded macro in the glossary.

EDITING THE GLOSSARY

Although it is a bit tricky, you can check out the code in the Glossary and edit it. To do that, open the Glossary file as a text file—by pressing the **Ctrl-F3** keys and by entering Letterhd.spg. The result is reproduced in Figure 1.6.

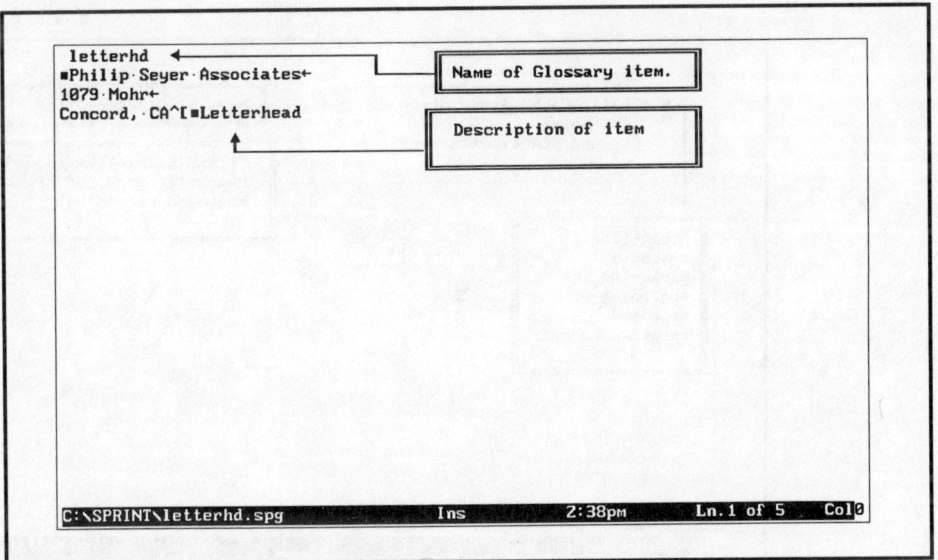

Figure 1.6
Viewing the Glossary code as a text file.

Notice that this keyboard recorded item in the figure does not begin with a % sign like the coded macros we looked at earlier.

If a glossary item does not begin with a % sign, Sprint writes the characters after the name to the screen when the glossary executes.

Now we can draw a distinction between keyboard recorded macros and coded macros. In the glossary, at least, coded macros begin with a % sign and signal Sprint to execute a series of commands. Keyboard recorded macros begin with character 254, the block-like character you see in Figure 1.7.

Control Characters in .Spg Files

Extensive editing of the .spg files is not currently practical because Sprint inserts a lot of control codes. Here is a list of some of the important control code conventions:

- The name of a glossary entry must be surrounded by the null, ASCII character 255, which is not visible on screen and is not reproduced by printers. Next comes a hard return and line feed combination (ASCII 13 and ASCII 10).

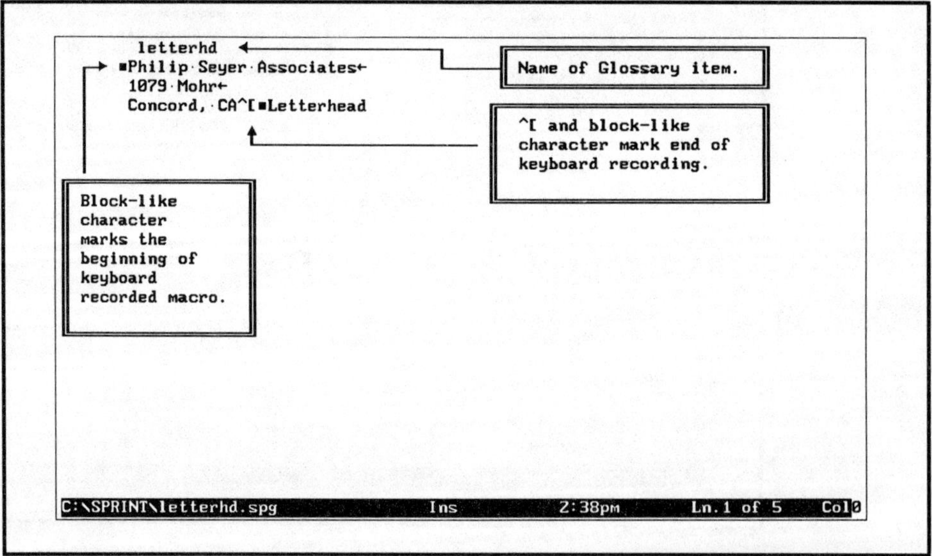

Figure 1.7
Block-like character in keyboard recorded macro.

- Carriage returns in keyboard recordings are shown on screen with a left arrow. (This is an ASCII 13 without an accompanying ASCII 10.)
- Coded macros begin with a % sign and signal Sprint to execute a series of commands. A coded macro appears all on one line.
- Keyboard recorded macros begin with ASCII 254. The end of the keyboard recording is marked by ASCII 27 together with an ASCII 254. (ASCII 27 appears on screen as ^[.)
- Immediately following the ASCII 27 and ASCII 254 comes the description of the keyboard recording, which ends with a hard return and line feed (ASCII 13 and ASCII 10).

Although we don't recommend extensive editing of glossary items, you can edit text within a glossary macro—but be careful not to delete any control codes.

Let's try it. Open the Letterhd.spg file with the **Ctrl-F3** keys. After the street address, 1079 Mohr Lane, type the suite number, **D-14**. Also add a zip code **94518** to the last line. Remember when you are editing Letterhd.spg, Sprint is not evaluating the codes and commands in the file. Also remember that if you throw some zany control characters into the text file, the file will do unusual things when it is invoked through the glossary commands.

To make our changed glossary file work, Sprint must *read* the revised .spg file. You can make this happen by going to the Glossary menu and selecting the List or Recall command. Try this:

1. Edit the .spg file and be sure the new version is saved to disk.
2. Choose the List command on the Glossary menu. (This is to ensure the new version of the macro will work if you want to launch it with a hotkey.)
3. Test the revised macro.

The revised glossary code is in Figure 1.8.

Merging Glossary Files

Once you have the *letterhd* Glossary item working, you may want to merge it with Standard.spg. That's easy:

1. Pick the Glossary command on the Glossary menu and switch to your Test.spg file. (Be sure to save the changes you have made to Letterhd.spg, if you haven't done so already.)

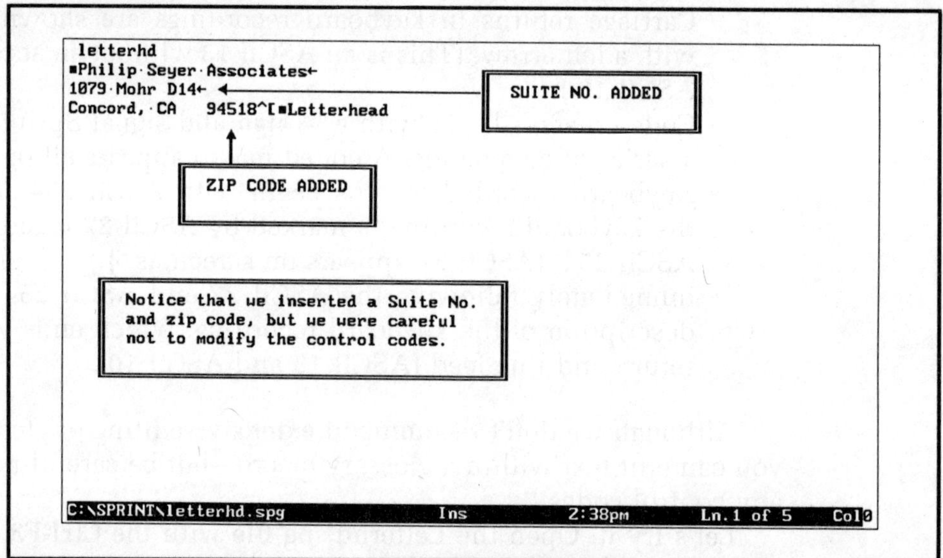

Figure 1.8
Modified keyboard recording code.

2. Pick the Merge command on the Glossary menu. Sprint will ask you for the name of another glossary. Enter **Letterhd**. Now your *letterhd* glossary item has been added to your Test.spg file.

Remembering the Three Variations

As you have seen, there are basically three kinds of glossary items. Let's review them and compare their structures.

Block Select Text Macros

You create these by highlighting an existing block of text in a file and picking the Define command on the Glossary menu. This item has a simple structure in the Glossary file, which is shown in Figure 1.9.

As you can see, first comes a null character (ASCII 255), followed by the item name. The name is terminated by another null character. Following that we find a hard carriage return, which appears in the file as a return and line feed (ASCII 13 and 10). Next comes the actual text that was originally block selected. The end of the block selected text is marked by a hard carriage return (ASCII 13 and 10).

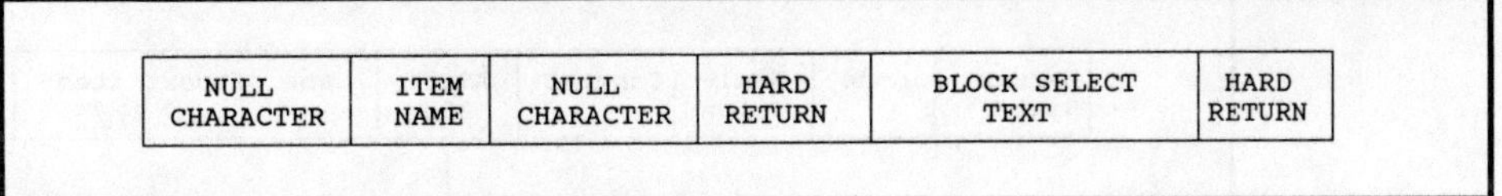

Figure 1.9
Structure of block select text macros.

Keyboard Recorded Macros

You create these macros by turning on keyboard recording and then typing away. You can open menus and make selections in the course of making these macros. When done recording, you press **Esc**, name your macro, and give it a description. In the .spg file, keyboard recorded macros have the structure shown in Figure 1.10.

Coded Macros

Coded macros are macros created by writing code rather than selecting or typing text. To put a coded macro into the glossary, you:

1. Prefix the code with %.
2. Highlight it.
3. Go to the Glossary menu and pick Define.

Coded macros have the structure shown in Figure 1.11.

As a power user and programmer, it's useful for you to understand the structure of these macros. This will enable you to do skillful surgery on the developmental versions of your .spg files and keep them healthy. In the coming chapters we will go into more detail on how you can develop your own coded macros.

Figure 1.10
Structure of keyboard recorded macros.

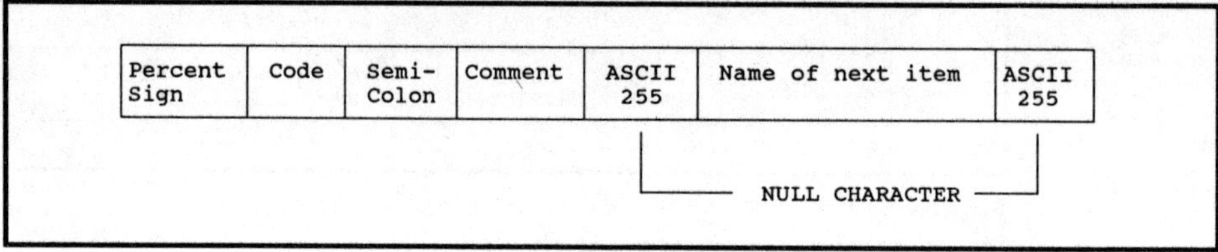

Figure 1.11
Structure of coded macros.

A CHALLENGE

Here is a programming challenge for you. Make a letterhead that includes the current date when it is printed. Put the macro into the glossary and set up a hotkey for it, such as **Shift-Alt-L**.

Some Hints and a Suggested Approach

You can have a coded macro insert text into the current file simply by putting the text in quotation marks. Whenever you want a carriage return, include \n at the end of your text. For example, to create a coded macro that inserts her name and address into a file, Elizabeth Taylor could write

```
% "Elizabeth Taylor\n"
"362636 Wuz Lane\n"
"Hollywood, CA 94518\n"
```

To put this into the Glossary, she could just highlight the text and then pick Define on the Glossary menu.

But that wouldn't give her the current date. However, there is a useful built-in Sprint macro called *timedate*. *Timedate* is not documented. We discovered it by browsing through the Standard.spg file. The *timedate* macro inserts the current date into a file in this format:

```
"January 1, 1998\n"
```

By putting together this information, you should find it easy to create a useful letterhead macro. Here's the basic structure:

```
% "Line 1\n"
  "Line 2\n"
  "Line 3\n\n"
  timedate "\n\n\n"
```

> **Where We've Been, Where We're Going**
> In this chapter, we reviewed operations of the glossary to show how it uses the macro language and how it can save programming time. We looked at a few coding methods and some editing techniques. In Chapter 2 we'll use a more direct method to load and run macros; we'll discuss ways to control key assignments and to customize or restore the Sprint editor.

Chapter 2
Fun With The MatchPair Macro

The fastest and easiest way to learn about coded macros is by using and imitating them. Coded macros—as opposed to keyboard recorded macros—are particularly effective tools. They capitalize on Sprint's ability to compile and run macros written in a full-blown programming language—a language complete with variables, integer math operations, looping and control structures, and I/O. Coded macros also keep well. After leaving them for a while, you will find on returning that they still have a quick efficiency. And if you document them well, you will find you can even remember how they work!

Because you already have a robust base to work from (Sprint itself), it is easy to develop your own productivity improvement system with just a few lines of Sprint code. This capability sets Sprint apart as a word processor and justifies its existence. It's the reason you will find yourself always coming back to Sprint. With Sprint you don't have to do things the way some remote programming team decided. You can have it your way! In this chapter you'll learn how to compile, load, and use an interesting coded macro called *MatchPair*.

THE MATCHPAIR MACRO

Sprint macros are stored in files that end with the .spm extension. A handy macro that comes with Sprint is called *MatchPair*. What *Match-Pair* does is a wee bit difficult to describe, but it is fun to watch, and it's a useful tool.

To appreciate *MatchPair*, you need to understand the concept of a delimiter. If you already understand delimiters, you may want to skip ahead to the next section on loading the *MatchPair* macro.

A delimiter is just a character or a symbol that marks a section of text or code. Delimiters come in pairs. The first delimiter marks the beginning of a section and the second delimiter shows the end. A simple example of this is a set of parentheses. The open parenthesis "(" marks the beginning of a parenthetical expression, and the closing parenthesis ")" marks the end. Delimiters are crucial in fields such as medicine, law, mathematics, writing, and programming, because when one or both are missing, the meaning of a passage can be changed. A missing delimiter is sometimes hard to spot—and a missing delimiter can ruin a macro that otherwise works fine.

When you execute *MatchPair*, the cursor will jump back and forth between a set of matching delimiters. If you are missing a delimiter, the macro will tell you so. If what you seek isn't considered a delimiter, it will tell you that, too.

MatchPair is stored in a file called Match.spm. It may take a little detective work to find the Match.spm file. We found Match.spm on the Sprint Thesaurus diskette. Unless Borland has recently changed things, you'll probably find it there, too.

Loading the *MatchPair* Macro

Follow these steps to compile and load the Match.spm file.

1. Copy Match.spm into your Sprint subdirectory. As you develop macros, you may develop your own .spm subdirectory, and copy Match.spm there.

2. Press **ALT-U M L**. These keystrokes may be easier to remember if you think of them as: Utilities, Macros, Load.
3. After you press **M**, and then **L** from the Utilities menu, Sprint will show you a list of all the Sprint macro files in the current directory. For *MatchPair*, put the selection bar on Match in the Macro menu and press **Enter**.

This sequence may not work if Sprint is in not in the subdirectory that the Match.spm is in. Sprint will search the current directory for all .spm files. It will also search for .spm files in all subdirectories that are in the DOS path statement. **Note:** You can press **Alt-F F C** to change directories.

Notice that you are selecting the file that contains the macro—not the name of the macro itself. Figure 2.1 shows how our Sprint menus looked when we selected Match. There are other macro names in the menu because we were working on a number of different macros. Also notice that the filename extension .spm does not appear in the filenames on the menu. It's important to know, however, that the .spm

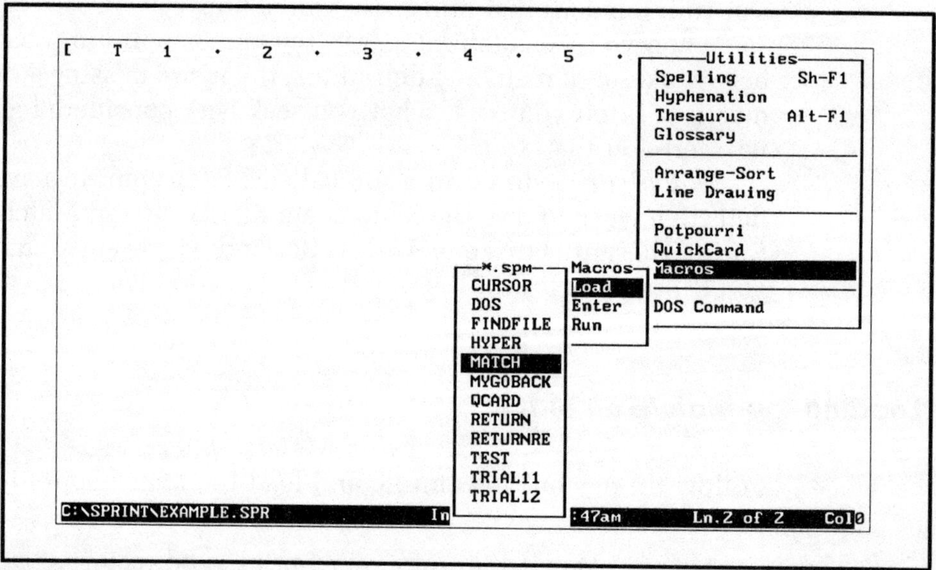

Figure 2.1.
Loading the MATCH.SPM file.

extension is required for Sprint to recognize a file as a macro. All the files Sprint puts in the menu after a macro Load command have .spm extensions. But only the root of the filename is shown.

Sprint will now display a message alerting you that it is compiling the macro. The code in the .spm file is not executable. It has to be translated into binary and loaded into the Sp.spm file; that's what the Load command does.

If there are any problems, Sprint may display an error message. If Sprint successfully compiles the macro, the menus will disappear. The status line will flash a message—so quickly you likely will not see it—"**Alt-M** has been reassigned to find matching delimiters." Once the menus pop off the screen, you know that your macro has been loaded into Sprint.

Macros that you load in this way are top dogs; that is, they replace any existing key definitions, including those defined for glossary items. Existing macros that do not conflict with the new macro are left undisturbed.

Activating *MatchPair*

Most macros are designed so you can activate them with a hotkey. Such is the case with *MatchPair*. You activate *MatchPair* with **Alt-M**. But wait—don't press **Alt-M** yet! To test *MatchPair*, we suggest you load in a file that contains some matching delimiters. (If you program in C or Pascal, you might want to load in one of your favorite programs.)

If no such file is handy, just type in a short test example, such as this one:

```
(This is just a (simple) test (tryout)).
```

Once you have some text that uses matching delimiters, put the cursor on a delimiter such as "(". Then press **Alt-M** and watch the fun. The cursor will bounce back and forth between matching delimiters. To exit the macro, press **Esc**.

What good is the macro? Well, as we said earlier, sometimes a matching delimiter is missing. For example, try deleting one of the parentheses in the test shown earlier, so that it looks like this:

```
(This is just a (simple) test (tryout).
```

Put the cursor on the first parenthesis and press **Alt-M**. What happens? Apparently nothing. Some of your keys may not immediately respond, as if there was keyboard lockout. Actually, the macro is searching and searching for the matching delimiter. It will search an entire file of any length. There can be a delay of several seconds, but eventually, on the status line, you'll see this message: "Mismatched or missing delimiter."

That actually is good news. If you had been nervously pressing keys while waiting for a reply, the message would just flash on your bottom status line—you may not even notice it—and the characters you were pressing would jump onto your screen. So be patient; wait until the macro has done its work and watch for the message it returns. Discovering one little missing delimiter can save you an afternoon of work. If you lack patience, you might just press **Esc** to cancel the macro operation.

If you put the cursor under a character that is not a delimiter, such as T, you'll get the error message: "Not a delimiter," as shown in Figure 2.2.

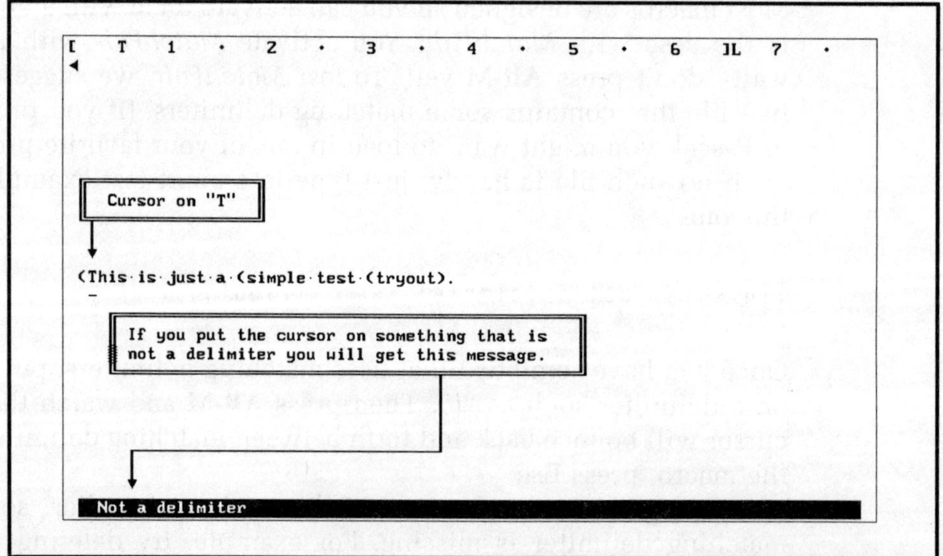

Figure 2.2.
"Not a delimiter" message from *MatchPair*.

HOTKEYLESS MACROS

You may encounter a macro that was not designed to be activated by pressing a hotkey. In that case, you can activate the macro by pressing **Alt-U M E**, and then entering the name of the macro. Try it with *MatchPair* as shown in Figure 2.3:

1. Put the cursor on a delimiter.
2. Press **ALT-U ME**.
3. When prompted, enter **MatchPair**.

Remember: You *invoke* a macro by its name, but you *load* a macro by selecting the filename that contains it. The file should be in the current subdirectory or a subdirectory reached through the DOS PATH statement.

Assigning a Macro to a Hotkey

To assign a macro to a hotkey, just follow these steps:

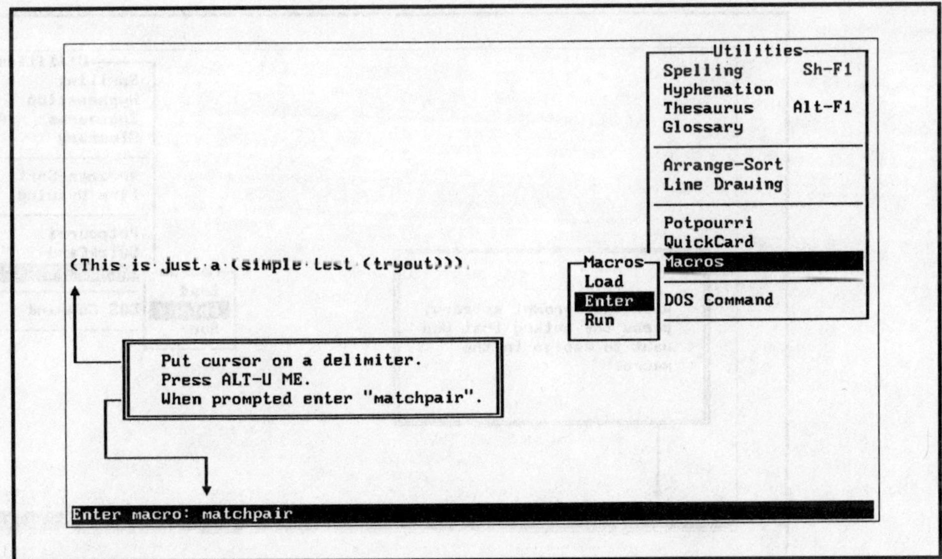

Figure 2.3.
Launching *MatchPair* by entering its name.

1. Press **Alt-U M E** (for Macro Enter).
2. Enter the name of the macro, **MatchPair**.
3. Press **A** to assign a special key to the macro.
4. At the prompt, press the desired hotkey (such as **Alt-9**).

Figure 2.4 shows the Sprint menus that appear when you follow these steps to assign a hotkey to a macro.

Now *MatchPair* responds to two hotkeys—**Alt-M**, a hotkey that was hard coded into the macro, and **Alt-9**, another hotkey assigned when *MatchPair* was loaded. You could assign a third hotkey as well.

MANAGING YOUR MACROS WITH QCARD

Sprint can create a Quick Reference Card for you that lists all of your coded macros and the hotkeys they are assigned to. The information is stored in a file text called Qcard.spr. To compile Qcard.spr, just press **Alt-U** and choose QuickCard from the menu.

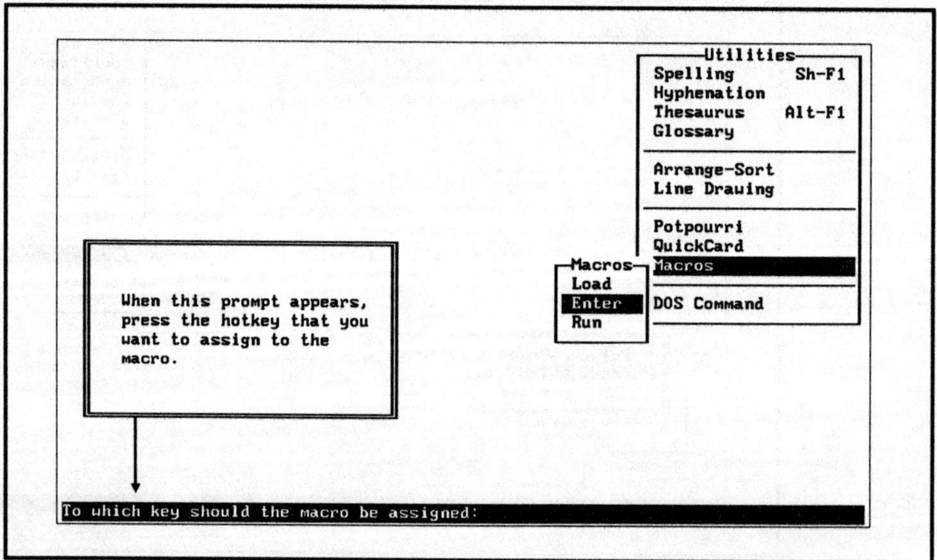

Figure 2.4.
Assigning a hotkey to a macro.

Sprint will scan your existing keys and build the Qcard.spr file. When Sprint finishes, you will be left in the Sprint editor with Qcard.spr loaded. You can then print a copy for your reference if you like, or close the file without saving it.

Note: *Qcard* is the name of the Sprint macro that creates Qcard.spr. The *Qcard* macro is built into Sprint, so you need not explicitly invoke it as a macro—just pick QuickCard from the Utilities menu. Later, in Chapter 3, we will show you how you can put your hands on the source code to Sprint. Then you may find it interesting to study *Qcard* and see how it works.

Before you loaded *MatchPair*, **Alt-M** meant to place a mark in a text, a function from the Edit menu. But now (if you actually loaded *MatchPair*) it means to execute *MatchPair*. Figure 2.5 shows a part of our Qcard.spr file. Notice that it shows that **Alt-M** has been assigned to *MatchPair*.

How did this change occur? Within *MatchPair* was some code that took the **Alt-M** key away from the Edit menu and gave it to *MatchPair*. The code in *MatchPair* that does this is

```
~M : MatchPair
```

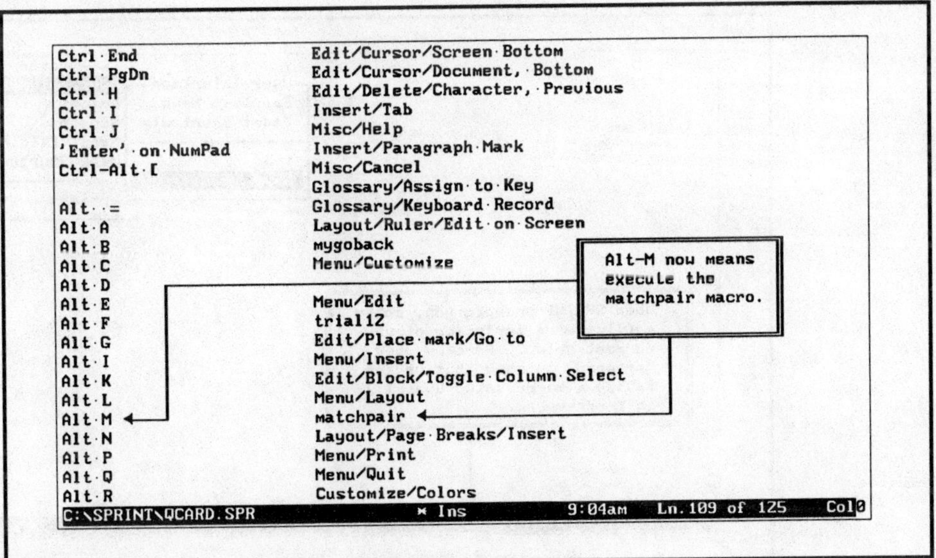

```
Ctrl·End                Edit/Cursor/Screen·Bottom
Ctrl·PgDn               Edit/Cursor/Document,·Bottom
Ctrl·H                  Edit/Delete/Character,·Previous
Ctrl·I                  Insert/Tab
Ctrl·J                  Misc/Help
'Enter'·on·NumPad       Insert/Paragraph·Mark
Ctrl-Alt·[              Misc/Cancel
                        Glossary/Assign·to·Key
Alt··=                  Glossary/Keyboard·Record
Alt·A                   Layout/Ruler/Edit·on·Screen
Alt·B                   mygoback
Alt·C                   Menu/Customize
Alt·D
Alt·E                   Menu/Edit
Alt·F                   trial12
Alt·G                   Edit/Place·mark/Go·to
Alt·I                   Menu/Insert
Alt·K                   Edit/Block/Toggle·Column·Select
Alt·L                   Menu/Layout
Alt·M                   matchpair
Alt·N                   Layout/Page·Breaks/Insert
Alt·P                   Menu/Print
Alt·Q                   Menu/Quit
Alt·R                   Customize/Colors
C:\SPRINT\QCARD.SPR                  ×·Ins          9:04am    Ln.109 of 125    Col0
```


Figure 2.5.
Reassignment of **Alt-M** shown in QCARD.SPR.

This code should appear on a line by itself—not within *MatchPair*. We'll discuss this in more detail later in Chapter 5. For now, just remember that when you load certain macros, they may cause key reassignments. You can control this by removing or editing the key reassignment code in the macros.

Any coded macro you load into Sprint is immediately a part of the current user interface. Sprint will save it to the Sp.ovl file when you exit Sprint. But what if you don't want your macros saved permanently? What if someone else will be using your computer—someone who does not know about your macros? (That could be a nice practical joke, or it could cause a headache.) Consequently, it's important to know how to save and clear macros that you have loaded.

SAVING MACROS IN A CUSTOMIZED USER INTERFACE

If you have a setup you like, you can save it before you clear out the macros, as shown in Figure 2.6. Use these steps:

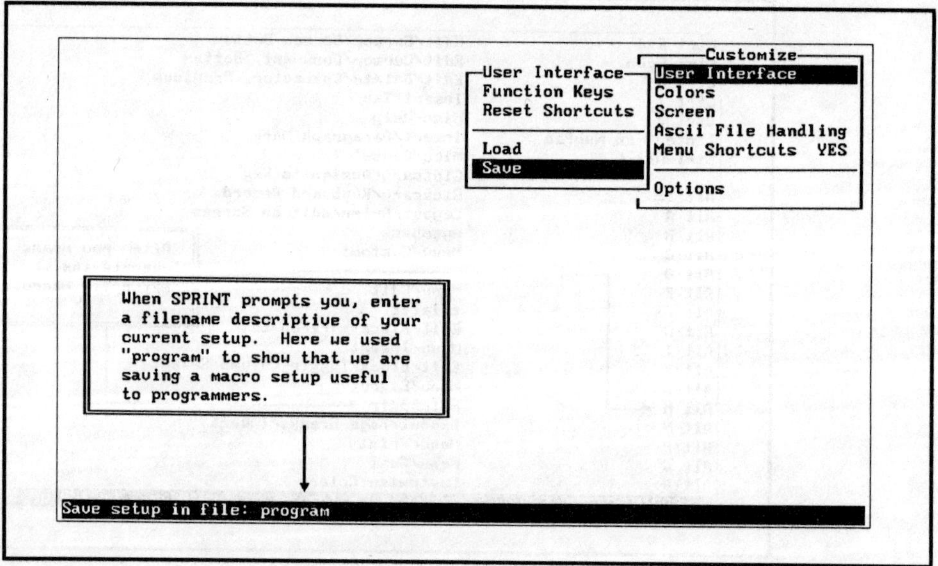

Figure 2.6.
Saving macro setups.

1. Press **Alt-C** to get to the Customize menu.
2. Press **U** to reach the User Interface menu.
3. Press **S** to save the key assignments.
4. When Sprint prompts you, enter a filename that is descriptive of your current setup. Later you can reload this customized interface whenever you want to.

The process bears repeating. You probably don't want to reload macros and assign them to keys every time you start Sprint! By saving your macros and key assignments to a special file during a session, all the changes to a *personal* version of Sprint are recorded, and you can return to Sprint later, with your selected keys still doing your favorite macros.

Sprint accomplishes that with its User Interface files, the .ui files. When you pick the Save command on the User Interface menu, Sprint asks you for a special filename. If you enter something like MatchTst to signify that you are testing a user interface with a new key for *MatchPair*, Sprint will record all the standard editor macros, as well as the *MatchPair* macro just added, and give the whole shebang the name MatchTst.ui. The next time you return to Sprint, it will load that interface if you press **Alt-C, U L**, and then choose MatchTst from the menu.

Important

When you choose a user interface, Sprint copies it to *Sp.ovl*. It then becomes the default user interface. Sprint always looks to *Sp.ovl* for its interface.

CLEARING TEMPORARY MACROS

Once your macros are saved, you can clear them from Sprint and return to the original user interface. The best way to do this is to

1. Press **Alt-C** to produce the Customize menu.
2. Press **U** to reach the User Interface submenu, then press **L**.
3. Enter the name of the original interface.

Where We've been, Where we're going

You are now able to
- Load a macro (or group of macros) defined in an .spm file;
- Assign a macro to a hotkey;
- Activate a macro with or without a hotkey;
- Save a set of macros in a new User Interface file;
- Clear newly created macros from Sprint by reloading the original interface.

In Chapter 3, we'll be using source code to produce small programs. You'll see how you can copy code from a file and modify Sprint to suit your own purposes.

Chapter 3

Learning from Sprint's Source Code

In this chapter we're going to build on what you learned in the previous chapter about Sprint macros (the coded kind). When you finish it, you'll be able to:

- Search for and capture good Sprint source code.
- Develop new macros from existing code.
- Compile and execute macros with a "secret" technique.
- Create a macro that displays a customized menu.
- Identify different categories of Sprint macros.
- Permanently install new macros you have created.

Let's begin by learning how to unpack the source code that Borland so freely supplies to all Sprint users.

UNPACKING THE BORLAND MACROS

One of the programs Borland supplies with Sprint is Unpack.com. We found Unpack.com on disk 3 of our version of Sprint. You'll probably find it there, too. Unpack.com is your program to unpack the source code to Sprint. The code is archived in a file called Spmsource.arc. Archiving saves space and reduces production and shipping costs. It's easy to expand the code with Unpack.com. We assume that you are using a hard disk designated as Drive C:. Just follow these steps:

1. Insert the Sprint disk containing Unpack.com in Drive A.
2. Make a subdirectory on your hard disk, such as Spmacros, by entering these commands at the DOS prompt: CD\and MD Spmacros.
3. Change to the new subdirectory. Press **CD \Spmacros**.
4. Log on to Drive **A:**.
5. Enter the command. **unpack Spmsourc.arc C :**

This will unpack all the macros that are archived on Drive A: and put them in the Spmacros subdirectory on drive C:.

If you want to see the different options you have with Unpack, just enter **A:Unpack** (with no DOS command line arguments). Unpack will then display a copyright notice and some brief documentation, as you can see in Figure 3.1.

As you can see, there are five options (switches) with Unpack, as well as a path and a file destination. But it isn't all that complicated.

```
C:\SPMACROS>unpack  ◄─── NOTE: UNPACK command given without arguments.

UNPACK program, version 1.50.  Copyright (c) 1987 Borland International.
UNPACK extracts files from an archive.

Usage: UNPACK [options] arcfile [destpath] [files...]
Options:
  /r = replace existing files            /v = verbose listing of archive(s)
  /c = extract file(s) to the console    /p = extract file(s) to the printer
  /t = test archive integrity

arcfile    Archive file name, wildcards *,? ok.  Default extension is .ARC
destpath   Destination for extracted files.
files      Name(s) of files to extract.  Wildcards *,? ok.
           Default is ALL files.

Examples:
  unpack examples                    - Unpack all files in EXAMPLES.ARC to
                                       current drive and directory.
  unpack examples a:\bin             - Unpack all files in EXAMPLES.ARC to
                                       A:\BIN directory.
  unpack examples a: *.pas *.inc     - Unpack all .PAS and .INC files in
                                       EXAMPLES.ARC to drive A.
```

Figure 3.1
Options shown when you enter UNPACK with no arguments.

Practically, it's best just to unpack all your macros and tuck them in one place, such as a subdirectory on your hard disk or on a diskette if you prefer. If you want to store the macros in a subdirectory called Macros on a diskette in Drive B, you could use this command:

```
A:Unpack Spmsourc.arc B:\Macros
```

The chief .spm file is Sp.spm. Probably the easiest way to start making customized menus is to modify excerpts from Sp.spm. It's a fairly long, 74K file, and it provides the principal Sprint macros as well as the main elements of the user interface. You can modify Sp.spm and then load it into Sprint. If you load the Sp.spm file, or any other .spm file, Sprint writes the new file in binary code to the overlay file, Sp.ovl, which holds the current user interface.

If you haven't unpacked the Sp.spm file yet, please do so before trying to carry out the next exercises.

Extracting Sp.spm Code

To find code in the long Sp.spm file, we suggest you press **F7** to start Sprint's search function. Then type in a word or phrase that you want to find and press **Enter**. Once you find the parts of Sp.spm that you want, you can copy them to a new file. There are several ways. Here is one effective technique:

1. Load Sp.spm into Sprint.
2. Open another window by pressing **Shift-F3**. Press **Ctrl-F3** and enter the name of some other work file.
3. Shift back to the first window with **Shift-F6**. Find the code that you want to use. Then highlight it.
4. Shift to the window containing your target file by pressing **Shift-F6**. Paste in the copied code by pressing **F6**. Then save the new file with **Ctrl-F2**.

You will probably want to open and close windows often as well as jump back and forth between them. See Figure 3.2, which summarizes the Sprint window manipulation functions.

You can close a window by pressing **Shift-F4**. If you close a window containing a file, the file will stay open unless you explicitly close the

Figure 3.2
Keystrokes for Manipulating Files in Sprint Windows.

If You Want To:	Then Press:
Open a new window	Shift-F3
Close a window	Shift-F4
Jump to a different window	Shift-F6
Load an open file	Ctrl-F9
Open a file in a new window	Shift-F3 then Ctrl-F3
Close a file	Ctrl-F4
Save a file	Ctrl-F4
Zoom a file	Shift-F5

file. It can be useful to leave a file open. To jump back to it, just press **Ctrl-F9** and move the selection bar over the file name and press **Enter**.

The Sp.spm code runs and it runs fast. If you copy excerpts from it and modify them, you'll get some modules of code that will run after a couple of trials. It's a lot faster than trying to write code using only a book as a guide.

Cautions

Remember that when you work with the Sp.spm file, you are programming the editor, not the formatter. Sprint filenames that end with the extension .spm affect the editor, a part of which is the user interface. Sprint filenames that end with the extension .fmt affect the formatter, which basically is the print utility. Both .spm and .fmt files are macro code. Keep editor .spm macros separate from formatter .fmt macros.

As another caution, we suggest you load the Sp.spm code into Sprint *so you can copy from it*. But you do not want the system *interpreting* the draft Sp.spm code, because the system already is interpreting your standard user interface. So be careful in naming files while manipulating Sp.spm code. We now keep our draft Sp.spm file in a separate directory. We decided it was best to keep Sprint from reading our Sp.spm test code as program code. We learned the hard way so you could benefit from our experience.

MAKING A CUSTOMIZED MENU

We will make a customized menu that will pop up on the screen when we call it. The menu will use a few of the Sprint functions already available, and it will offer a new function or two. So we will copy existing code and modify it. Let's go through this step-by-step:

1. Make a copy of Sp.spm and put it in a subdirectory, called, say, SPM. Open your copy of Sp.spm *as a text file*.
2. Open a second window by pressing **Shift-F3**. Then open a file called Mykeys.spm by pressing **Ctrl-F3** and entering **Mykeys.spm**. Once the file is open, press **Shift-F6** to return to the window containing Sp.spm.
3. Search for the Main menu section of the Sp.spm file. A good way is to press **F7** and enter **Main Menu**. Mark the first few lines of code through the line that begins with "Typestyle menu."

Figure 3.3 shows the code that we want you to copy into the Myin-

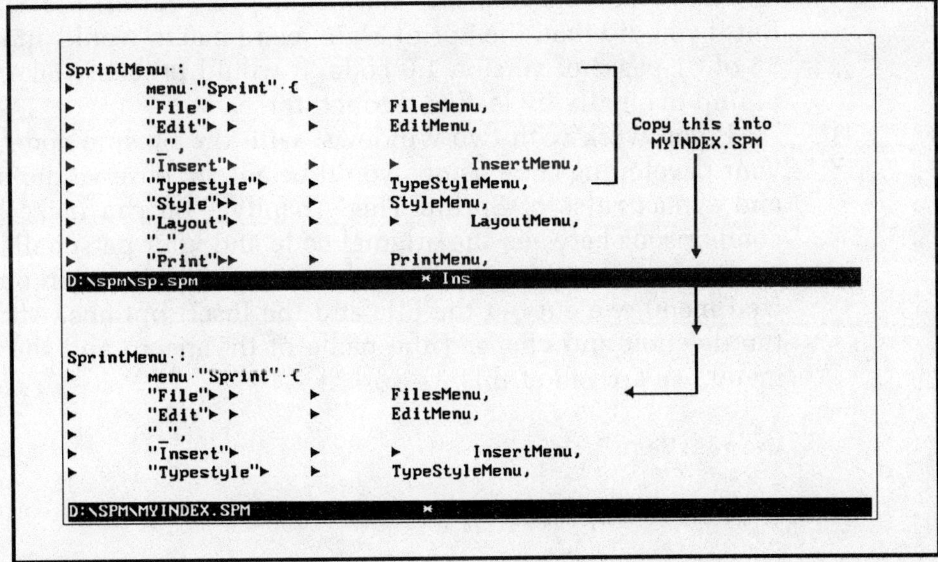

Figure 3.3
Copying code from SP.SPM into MYINDEX.SPM.

dex.spm window. This figure also illustrates the split screen technique. Notice that we have Sp.spm loaded into the top window and MyIndex.spm into the bottom window.

We suggest you put a mnemonic name on your macro—in this case, let's use the name *MyIndexMenu:*. As a rule of thumb, put macro names flush left and follow them with a colon. That enables the compiler to recognize the text as a macro. (As you may recall from Chapter 1, macros in the Sprint Glossary have a different format than that discussed here.)

There is no particular filename specification for macro names, unlike the xxxxxxxx.xxx format required by DOS. The only restrictions on macro names are

- Do not use the names of other program macros.
- Do not embed spaces in macro names.
- Do not begin the name with a number.

The Sprint menu macro we are using appeared as line 2884 of 3,156 lines in version 1.0 of the Sp.spm code. So it's a little more than three-fourths of the way through more than 3,000 lines of code. That's why we recommend you make heavy use of the find, block, and copy functions built into Sprint. You could print out all the Sp.spm code. But if you did that, the Sprint Main menu macro would appear on page 56 of 61 pages of version 1.0 code. It would probably take a half hour to find manually by leafing through the code.

If you work with two windows, with the Sp.spm code on top and your developing code below, you'll be able to observe the punctuation and syntax rules of Sprint. That's handy. You can make line-by-line comparisons between the original code and your personalized version.

Because we didn't want all the Main menu items in our personalized menu, we cut out the File and the Insert options. After we made the deletion and changed the name of the macro and the title of the menu, we arrived at this:

```
MyIndexMenu :


    menu "My Menu" {


        "Edit"              EditMenu,


        "Typestyle"         TypestyleMenu,
```

Important
____

In this example, we need to drop the comma after Typestyle
Menu, and finish the menu list with a closing brace.

So edit the macro again to look like this:

```
MyIndexMenu :

    menu "My Menu" {

        "Edit"              EditMenu,

        "Typestyle"         TypestyleMenu

    }
```

Here are some important points to notice about this macro:

- The code below the macro name is indented. The compiler will
  not recognize the macro code unless each line after the title is
  indented.
- Commas are used to separate menu items.
- All the menu items are enclosed with braces. (The Sprint compiler treats the expressions between the braces as a word.)

Notice that the closing brace is indented, although it ends a paragraph of code. That punctuation convention is in the style of the C
and Pascal languages. Typically, the closing brace appears on the line
below the final macro expression. Notice that in the Borland style, the
opening brace does not appear on its own line and it is not aligned with
the closing brace. You may have your own style for placing delimiters.

Those of you who hunt and peck on the standard IBM keyboard
will find the braces as uppercase characters on the upper-right. You
could use other delimiters, but braces will make the code clearer for
other programmers.

Now let's return to Sp.spm to find more code. Suppose you want
to include the code that goes with the Index option on the Style menu.
Here's how you might find the appropriate code and use it to build
your own menu option.

First, toggle to the window with the Sp.spm code. We are looking for the code for the Style menu. Because spaces are not allowed in macro names, we can guess that macro name is probably *StyleMenu*. Before beginning the search, be sure to go to the top of the target file by pressing **Ctrl-PgUp** (or **Ctrl-QR**), so you search the entire file. In this case, you need to repeat the search for stylemenu, because the first match by the editor will put you on TypestyleMenu. You can press **Ctrl-L** to continue the search.

We suggest you set Sprint to ignore distinctions caused by capital letters when doing a search. You can do this by setting CASE SENSITIVE to NO. Press **Alt-E S C**. Then press **Enter** to toggle the choice to NO. Finally, press **Esc** to exit from the Edit menu.

When you've found the Style menu, you'll see a menu option for *IndexMenu*—that's the one we want because in this hypothetical example, we want to put an Index Word option in our custom menu. Figure 3.4 shows the call to *IndexMenu*.

We really want the code from *IndexMenu*. You might want to try to search for *IndexMenu* by pressing the **F7** and entering **indexmenu**. But if you look forward from where you were in the Sp.spm file when you found the *StyleMenu*, you won't find *IndexMenu*. Again, you need to go to the top of the file before beginning a search.

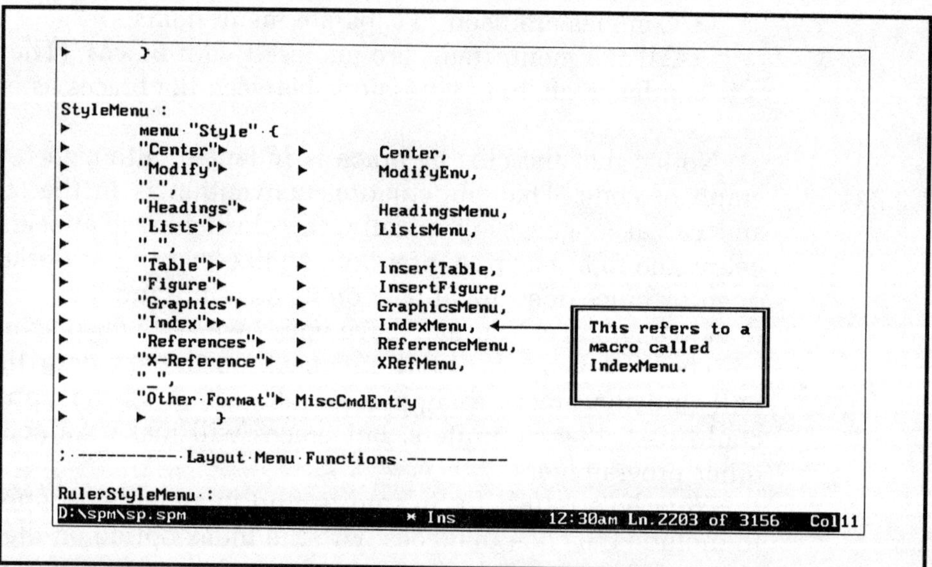

Figure 3.4
The reference to "IndexMenu" in the StyleMenu macro.

When you find the target, the first few lines will look like this:

```
IndexMenu :

    menu "Index" {

    "Word"                    IxWordHelp if !select SelectWord

                              '^D' CharFormat,
```

Use the **F3** and **F4** keys to mark the two lines beginning with "Word". Toggle into the window with the Sp.spm code by using **Shift-F6**, and paste the code fragment onto the developing menu on the line right after the opening brace. Notice in the two-line expression the word *IxWordHelp*. That's a macro to start the context-sensitive help system. We won't use it in this exercise, so edit it out. Also change "Index" to "Please index this word". Figure 3.5 shows how the developing macro should appear.

```
MyIndexMenu :
    "My Menu" {
    "Please index this word" if !select SelectWord
                '^D' CharFormat,
    "Edit"          EditMenu,
    "Typestyle"     TypestyleMenu
}
```

Figure 3.5
Our developing macro.

Avoiding Ruler Lines

Did Line 3 of the code wrap to line 4 on your screen? If so, it may be because you have a ruler line in your file. *You must get rid of any ruler lines in macro code and work with text in ASCII only.* Remember that in ASCII every line ends with a carriage return. To be sure this is the case, it helps to have Sprint set up to show carriage returns. To do that:

1. Press **Alt-C** to activate the Customize menu.

2. Select Screen.
3. Set Paragraph Marks to ON.

A "Secret" Method for Testing the Macro

Once you have finished the macro code in the MyKeys.spm window, be sure to save that file by pressing **Ctrl-F2**. After saving it, you are ready to test it. Here's a "secret" method for testing macros (known only to serious Sprint macro hackers).

Right after you finish typing the macro, press **Shift-Alt-R**. Sprint will then start compiling the macro currently in the editor. If the compiler detects an error, it may be displayed on the status line. If all goes well, no error message will be displayed and you will know that your macro compiled. To eXecute your new macro, press **Shift-Alt-X**. (We capitalized the X in eXecute to help you remember **Shift-Alt-X**.) Sprint will prompt you for a macro name. Just enter name of your macro, which in this case is **MyKeys** (without quotes).

Standard Method for Loading Macros

You can load and execute macros in different ways. The usual way is to start with the Sprint Utility menu. We covered that procedure in Chapter 2, but let's review it briefly here:

1. Make sure the MyKeys.spm file is in the Sprint subdirectory.
2. Press **Alt-U** for the Utilities menu, then choose Macros and Load.
3. Select MyKeys, which should appear on the menu after you select Load.
4. Return to the Macros menu. (Press **Alt-U** and choose Macros.) This time select Enter.
5. At the prompt, enter the name of the macro: **MyKeys**.
6. Sprint will now ask you whether you want to execute the macro or assign it to a key. For now, just execute it by pressing **E**.

Using a Hotkey

To assign a macro to a hotkey, repeat the six steps listed previously, but this time, in the last step, assign the macro to a hotkey by pressing

A instead of **E**. Then test the macro by pressing the hotkey. A good out-of-the-way hotkey for testing is **Shift-Alt 0**.

As we mentioned earlier, another way to assign a macro to a hotkey is to include a line like this in your macro file:

```
~A : myindexmenu
```

Figure 3.6 illustrates this approach in the *MatchPair* macro. Note that the line that binds a hotkey to a macro must not appear within a macro. A good place for this line is at the end of the file containing the macro. ~A : myindexmenu assigns the macro to **Alt-A**. To work, that assignment statement must appear below the macro name. For example, to assign the macro to **Alt-B**, you would write below the macro label:

```
~B: MyIndexMenu
```

In this example notice that there must be a tilde symbol in front of the letter ~B. It is followed by a colon, a space, and then the name of macro, which here is *MyIndexMenu*.

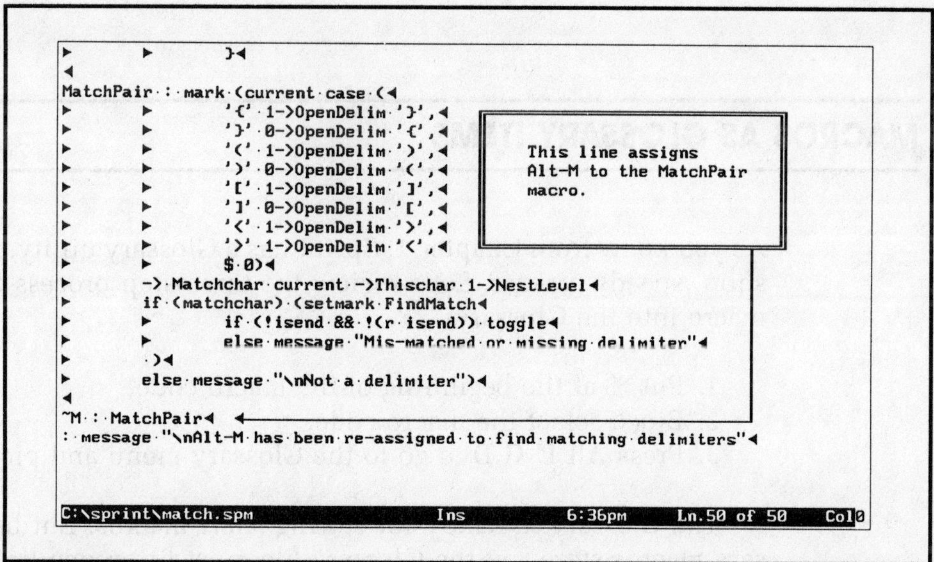

Figure 3.6
A key assignment within a macro.

SAVING AND ERASING MACROS

Whenever you compile an .spm files with **Shift-Alt-R**, it immediately becomes part of Sprint. When you exit Sprint, any macros you have compiled in this way are saved in the Sp.ovl file. That makes those macros a regular part of the current interface. To make a backup copy of this version of Sprint, press **Alt-C U S** and enter a unique name.

You can erase the macros you have just compiled by going back to an earlier interface. Press **Alt-C U L** and select the interface you want from the menu. Remember: whatever interface you load gets copied over the existing Sp.ovl file.

But what if you don't have an earlier interface to go back to? Fortunately, there is another way to erase macros you have just compiled and loaded into memory. Press **Shift-Alt-X** and enter **0 → ovlmodf**. Then exit from Sprint. Now, the macros you have compiled in your current session will not be saved to the Sp.ovl file. This works because *ovlmodf* is an internal global variable, *ovlmodf* which is short for "overlay modification flag." If *ovlmodf* is set to 1, Sprint will modify Sp.ovl, but when ovlmodf is set to zero, it won't. Note that the expression "0 → ovlmodf" sets *ovlmodf* to zero.

MACROS AS GLOSSARY ITEMS

As you know from Chapter 1, Sprint has a Glossary utility, which holds short, speedy macros. Let's review the three-step process for putting a macro into the Glossary:

1. Put % at the beginning of the macro code.
2. Block select the macro code.
3. Press **Alt U-G D** to go to the Glossary menu and pick Define.

The Glossary is handy for storing *short* macros. But because Glossary macros stored in the Glossary file must fit on one line, they can't be longer than 256 characters. Long macros won't fit in the Glossary.

You can still have some Glossary macros that have multiple lines *when they appear in your source code*. But when you highlight a macro and press **Alt U-G D**, Sprint removes the carriage returns and moves the macro into the Glossary file so it appears on one line.

ELEMENTS OF THE SPRINT LANGUAGE

Primitives and Other Beasts

The menu example shows the differences among macros in the Sprint language and the use of macros in combination. *Menu*, *imenu*, and *exitmenus* actually are macro primitives that are already compiled. The source code for the primitive is **not** available and we can't modify macro primitives. An example of a primitive macro is *menu*. When we invoke the *menu* macro, for example, on the second line of *MyIndexMenu*, Sprint automatically:

1. Draws a box.
2. Gives it a title.
3. Lists the menu items.
4. Establishes a light bar.
5. Highlights the first letter of each box.
6. Places the menu slightly below and to the left of any other menus on the screen.

That's a powerful routine for a one-word primitive!

There are other macros, which we can also think of as being built-in macros. They are built-in because we can instantly execute them without having to compile them; they already exist in Sp.ovl. An example is *InsertFile*, which you can find in Core.spm. You can instantly execute this built-in macro by pressing **Shift-Alt-X** and entering **InsertFile**. But *InsertFile* is not a primitive because we can look at the source code and see how it is broken down into smaller macros. When we call the macro *MyIndexMenu*, we are calling code comprised of other macros. So it's a coded macro. Once we compile it, it becomes part of Sp.ovl, too. Names of coded macros usually appear in upper and lowercase.

Names of primitives are given in lowercase. This is just a convention, not a requirement of the compiler. Not all programmers follow this rule.

Primitives are not necessarily elementary commands without options. For example, with the *menu* primitive, you can create division bars in the menu with a single underline character among the menu items. The menu macro will execute the command or menu item that the user selects, then redraw the screen.

Some primitives are error-tolerant. If a command in a menu doesn't execute for some reason, the *menu* macro will present the choices again, so the user can choose another item.

Macro Variables

A second group in the macro language are the macro variables. For example, the *tabsize*, *cleartab*, and *settab* variables manipulate tabs when there is no ruler line or when there are no tabs set in the current ruler line. A typical tabsize command might be

```
10 -> tabsize
```

This moves the value ten into the *tabsize* variable. It's like tabsize = 10 in Basic. This establishes ten units between each tab when printing or writing to the screen. Some variables are primitives, but you can still assign values to them.

The value a variable contains is critical, because it often determines the destiny of a macro—what path it will follow. Here are some important rules about how variables take values.

A variable that you declare with int *after a macro name* takes on the value of the current argument. That is an important rule to remember. The current argument is some value that has been returned by the previous command. Each command in Sprint returns an argument. If a returned value is non zero, Sprint regards it as True; if zero, Sprint regards the value as False.

Global Variables

A variable that you declare *at the top of a file*, before declaring any macro names, is a global variable. This means you can use the variable in any macro and you don't (and can't) define it within a macro. When you define a global variable you may initialize it to a specific value as in

```
int trois = 3.
```

Even though you have initialized a global variable, you can still set it to a new value with the -> operator. For example, to set trois to four, you would write

```
4 -> trois
```

Local Variables

You can also define a variable within a macro using int. However, in this case you do *not* initialize it using the equal sign =. *A local variable takes on the value of the current argument.* Remember, in Sprint Macro programming every command returns a value. We call that value the current argument. Sprint passes that argument on to the next command. Here is a simple example:

```
cube:  int x

       x * x * x
```

In this tiny macro, we don't initialize x. But we do define it with "int". If the incoming argument is 3, cube will return 27 (3 times 3 times 3).

To pass a specific value to cube, we can just hard code a number in front of cube, like this

```
3 cube
```

Note: The cube macro (as we've just presented it) would not display anything. It just returns the cube of whatever number you feed it. To see the returned argument you have to do something with it—like feed it into the *message* macro. Here's an example:

```
3 cube

message "\nCube of 3 is %d"

ask "Press Y to continue. "
```

The %d just tells Sprint to print the value returned by the previous command in decimal form on the status line. You could use %x to see the value in hexidecimal format. The \n causes a carriage return. We do this just to clear the status line. The *ask* macro just forces the system to pause until the user presses **Y** or **N**. That allows us to read the message on the status line before the macro finishes.

If you're not sure what value a global variable represents at any given place in a macro, you can insert an *abort* macro and then press **Shift-Alt-X**. Then enter the variable name, and the equal sign, as in

```
SearchOpt  =
```

Sprint will then display the value of the variable on the status line. Note that *abort* is a macro primitive so it appears in lowercase.

For local variables, you need to use another approach because once a macro ends, you can't get to its local variables. In this case, you can insert a *message* macro and an *ask* macro where you want to know the value of an argument, just as we showed you with the cube macro. Here's another example. Inside a macro you might put in these lines:

```
trois message "The value of trois is %d" ask "Press Y to continue."
```

Sprint has a number of predefined (primitive) global variables that return useful information. Here are examples:

- *cd* returns the name of the current directory.
- *current* returns the ASCII value of character that the cursor is currently on.
- *column* returns the cursor column position. (Starting column = 0.)
- *dcolumn* returns the column where the cursor was before the current macro started executing.
- *line* returns the current file line number. If you set *line* to some value, the cursor will jump to that line.
- *dline* returns the current line relative to top of the current window. You can move the cursor to a specific line of a window by setting dline to the desired value.

Appendix E contains a listing of the global Sprint variables with descriptions of their purposes.

If you're not sure how the Borland Advanced User Interface uses a

Sprint global variable, search for it in the core.spm and the sp.spm files. Then backtrack until you are led, inevitably, to its associated menu item. Sometimes you can manipulate a variable directly from a menu.

Math Functions

We need variables to do math functions in Sprint. Sprint has a few calculating functions and a full range of the Boolean operators that programs use to handle logic. There's more explanation of the functions in later chapters and appendices. For now, we'd just like to demonstrate that Sprint can add and subtract and that simple math functions can be used as building blocks for higher math functions.

Figure 3.7 is a listing of the macro *DoSomeMath* that illustrates global variables, an assignment statement, math functions, and Boolean operators.

The statements above the macro name *DoSomeMath* initialize or declare variables. Because the variables are above the macro label, they are available to any other macro running in Sprint— another macro could use the variable *remainder*, for example. The first statement in the macro both declares a variable *trois* and sets it to 3; it is a declaration and assignment in one.

You can type and load *DoSomeMath* and it will do math for you on the status line, displaying variable values and results as it goes. So that all the information will not flash by, two-second delays are built in with the "2000 delay " statements.

A higher math function such as a cube, available in other languages, is not available in Sprint, but you can build a cube macro as we illustrated earlier.

DoSomeMath shows a sum with the + operator and assigns the results to another variable. We list Sprint operators and explain them in Appendix C.

The third math function, illustrating division, uses variable names in the messages. There are two format specifiers. One refers to the value of the variable *cube* and the other refers to the value of the variable *quotient*. The math functions end with a subtraction statement.

We explain Sprint's bitwise operators in Appendix C; we also discuss them in the coming chapters. (For more details on these bitwise operators, you may want to see a beginning book on assembly language programming or a computer science textbook.)

```
        ; Declaration of global variables

        int trois = 3
        int cube
        int sum
        int remainder
        int quotient
        int bitwiseAND
        int bitwiseEOR


        ;**************************** DoSomeMath ****************************

        ;USE: Demonstrates how to do simple math and "bit fiddling"
        ;     Shows how you can declare and initialize global variables.
        ;     Also, shows how you can assign values to variables with the
        ;     "->" operatior and use the message statement to display their
        ;     values.


        DoSomeMath:

            (trois*trois*trois) -> cube
            message "\n The cube of trois is %d"
            2000 delay
            (trois + trois) -> sum
            message "\n The sum of trois and trois is %d"
            2000 delay
            (cube/trois) -> quotient
            cube message "\n %d divided by trois is" quotient message " %d"
            2000 delay
            (quotient - trois) -> remainder
            quotient
            message "\n Trois subtracted from %d is" remainder message " %d"
            2000 delay
            (trois & trois) -> bitwiseAND
            bitwiseAND message "\n Bitwise AND of trois with itself is %d"
            2000 delay
            (trois^trois) -> bitwiseEOR
            bitwiseEOR
            message "\n Bitwise exclusive OR of trois with itself is: is %d"
            2000 delay
            (trois|trois) -> bitwiseEOR
            bitwiseEOR
            message "\n Bitwise inclusive OR of trois with itself is %d"
            2000 delay
```

Figure 3.7
Math functions in Sprint.

The bitwise AND, &, evaluates two expressions (or variables). Then it makes a bit-by-bit check of the returned values. If both corresponding bits are set to 1, then the bit in the resulting number will also be 1.

The bitwise exclusive OR, ^, also evaluates and then makes a bit-by-bit check. It sets a bit to zero in the result if the corresponding bits in the two values are set to 1. But if either bit is set to 1, then the resulting bit will be set to 1. If both bits are zero, then the result is also zero. Because the corresponding bits in our example are always both 1 or both zero, the result is zero.

The | operator does an inclusive OR. If either bit is set to 1, then the bit in the result will be 1. Also, if both bits are 1, the resulting bit will be set to 1.

Macro Directives

Directives are instructions to the Sprint editor, acting as a compiler, rather than instructions to the CPU. For example, macro code often uses include files to tell the compiler that other macros are coming. In the Sp.spm file, for example, we find these include directives:

- #include "core"
- #include "column"
- #include "gloss"
- #include "mouse"
- #include "sort"
- #include "drawline"

Automatically Called Macros

An automatically called macro is implicitly called prior to or after a specific action—usually on start-up or when Sprint needs some special service. *Init*, for example, reloads the user interface if the user has exited the program and enters it again, or chooses to refresh the interface. The automatically called macros are mechanical and often transparent to the user.

There are 156 small, fast built-in primitive macros, 52 built-in macro variables, a couple dozen math and logical operators, only 4 macro directives, and 9 automatically called macros. They comprise the basic vocabulary of people who want to work in the Sprint macro language and take as many shortcuts as possible. In addition, you will find other global variables in Core.spm. Sp.spm and Core.spm also have coded macros that act just like primitives—the difference is that you can see the source code. You can even make modifications and then recompile Core.spm and Sp.spm to more fully customize Sprint. We don't recommend you do this until you've had a lot of experience just writing and compiling your own macros.

USER FRIENDLY CUSTOMIZING WITH MACROS

Figure 3.8 shows an example of a fairly large menu, the File menu—one of the first options on Sprint's Main menu. When you pick the command New, the program executes *NewFile*, which prompts for a filename and opens the file. Figure 3.9 shows the macro code for the Sprint File menu. Notice how the underline character is used to create the division bars you see in Figure 3.8.

The File menu is a macro; the Main menu calls it and the File menu in turn can call several other macros, such as *NewFile*. Sprint is a construct of macros upon macros.

Figure 3.10 shows an imaginary menu—one we might use in the office to improve our productivity. The basic structure of the menu is in place. It won't work just as it is, though. Can you explain why?

This example shows how easily you can lift an existing, working menu and put the things on it that you may need to work with frequently. You can do this and give menus and commands familiar,

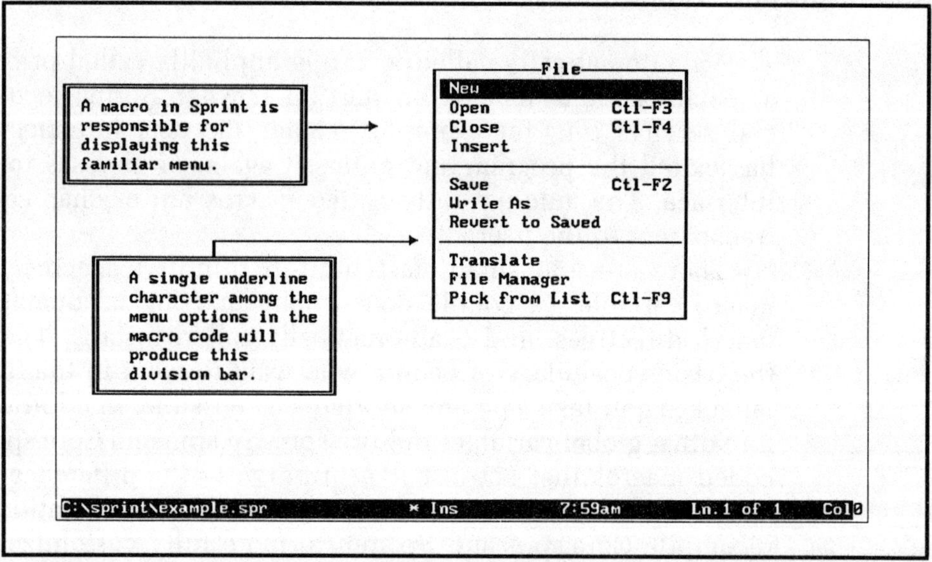

Figure 3.8
The Sprint file menu.

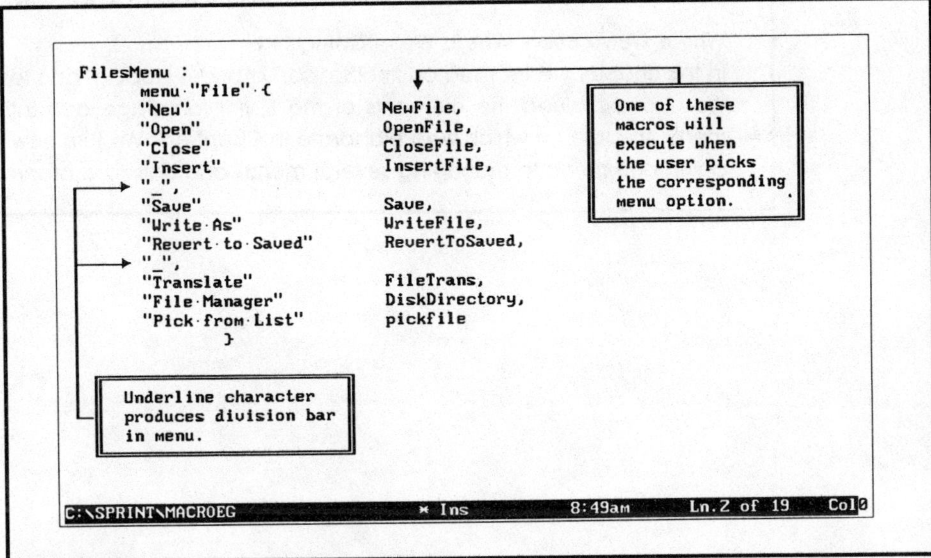

Figure 3.9
Macro code for the Sprint file menu.

intuitive names. But the menu is not yet complete. It won't compile because we still need to write: Doit, Delay, Delegate, Drop, Income, Expenses, Deadlines, Promo, Cust, and Prospects Once those macros are written, the menu choices on the left will actually do something. For example, the *Income* macro might start up dBASE, or even better, launch Paradox, a powerful database program from Borland.

```
ToDo :
     menu "Office Productivity" {
     "A. Do (Plan of the Day)"      Doit,
     "B. DeLay"                     Delay,
     "C. Delegate"                  Delegate,
     "D. Drop"                      Drop,
     " ",
     "E. Income"                    Income,
     "F. Expenses"                  Expenses,
     "G. Deadlines"                 Deadlines,
     " ",
     "H. Promotion/Advertising"     Promo,
     "I. Customers"                 Cust,
     "J. Prospects"                 Prospects
          }
```

Figure 3.10
Imaginary Office Productivity menu.

Where We've Been, Where We're Going
In this chapter we focused on finding, copying, developing, and testing code. We also explained the elements of the Sprint language and introduced a menu structure on which we'll elaborate in Chapter 4. We turn now from managing one menu to managing several menus and calling a program.

Chapter 4
Building Your Own Interface

When we first learned that Sprint menus and macros could be used to build an interface, we were a little put off by the apparently complex commands. But once we tried it, we discovered that with some coding and a little maneuvering around the menus, it's not hard to build an interface. Your own interface can empower, promote efficiency, and build bridges to other people and systems.

THE SPRINT MENU

Designing an interface begins with the Sprint menu, reproduced in Figure 4.1. There are some options on the Sprint menu that we like, and other options that we don't use very often. For example, we find the File menu and its children indispensable, whereas we infrequently use the Insert menu and the menus listed below it.

Developing an interface also begins with selecting those menu items you can do without. Of course, you could start from scratch, if you were willing to do a lot of coding. But we like to demonstrate successive refinement from a working model. To throw out the entire Sprint menu is to discard the baby with the bath water. And if we didn't start with

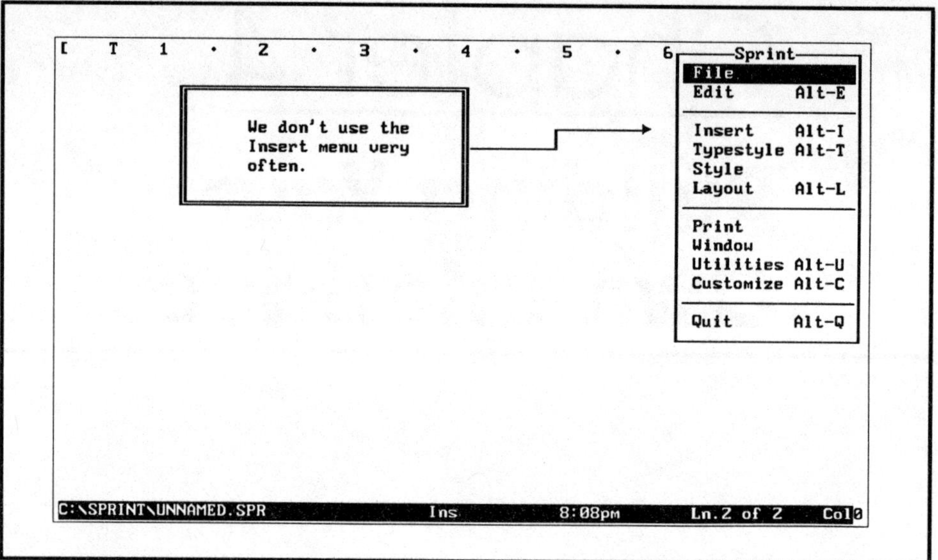

Figure 4.1
Sprint's main menu.

any of the Sprint menus, we'd need a scheme to open some of the menus that we eventually would need, as explained in the discussion about the Formatting menu.

THE SCHEME

Our new Main menu, illustrated in Figure 4.2, shows where we're going. It puts DOS services at the top of our priorities because we found that often we were leaving Sprint to format a disk, to check memory, or to get a DOS prompt. You may have received a DOS prompt attack: "Just give me my DOS prompt!"

All users have their preferences, so we don't expect you to agree with this arrangement. As you may have noticed in Chapter 3, we showed you another way to exit to DOS—through a hotkey.

The decision to put DOS services at the top of our Main menu

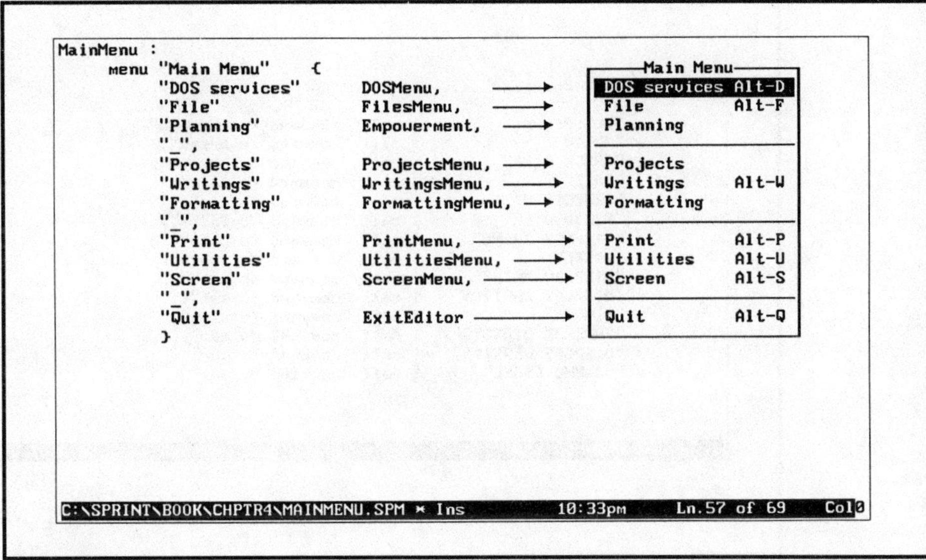

Figure 4.2
The new Main menu.

shows how personalized a Sprint environment can become. Let's look at the this personalized menu in more detail.

ATTACHING CODE TO A MENU ITEM

The coding for the DOS services appears in Figure 4.3. It begins with the macro name, a space, and a colon, as described in Chapter 3. Then comes the menu command, the title of the menu, and the menu items.

We present the DOS menu coding to show that you can put macro coding in a menu macro, on the same line as a menu item. For example, if we want a DOS prompt, we just pick DOS and then DOS Prompt; the code that follows will execute. Here, it is a call to the DOS command processor—more on that is presented in Chapter 6. *Note:* Although it appears pleasant enough on the screen, as reproduced in Figure 4.4, we caution you that the DOS menu is a little harder to build than it looks.

```
DosMenu :
     menu "DOS Commands" {

          "DOS Prompt"           1 call "command /c command",
          "BREAK"                1 call "command /c break",
          "CHECK DISK"           1 call "command /c chkdsk",
          "DATE"                 1 call "command /c date",
          "DIRECTORY"            1 call "command /c dir",
          "FIXED DISK"           1 call "command /c fdisk",
          "DISPLAY JOINS"        1 call "command /c join",
          "LABEL"                1 call "command /c label",
          "DISPLAY PATH"         1 call "command /c path",
          "DISPLAY ENVIRON"      1 call "command /c set",
          "TIME"                 1 call "command /c time",
          "TREE OF DIRECTORY"    1 call "command /c ver",
          "DISPLAY VERSION"      1 call "command /c ver",
          "VOLUME LABEL"         1 call "command /c vol"
          }

C:\SPRINT\UNNAMED.SPR                  × Ins              8:45pm      Ln.2 of 23      Col0
```

Figure 4.3
The DOS *menu* macro.

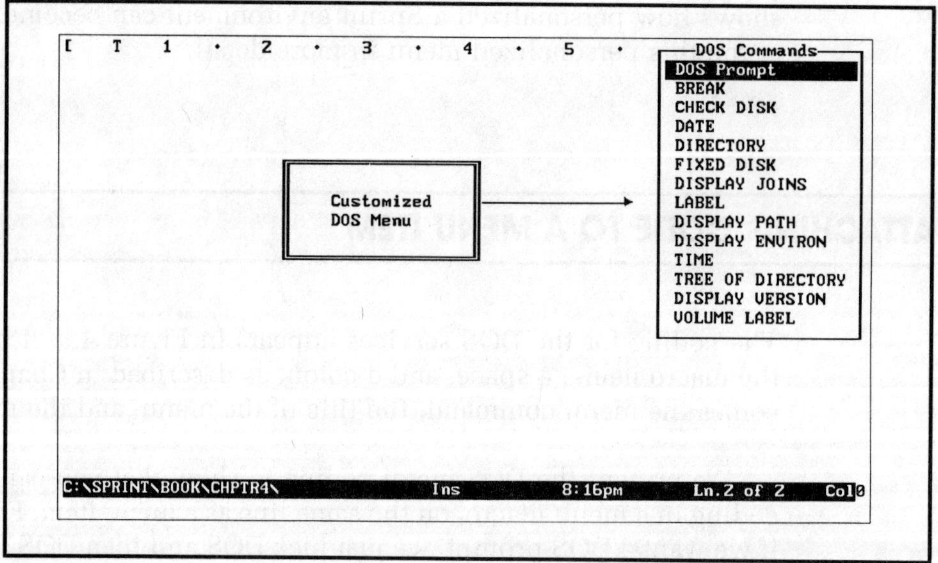

Figure 4.4
The DOS menu.

COMMAS, STRINGS, AND SEMANTICS

The Sprint editor, while acting as a compiler, is extremely intolerant of misplaced commas. One misplaced comma results in code scrambled all over your screen, abnormal ends, and other calamities. Yet scrambled code is easy to fix. When we built menus, almost every failure was due to a misplaced comma or a menu option that couldn't execute because the command processor couldn't locate the file. You'll be throwing together menus in no time if you:

- Put a comma on the end of every menu item but the last one.
- Enclose the menu command in delimiters.
- Use quotation marks carefully.
- Test your macro occasionally.

We listed as DOS commands only those that did not require a modifier, string, switch, or argument, in addition to those not transparently available through Sprint menus. It's an odd lot of DOS commands that serves as a suggested starting point for you.

There's one other qualification. In the DOS menu (just as an example), we could have included a badly needed command, *mkdir*, the make-directory command that is absent from the interface and so often needed. We began construction of the DOS menu, in fact, to work on that command. But *mkdir* is one of those DOS commands that requires an argument, such as mkdir c:\sprint\walk, which would produce walk as a subdirectory of sprint. We decided to keep our example simple here.

To pass a string in a menu command, it must be a constant, as illustrated in the DOS menu code, or we would have to accept input from the user. It's not hard taking input from the user—it just requires a Q buffer, a prompt, some coding, and some error-handling. We spared ourselves those arrangements to simplify this exposition. We worked around the problem of adding strings to DOS commands by making the DOS prompt the first option on our DOS menu. If a string must be passed, we can choose that option, then type the entire command on the DOS command line. Such decisions and workarounds will shape your environment design and your menus.

Our next menu item is *File*, and we lifted it from the Sprint menu.

There is no coding required here; if we just insert the words "File" and "menu" into our menu macro, it in turn calls a macro in Sp.spm that provides Sprint's file services. We positioned the _Files_ menu item so it would complement the DOS menu—between these two menus, most of the critical DOS functions are covered. It's just another of our preferences; that is, to keep system commands and file functions close together and high in our personalized menu system.

Before we go too much further with menus, we'd like to clarify some language. The word _File_ in our Main menu is what we call a menu item. If we highlight that item with the selection bar and press **Enter**, the editor looks in the Main menu macro for the string after the word _File_. We refer to that string as code, or a macro. When you pick _File_, the editor calls the macro _FilesMenu_. _FilesMenu_ is another menu, a submenu in fact, and it's also a macro. All macros are not menus, but all menus must be macros, because macros are the language of Sprint.

Also, we sometimes refer to the _MainMenu_ macro or the Main menu. Here, we include the macro that writes the Main menu to the screen, and related, subsidiary macros that produce the menus and commands derived from the Main menu.

TESTING AND COMPILING

Now, we have two working menu items in our Main menu. The coding for our Main menu appears in Figure 4.5. Note that it does not matter that most of the macros for most of the menu items are incomplete. If we don't select those menu items, and thus don't call those macros, there won't be any abnormal end. The _MainMenu_, in other words, will write to the screen because the _MainMenu_ macro appears to be complete, even though most macros for most of the submenus are incomplete. If we avoid calling incomplete menu items, we can examine the way the Main menu writes to the screen, and reorganize it before we get mired in deeply nested menu code.

And so it's time to test our code. We put together the DOS menu coding and the _MainMenu_ coding, with the Main menu just below the DOS menu. The organization is reproduced, in part, in Figure 4.6. We compressed the coding with ellipses to show how two menu

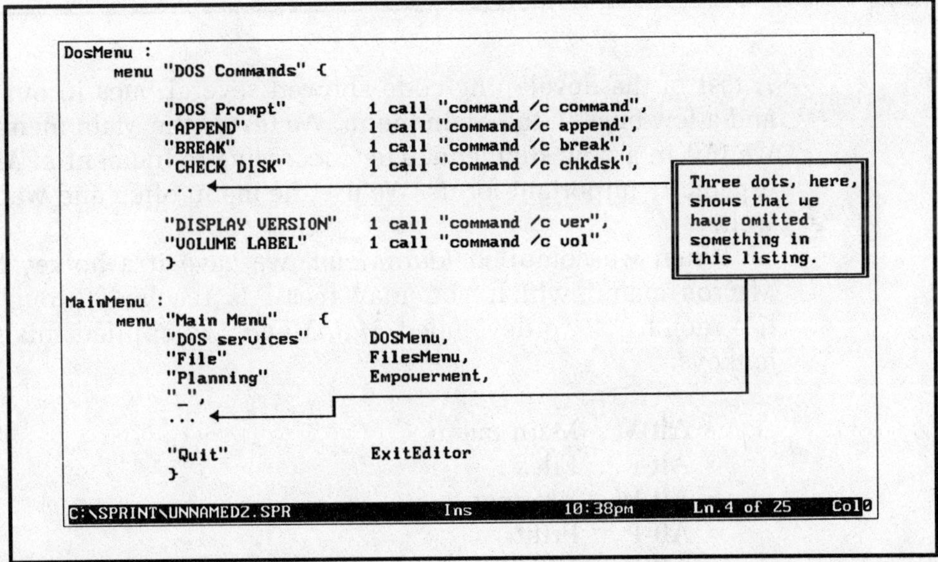

Figure 4.5
Developing code for customized Main menu.

```
DosMenu :
    menu "DOS Commands" {

        "DOS Prompt"        1 call "command /c command",
        "APPEND"            1 call "command /c append",
        "BREAK"             1 call "command /c break",
        "CHECK DISK"        1 call "command /c chkdsk",
        ...

        "DISPLAY VERSION"   1 call "command /c ver",
        "VOLUME LABEL"      1 call "command /c vol"
        }

MainMenu :
    menu "Main Menu"    {
        "DOS services"      DOSMenu,
        "File"              FilesMenu,
        "Planning"          Empowerment,
        "_",
        ...

        "Quit"              ExitEditor
        }

C:\SPRINT\UNNAMED2.SPR          Ins         10:38pm       Ln.4 of 25    Col0
```


Figure 4.6
Partial listing of customized menus.

macros are in effect one macro. The *MainMenu* macro is below the *DOSMenu* macro, which we usually regard as subordinate to a Main menu. That may seem unusual. You'll see the same thing in the main Sprint program, stored in the Sp.spm file; that is, the Sprint menu appears last, below all the other menus, the submenus. It is all one large system, one large macro, but with each menu a macro unto itself, and with the top menu compiled last. Otherwise the editor will stop for an apparent error. If the *MainMenu* is first in the system, the editor will encounter menu macros that have not yet been compiled. The editor will stop and put a message on the status line that a menu item macro is not recognized. When menu macros are organized so the lowest menus (submenus) are compiled first, by the time the editor gets to the Main menu, it recognizes menu calls. There is no compile error. Using this strategy, we don't need to make forward declarations as we did in Chapter 3.

A HOTKEY SCHEDULE

A test of the developing code showed several bugs in our DOS menu and a few bugs in the Main menu. We tested the Main menu every time we put in a new submenu. The successive refinement of *MainMenu* is especially important for us. We use the menu often and want it to work well.

When we compiled *MainMenu*, we gave it a hotkey through the Macros menu, which you may recall is reached through the Utilities menu. As we developed *MainMenu*, we applied this schedule of hotkeys:

- **Alt-M**   Main menu
- **Alt-F**   Files
- **Alt-W**   Writings
- **Alt-P**   Print
- **Alt-U**   Utilities
- **Alt-S**   Screen
- **Alt-Q**   Quit

You may remember that you can assign hotkeys to a menu item by highlighting the menu item, pressing **Ctrl-Enter**, and pressing the desired hotkey at the prompt. Our hotkeys may appear rather humdrum. But **Alt-S**, which produces the Screen Codes menu, does what otherwise might take two or three keystrokes. We need that type of quick, clean access to make our system efficient. Mind you, the **Alt-Z** combination in the original interface toggles the Codes off command from the Screen Codes menu to reveal word processing codes, but we want the entire Screen Codes menu available quickly.

MENU ITEMS THAT CALL PROGRAMS

The next item on our Main menu, *Planning*, shows that a program can be called from Sprint, indeed, from a menu item. As illustrated in the *MainMenu* code in Figure 4-5, the macro *Empowerment* is called when the menu item *Planning* is selected. The coding for *Empowerment* is

```
Empowerment :

    set QN "c:\\empower\\empower"

    set Q0"sp.exe"

    16 call"command /c" QN
```

Here's a line-by-line explanation of the macro. The first line is the macro name. The second line puts the name of a directory, empower, and a program, also named empower, in a memory buffer. Memory buffers are explained in Chapter 5. The third line loads the Sprint editor. The 16 in the last line is an argument that tells the *call* macro to free memory Sprint otherwise would use; this gives the called program plenty of room.

Detailed explanations of the various commands are in Chapters 5 and 6. We reproduce this code only to show that Sprint can call an external program directly from a menu. The program, developed by

Seyer Associates, organizes business and personal matters, so we call the menu item *Planning*. When *Empowerment* finishes, Sprint restarts itself and reclaims the memory it needs.

OPENING DIRECTORIES AND FILES FROM MENUS

The *Projects* item from the new *MainMenu* starts the *ProjectsMenu* macro. Figure 4.7 shows the code loaded into the Sprint editor. This menu item shows how you can call a directory from a menu. The purpose of the menu item is to quickly provide a directory suited for any of three projects, so any relevant file in a directory can be opened. That way we don't need to remember file names for our projects, or even directory names. Note that in this menu, as in the previous example, coding directly follows menu items. *Sprint book*, for example, is

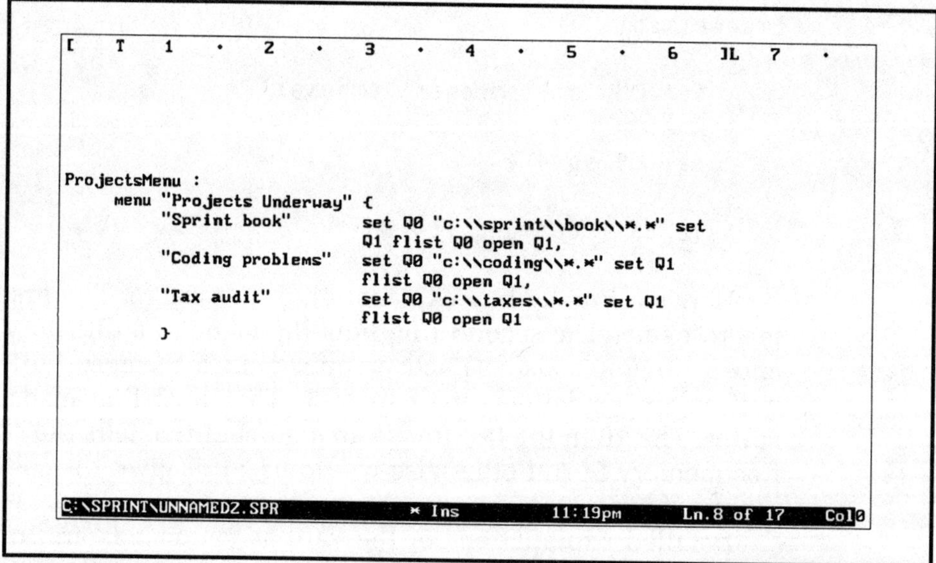

Figure 4.7
Code for *ProjectsMenu*.

directly followed by macros that put a directory for the book in a memory buffer, then draw a menu of files from which we select one that the macro opens. The same coding is used for the two other menu items in the Projects menu.

On the screen, the *Projects menu* looks like Figure 4.8. The figure shows cascading menus, that is, one menu opening below another.

So far, just a little coding and organization have produced, a customized Main menu, a second menu that pulls together rather dissimilar projects, and a subdirectory listing for one of the projects, from which we can be reminded of unfinished files or quickly select another file for work.

The *Writings* item on the Main menu copies the idea in the *Projects* item. Subdirectories are called by the macros after the menu item, as shown in Figure 4.9. A point to remember when working with macro code is that the backslash that signifies a directory or subdirectory in DOS must be a double backslash, \\ , in macros, because the single backslash is a reserved character in Sprint. For example, we use \n to indicate a newline character.

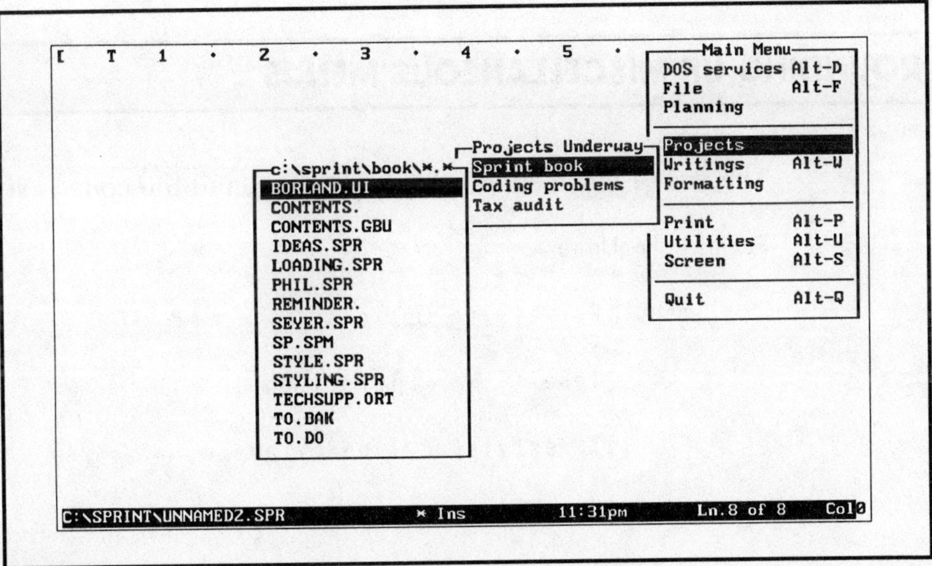

Figure 4.8
Cascading menus.

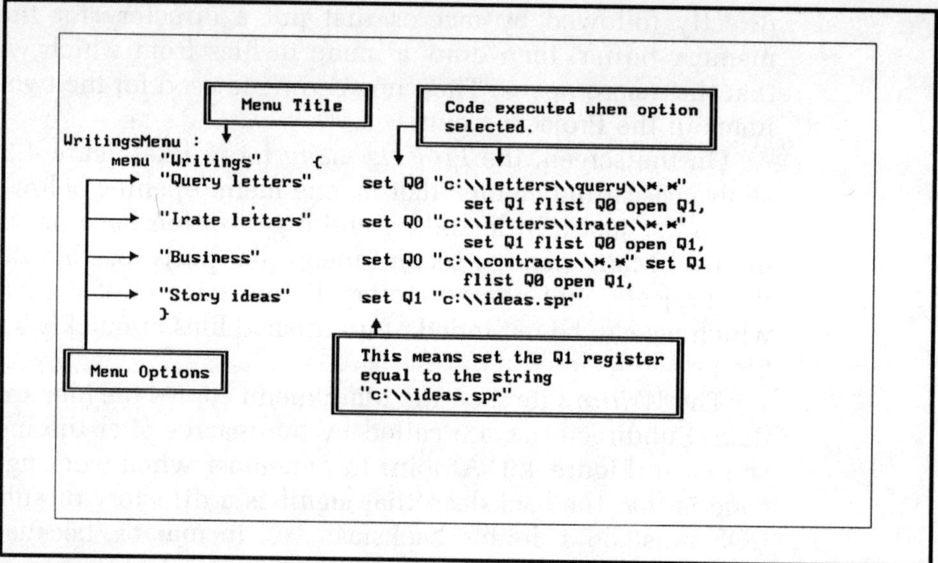

Figure 4.9
Code for the *WritingsMenu*.

ROUNDING UP MISCELLANEOUS MENUS

The last of our menus is for formatting, and the code is simple:

```
FormattingMenu :

    menu "Formatting Options"{

        "Insert"        InsertMenu,

        "Typestyle"     TypeStyleMenu,

        "Style"         StyleMenu,

        "Layout"        LayoutMenu

    }
```

Figure 4.10 shows how all of the code fits together in a single .spm file.

If we did not include this menu, which incorporates items found in the Sprint menu, we couldn't get to the Variable command, because we couldn't open the Insert menu. (Well, we could issue a command for the menu from the status line by using **Shift-Alt-X**, but someone else on our system certainly wouldn't know that.) Only by opening the Insert menu, or assigning the Variable menu to a hotkey in advance, could we get to the Variable menu. Figure 4.11 shows the chain of menus involved—the Insert menu and two of its three children. Refer to Figure 4.10 for a listing of all of the macros we have discussed. We may want to type it into a file called Custmenu.spm, for example, and then compile it.

We couldn't show you all three menus that open below the Insert menu because the second one erases when the third one is called. The Pick Variable menu is followed by a Template menu. The point is that visual access to all those menus is lost if the Insert menu is dropped from a customized user interface. We could:

- Copy the coding for the Insert menu and its children from the original code.
- Separately compile the menus.
- Give them names.
- Call them at will with a menu shortcut hotkey.

But why bother? By including one menu item in our new Main menu, called *Formatting*, we can open a window to all of the menus: Insert, Style, Typestyle, and Layout—and all the children of these menus.

This technique has consigned about a third of the Sprint standard interface to a single menu item, *Formatting*. We think it's fitting, because we get into those menus infrequently. Conceivably, we could organize all the Sprint menus below a single Main menu item, *Sprint*, and dedicate the rest of the customized menus to special applications.

We recommend that you leave intact our final Main menu item, *Quit*. Otherwise you would have to separately compile and execute the *ExitEditor* macro called by the *Quit* menu item. If you don't make an orderly exit from Sprint via the *ExitEditor* macro, your overlay, swap, and glossary files won't be updated, and you would lose work, or you could overwrite good work with outdated material.

```
        DosMenu :
              menu "DOS Commands"        {

                        "DOS Prompt"              1 call "command /c command",
                        "APPEND"                  1 call "command /c append",
                        "BREAK"                   1 call "command /c break",
                        "CHECK DISK"              1 call "command /c chkdsk",
                        "DATE"                    1 call "command /c date",
                        "DIRECTORY"               1 call "command /c dir",
                        "FIXED DISK"              1 call "command /c fdisk",
                        "GRAPHIC CHARS"           1 call "command /c graftabl",
                        "GRAPHICS"                1 call "command /c graphics",
                        "DISPLAY JOINS"           1 call "command /c join",
                        "LABEL"                   1 call "command /c label",
                        "DISPLAY PATH"            1 call "command /c path",
                        "DISPLAY ENVIRON"         1 call "command /c set",
                        "TIME"                    1 call "command /c time",
                        "TREE OF DIRECTORY"       1 call "command /c ver",
                        "DISPLAY VERSION"         1 call "command /c ver",
                        "VOLUME LABEL"            1 call "command /c vol"
                        }


        ProjectsMenu :
              menu "Projects Underway"           {
                        "Sprint book"            set Q0 "c:\\sprint\\book\\*.*"
                                                 set Q1 flist Q0 open Q1,
                        "Coding problems"        set Q0 "c:\\coding\\*.*"
                                                 set Q1 flist Q0 open Q1,
                        "Tax audit"              set Q0 "c:\\taxes\\*.*"
                                                 set Q1 flist Q0 open Q1
                        }

        WritingsMenu :
              menu "Writings" {
                        "Query letters"          set Q0 "c:\\letters\\query\\*.*"
                                                 set Q1 flist Q0 open Q1,
                        "Irate letters"          set Q0 "c:\\letters\\irate\\*.*"
                                                 set Q1 flist Q0 open Q1,
                        "Business"               set Q0 "c:\\contracts\\*.*"
                                                 set Q1 flist Q0 open Q1,
                        "Story ideas"            set Q1 "c:\\ideas.spr"
                        }


        FormattingMenu :
              menu "Formatting Options"          {

                        "Insert"                 InsertMenu,
                        "Typestyle"              TypeStyleMenu,
                        "Style"                  StyleMenu,
                        "Layout"                 LayoutMenu
                        }

        MainMenu :
              menu      "Main Menu"        {
                        "DOS services"           DOSMenu,
                        "File"                   FilesMenu,
                        "Planning"               Empowerment,
                        " ",
                        "Projects"               ProjectsMenu,
                        "Writings"               WritingsMenu,
                        "Formatting"             FormattingMenu,
                        " ",
                        "Print"                  PrintMenu,
                        "Utilities"              UtilitiesMenu,
                        "Screen"                 ScreenMenu,
                        " ",
                        "Quit"                   ExitEditor
                        }
```

Figure 4.10
Complete code for customized interface.

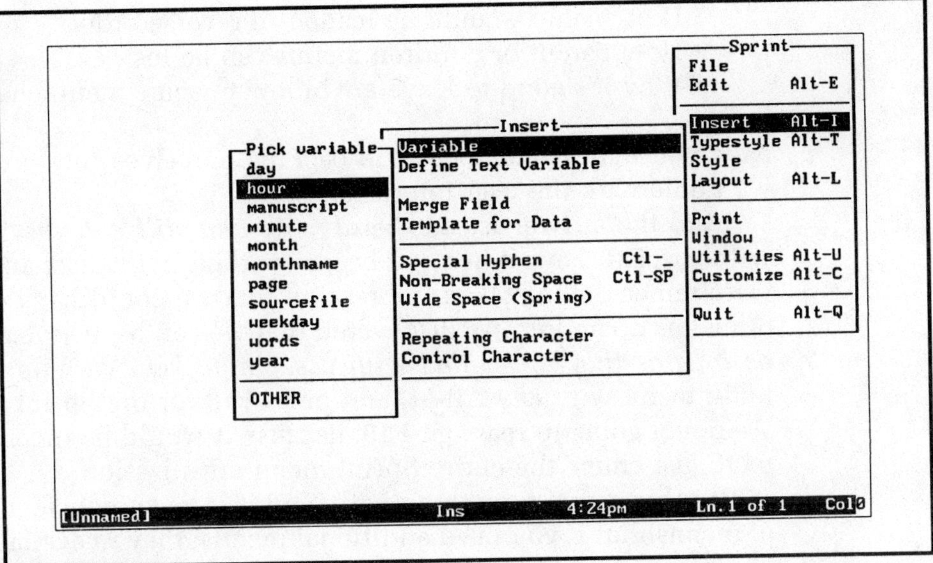

Figure 4.11
The insert menu chain.

PROMOTING A CHILD MENU

The last three commands on our new Main menu are straightforward. We borrowed the *Print* menu item and the *Utilities* menu item from the Sprint menu. They preserve the chain of related menus that we use frequently in program development. The *Screen* menu item in our new Main menu is a child of the Customize menu. We brought it to the top because we frequently turn on screen codes to look for coding mistakes, unexpected carriage returns, and ASCII characters creeping through the night.

We offer this arrangement as an example of sacrificing a parent menu to have the child menu. We made moderate use of the Customize menu and its children, but we made such frequent use of the Screen menu that we'd do without all of them just to get screen codes on and off quickly.

That completes our rearrangement of the Main menu. You've seen:

- How menus should be loaded in reverse order.
- How parent or children menus can be lost.
- Why it's good to leave a window to some menu chains.

Now you may wonder if we're backing ourselves into a corner when we fiddle with the user interface.

And the answer is, not hardly. *We can still call the Sprint menu with the* **F10** *key.* When we began working with user interfaces, we were under the mistaken impression that we could have only one set of menus operating. We discovered that we can have several menu sets *as long as they are called with a separate key.* We pop up our new Main menu with key **Alt-M**, and press **F10** for the Sprint Main menu. We're not going to reassign **F10**, because it would be inconceivable for us to just chuck the entire Sprint menu organization.

It takes a while working with Sprint to even consider another set of menus. But if you need additional menus, they're available, and you can keep your old system, too.

USING SPRINT WITH A HOST SYSTEM

We think the most interesting application of customized menus and personalized user interfaces is to make Sprint more compatible with systems that may not use DOS—in networks running the Tops program, in VAX and Honeywell systems, in systems that are operated by mainframes, or through Unix environments.

Our experience with these network issues suggests that if Sprint can pass or process ASCII strings, those strings can be evaluated or converted to system commands on a host machine. We found little difficulty, for example, customizing XyWrite to issue system commands for a VAX/VMS environment, or using WordPerfect as an offline line editor for ASCII files uploaded to an IBM CMS system, or creating ASCII files with FrameWork that eventually could be exchanged with a MacIntosh SE.

One advantage offered by Sprint is that certain functions and string-handling routines can be built right into the main menu. Even context-sensitive help can be added. So a sort routine or a database query, crucial for editing large indexes on a large systems, might be issued from the local word processor by a novice. Sprint has the potential to serve many needs with a variety of interfaces, and to serve many systems with simple menus and windows.

WHERE WE'VE BEEN, WHERE WE'RE GOING
In this chapter you learned how to customize menus within Sprint. In the next chapter you will learn to customize a file system. We'll take you through macro code that will summon often used files, at the push of a button. You will be well on your way to an electronic personal office.

Chapter 5

Cursor Control, Q Registers, and Hypertext

In this chapter we explain some of the mechanics of the Sprint language and also delve into some of the intangibles of Sprint macro programming style. We'll discuss cursor control, primitive and coded macros, and Q registers. Although you won't know all the rules of the Sprint language when you have finished this chapter, you will have enough expertise to begin expressing yourself as a Sprint macro programmer. Also, you'll have a productivity-boosting macro that you can use to transform Sprint into a hypertext editor. We think you'll find this chapter both amusing and informative.

MANAGING THE CURSOR

Before you can write effective macros, you need to be proficient at using cursors. In some macros, we use the cursor to mark a specific area of a file. In these macros we often evaluate an expression above the cursor. In other macros, we may want to move the cursor to an area of text that the user has previously selected, searched, or sorted.

We'll start by looking at some simple cursor commands. Although they may seem elementary to you, keep in mind that they are the nuts and bolts of strong, clean macros.

Moving Forward One Character

The simplest cursor macro is *c*. To tell the cursor to move forward one character, you simply write:

```
c
```

Let's test this macro. Press **Shift-Alt-X** and enter:

```
c
```

Notice that when you execute the macro the cursor will hop forward one space. You may want to repeat the macro a few times to watch the cursor animation.

Reversing the Cursor Direction

Now let's try another simple macro, which reverses the direction of cursor movement. The macro is simply *r*. To try this, press **Shift-Alt-X** and enter:

```
r c
```

You will see the cursor reverse—move one space to the left.

Extended Cursor Movement

You can make the cursor move several characters with a *to* macro. Sprint has several of these. A common one is

```
toeol
```

This just moves the cursor to the *end-of-line*. Test the *toeol* macro in the same way. Does the new macro move the cursor exactly to the last character on the line? (Check your answer with the discussion below.)

This macro may seem to take the cursor past the last character. For example, if you have Sprint set so it does not show spaces and carriage returns, you won't see the space or carriage return at the end of the line. But in fact, *toeol* does move the cursor to the end of the current line—but the end of the line is usually either a carriage return or space, which may be invisible. Recall that you can display spaces or carriage returns by issuing the Screen command on the Customize menu. **Alt-C S** will take you there. For now we suggest you set codes and spaces to On.

Checking the Current Character

When you are moving the cursor around, it is often useful to be able to tell which character the cursor is on. Here is a trick you may find useful. To find the ASCII code for the character pointed to by the cursor, just do this:

1. Press **Shift-Alt-X**
2. Enter **Current** =
3. Press **Enter**

Sprint will execute the macro called *current*, which returns the ASCII value for the character above the cursor. You can get it in hexadecimal format, too, if you want. Just enter **Current** = **"%x"** at the prompt. If you want it in octal format, then enter **Current** = **"%o"**.

Figure 5.1 illustrates how to check the current character. We executed the *toeol* macro and then the *current* macro by using **Shift-Alt-X**. Notice that Sprint displays the value 31. Sprint uses this code as a soft return.

The Point Concept

The Sprint Advanced User's Guide says that a *point* is "a position in the text where editing occurs." Actually, a point is a position *between* two characters. If there is only one character in a file, and the point is at the beginning of the file, the point will be before that first character.

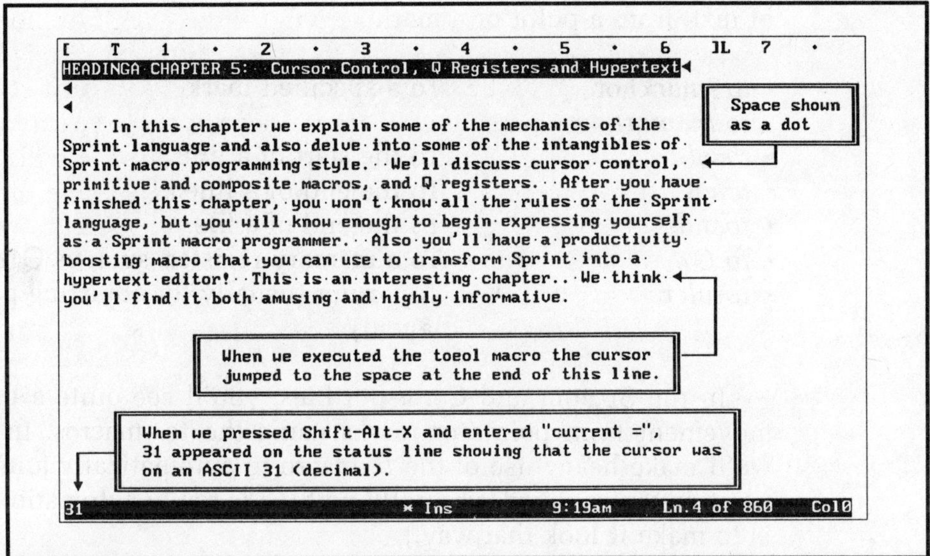

Figure 5.1
Testing the toeol macro.

The point moves with the cursor. The point is always just to the left of the character the cursor is on. If this seems a bit abstract, that's because it is.

The Point and the Mark

It's often necessary to mark a position in a file or a text so you can return to it later. Marks can help you sort, select, and edit data. To enable you to save your position in a file, Sprint provides 17 marks as well as several macro commands to manipulate marks. A mark, like a point, rests between two characters. You can assign Mark0 through Mark9, and MarkA through MarkF. There also is a special global mark, gmark. You can read more about marks and points in the Appendix D.

Handy Cursor Commands

You've already learned three cursor commands: *c*, *r*, and *toeol*. Here is a list of other handy cursor commands that handle lines or long strings of text, from a point or a mark:

- *to (mark)* or   To a specified mark.
  to themark
- *tosol*   To the start of a line.
- *toeol*   To the end of a line.
- *toend*   To the end of a file.
- *to Q1*   To a memory register, such as Q1.
- *toruler*   To a ruler (usually for adjusting page layout).

In the Sp.spm and Core.spm files, you'll see quite a bit of cursor movement from points or marks using the *to-* macros. In Chapter 7, we'll make heavy use of the *to* macro to automatically jump back to a position we've saved. (Actually nothing is really automatic, but our job is to make it look that way.)

Now let's do another cursor movement experiment. In a text file, use the **F3** and the **right arrow** keys to select and highlight one or more lines of text. When you highlight text in this way, Sprint will put the cursor just after the highlighted text and the point just to the left of the cursor, at the end of the highlighted text. Now using **Shift-Alt-X**, execute this command:

```
c to themark
```

When you execute the macro, the cursor returns to the beginning of the selected text, and the highlighting disappears. It is just as if you had pressed the left arrow key to back up the cursor to the beginning of the highlighting.
(Note: The select block function is still active, though. So if you move the cursor, you will again start highlighting text. To turn off highlighting, press **Shift-Alt-X** and enter:

```
0 ->Select
```

Select is a handy global variable that controls whether on-screen highlighting is active. The 0-› Select command moves a zero into *Select* and thereby turns off highlighting.

Now, let's consider what happened when you pressed **F3**. Sprint set Select to 1 and also saved your position in the file by setting a mark (which we can refer to as *themark*). When you moved the cursor to highlight the text, the point moved along with the cursor. When you finished highlighting the text, the point was at the end of the text. **Note:** The area between the point and the mark is the *region*.

Because *Select* was set to 1, Sprint highlighted the region. The cursor (and the point) reversed to themark when we issued the command:

```
c to themark
```

To- macros and *mark* macros can manipulate the cursor as effectively as *c* and *r* macros. Let's take a break now from cursor control and look at one of Borland's inventions: Q registers.

ABOUT Q REGISTERS

Sprint calls and passes filenames through Q registers. Sprint's authors call these Q registers string variables. You can think of them as places in memory that hold text or strings or the result of some operation. Whatever they're called, they're drawers in memory where Sprint can store text for current processing or for later use.

You can stuff an entire file of virtually any length into a Q register!

It's important to you, as a Sprint programmer, to understand how to use these registers. Some are dedicated to handling files or storing messages, while others are available for your own routines. You can find a listing of registers and their assignments on the first page of the Core.spm and the Sp.spm programs. There are 26 Q registers in all, as shown in Figure 5.2. Remember that there is a register Q0 (Q zero) as well as a register QO.

The primary register is Q0 (Q zero). Several macros use Q0 to store important file names. If you look inside this register from time to time (we'll show you how later), you'll often see Spedit.exe (also named Sp.exe in version 1.0). Spedit.exe is the main Sprint program.

Figure 5.2
Use of Q Registers.

Register	Use
Q0	Used for anything that requires a filename. Some macros use it as a work area.
Q1	Used for anything that requires a filename
Q2	Used to hold search string or string to replace
Q3	Used to hold replacement string
Q4	Used for environment modifiers, and formatter commands
Q5	Used for DOS commands and formatter calls
Q6	Used for DOS commands and formatter calls
Q7	Used for environment names and style dimensions
Q8	Used for getting text for footnotes and formatter commands
Q9	Used by help system
QA	Used by glossary and holds current name
QB	Used by glossary and holds glossary
QC	Used by glossary scratch
QD	Used as a general work area
QE	Used by spelling checker and holds bad word stack
QF	Used to collect keystrokes for replay
QG	Reserved by WordPerfect emulation macros
QH	Used by *column* macro
QI	Used for macro entry
QJ	Holds current Speller engine parameters
QK	Holds a record containing Spmerge
QL	Reserved
QM	Reserved
QN	Unassigned
QO	Unassigned
QP	Unassigned

At one time or another, Q0 holds the name of every file you use. Its companions are Q1 and QD. Q1 is a partner that also holds filenames. When Q0 and Q1 need to swap contents, QD holds intermediate results. QD also carries messages to the user.

Q5 is interesting; it holds the last DOS command executed. For example, if you go to the Utilities menu, choose DOS Command, and then enter a command, Sprint will save it in the Q5 register. (That's why Sprint is able to remember your previous DOS command.)

Sprint lets us peek into any register whenever we feel the urge.

Here's an experiment. Press **Alt-U D** and enter some harmless DOS command, such as **dir**. After you return to Sprint, press **Shift-Alt-X** and then enter **Q5**. Sprint will display the DOS command that you just gave.

Sprint uses Q2 and Q3 for string-handling. Q6 is for formatter calls.

If you look into Q6, you'll often see a filename such as spfmt, a formatting file. The rest of the registers are special-purpose, or unassigned.

We like to use the Q4, Q7, and Q9 registers for some macros. They're near the top of the register list and Sprint doesn't use them too often. Q4 and Q7, you can see from the register list, are for DOS environment variables; Q9 is usually available because you rarely have a help menu on the screen. We use the Q4 and Q7 registers to hold the character string from our last operation. They are rather unconnected to Q0, Q1, and QD, where most of the action is. We warn you not to imitate the Sprint coding practice and make extensive use of the Q0, Q1, and QD registers—if you do, you'll find it difficult to get unambiguous results.

For example, after an operation involving file-handling, you might expect to see some result in Q0; but if you try to peep into Q0, Sprint may have already changed its contents. Not so with the Q4, Q7, and Q9 registers; when you peer inside them, you can expect to find a value that you put there. To be on the safe side we like to use the QN, QO, and QP registers to do our hacking, because they are completely unassigned.

You can use **Shift-Alt-X** to look into registers. Then you can debug macros as you go, because you can build the code slowly, checking registers for accurate execution of experimental routines. If a register contains a lot of text, you may want to go all the way inside it. You can do that, too:

1. Press **Shift-Alt-X**.
2. Enter **to ‹register name›**.
3. Press **Ctrl-F9** and choose a file to return to.

We add one final note. A point is in every Q-register. If the register is empty, perhaps cleared with a command such as Set Q4"" (with nothing between the quotes), the point is at the beginning of the register. What if you wrote to the register with the line:

Set Q4 "Now is the time for all programmers to meditate."

The point still will be at the start of the register. That way, if you select the entire contents of the register, to move it elsewhere, Sprint will pick up everything from the start (the point) to the end (the mark).

CODED MACROS VERSUS PRIMITIVES

Remember, if a macro is built into Sprint, we call it a primitive. If we can look at the source code for a macro, we call it a coded macro. The Sprint editor uses coded macros extensively and calls nine of them automatically. Here is an example of the *Restart* coded macro:

```
Restart :

    NormalMode

    if (exist "log.$$$") {

        draw pageread "log.$$$"

        fdelete "log.$$$"

    }

        while keypressed key    ; eliminate type-ahead
```

After a pagination operation, *Restart* is called automatically.

The other eight automatically called macros are *Bell*, *DoHelp*, *EditKey*, *GetKey*, *Init*, *InitArg*, *Main*, and *MenuKey*. Notice that we start coded macros with a capital letter. We write primitives in all lowercase. You can find a listing of many of Borland's coded macros in the Core.spm and Sp.spm files.

Unfortunately there is some confusion among users talking about macros. Generally a macro is a series of actions that a user can start by pressing a single key. That's why we call Sprint Glossary items "macros" even if they are just keyboard recordings. Sprint documentation and the program refer to both primitives and coded constructs as macros. You can distinguish primitives from larger constructions only if you know most of the primitives, know some of the coded macros, or look for a capitalized letter in the name. Remember that you *cannot* get to the source code of primitive macros and modify them. You can, however, create and modify the coded macros.

If you load the Core.spm program, paginate it, and send it to your printer, you'll have a page-by-page listing of coded macros as well as a good syntax guide to the use of primitives. By using the *F7* search key, you can isolate useful coded macros. One that seems to recur in our work is

```
CheckWild : mark (qswitch ('*' csearch || ('?' r csearch)))
```

Like other coded macros, *CheckWild* must have its name flush left. Notice that the name contains capital letters and is followed by a colon. After the macro name comes a combination of other macros.

In this case, *CheckWild* marks a place in the text, switches to a register (specified earlier), and then moves the cursor through the register to look for any '*' wildcard character. Next it moves backward (toward the start-of-file) for the other '?' wildcard character. *Csearch* means search in the current direction with the cursor.

This macro also illustrates the levels of nesting possible in a command as short as one line. *'?' r csearch* is nested the deepest. See Figure 5.3. The *'?' r csearch* macro is within an expression that asks

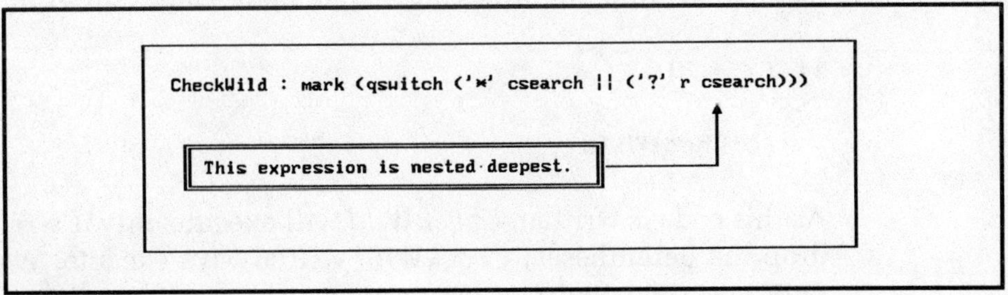

Figure 5.3
Nesting of '?' r csearch.

```
        SaveSetup :
           do   (
                set Q0 "" message "\nSave setup in file: " set Q0
                if (!length Q0)
                   stopped error "You must give the setup file a name."
                else if (0 CheckWild)
                stopped error "Wildcards are not allowed."
                else {
                   set Q0 fchange "%.UI" Q0
                   if (!(32 exist Q0) || ask "Overwrite existing file?")
                      {
                      ovlwrite Q0
                      break
                      }
                   }
                )
```

Figure 5.4
Extensive nesting.

Sprint to test for one condition ('*' csearch) and, if it is false, to test the other condition. Those tests, in turn, are nested within a *qswitch* macro, indicating the operations are to be performed in the register.

Figure 5.4 gives an example of extensive nesting. It is a coded macro that saves your setup in the overlay file. It is a good example of macros and macro strings.

There are three levels of nesting and a fourth level in which expressions such as *0 CheckWild* are enclosed in delimiters. *0 CheckWild* means: "in register Q0, check to see if there are any wildcard characters." The example is offered to show that in coded macros, or strings of macros, you must enclose some commands with delimiters (parentheses, braces, etc.). Use nesting and delimiters if you are looping a routine or if you are writing commands that require evaluation. It is especially important to use them after an if-statement so that the delimited commands will function as a single statement. Here's an example:

```
if (x = 3)


    (0 CheckWild).
```

As this code is written, *CheckWild* will execute only if $x = 3$. But if you drop the parentheses, *CheckWild* will always execute. Why? Because only one statement can be contingent on an if-condition. The syntax for an if-statement, here, is

```
if (condition) statement
```

This is identical to the syntax used in C. Even though you can have only one statement contingent on an if-condition, that statement can be compound and contain many commands. To make Sprint interpret a set of commands as a single statement, you must surround them with delimiters. In Sprint macro programming, the 0 is, in itself, a statement that sets the current argument to zero. So 0 CheckWild is really two statements. That's why we must write (0 CheckWild) so that Sprint interprets this code as a single compound statement.

We found many examples of delimiter usage in Core.spm and Sp.spm. The coded macros from these files are quite useful; we check the listings regularly for little routines we can use. For example, we frequently use this one:

```
AllCaps :                ; uppercase Qx

   mark {qswitch while  !isend ToUpper}
```

AllCaps simply marks our place in another routine, *qswitches* to a register, and while not at the end of the file, it converts the register contents to uppercase. Borland abbreviates this routine "uppercase Qx." Qswitches to a register means place the point at the start of a specified register. Which Q register will *qswitch* switch to? It will switch to the register specified by the current argument.

Programming Sprint macros, then, boils down to:

- Managing the cursor in text and in Q registers.
- Looking at the schedule of memory registers used by the code.
- Developing original tools.
- Knowing macro primitives.
- Knowing that some coded macros are important.
- Understanding how macros pass and receive arguments.
- Appreciating structure and syntax.
- Borrowing and modifying code whenever possible.

We're going to do that now, developing a hypertext macro we call *FindFile.spm*.

DEVELOPING HYPERTEXT WITH SPRINT MACROS

Introduction to Hypertext

Hypertext, simply defined, is nonlinear text on computer screens. More precisely, hypertext is a network of linked nodes. Think of a node as a chunk of text organized around a single topic or ideas. A node is often limited to a screenful of text, although this is not always the case. A node may correspond to a DOS file or it may be a part of a DOS file. Within each node there are special words or graphic images that act as buttons. When you put the cursor on a button and press a designated hotkey, the system brings up the node specified by the button. The new node may fill the entire screen or appear in a small pop-up window. Sometimes a button triggers a sequence of instructions; for example, a button may dial a phone number, display a graphic image or an animation sequence, and activate recorded or synthesized speech.

Many users are gravitating to hypertext because it allows them to organize data the way they think—in an associative way. For example, while typing notes to develop an idea about some project, one idea may trigger another related idea. Instead of having to disrupt work on the current project, the user can simply create a button that links the current node to related text in another node. Once the user forges a link between two nodes, it remains until the user decides to remove it. Later, while referring to a node, a user can easily pop into a linked node simply by putting the cursor on a node reference (a button) and pressing a hotkey.

Guide and HyperCard on the Macintosh were probably the first hypertext systems to appear on micro computers. Recently several PC application programs have begun to include hypertext capability. For example, HyperPAD, askSam, EMPOWERment, Guide 2, HyperTSR, LinkWay, Black Magic, Hyperbase, PC-Browse, and KnowledgePro all allow users to create hypertext networks.

It is interesting to note that the concept of hypertext is not new. In a 1945 article entitled "As We May Think," Vannevar Bush advocated the development of a hypertext system he called "The Memex." To get an idea of how hypertext works, imagine that you are reading some instructions on screen and that certain words are highlighted. This may mean that these words are buttons and that some extra text (hypertext) is hidden behind these buttons. Often a good use for hypertext is to explain key terms. That helps make the documentation concise. If readers need the definition of the highlighted words, they can easily get to it by pressing a hypertext button.

Using the power of Sprint macros, it doesn't take much code to transform Sprint into a useful hypertext system! (In a real sense, such a system is superior to many other hypertext systems because it is simultaneously a powerful word processor and a hypertext system.) In this and subsequent chapters we will show you how we did just that. With the *FindFile*, you will be able to put the cursor on any word in a master file and instantly jump into the file named by that word. This enables you to link one file to another in hypertext fashion. You can also put the cursor on a drive or path specification, like **A:** or, **C:\letters**, and *FindFile* will present a menu of files to choose from. You can also include wildcards if you like. After jumping into a related file, you can return to the original file by pressing **Ctrl-F4**.

If the named file doesn't exist, Sprint will ask you if you want to create it. With this capability, you can almost instantly increase your productivity. For example, create a control file. In the control file you can list several other files along with a description of each file. To jump into any one file, just point to it with the cursor and press the appropriate hotkey.

You may not appreciate the usefulness of this arrangement until you try it. The advantage is that you need not remember file names or memorize what they contain. Instead, you just:

1. Refer to an organized set of document descriptions.
2. Select the appropriate document by pointing to it with the cursor.
3. Press a hotkey.

Hypertext has other advantages. It helps you see the big picture. Because categorization and organization is so natural with hypertext, it could even change the way you think. In fact, some hypertext users find that their thinking and work become more organized.

```
OpenFile :
     if (1 checkwild)           ; if a default file mask exists
          set Q0 Q1
     else set Q0 ""
     do     {
          message "\nFile to open: " set Q0
          0 AllCaps
          ; a hack to allow '/foo/', and 'a:' to pop a directory up
          mark {
                    to Q0
                    toend r c
                    if (current = '\\' || current = '/' || current = ':') {
                              c insert "*.SPR"          ; add default mask
                              }
          } ; end of hack
          if length Q0
                    set Q1 flist Q0
          else set Q1 flist "*.SPR"          ; so Q0 remains empty
          if !length Q1     {                ; no files matched
                    set QD "No files match '"
                    mark (to QD toend insert Q0 insert "'.")
                    stopped error QD
                    }
          else
          if (buffind Q1) break
          else if (exist Q1) {
                    open Q1
                    StartFile
                    break
                    }
          else {   ; add extension of .SPR if none:
                    1 SetSPRext
                    if (buffind Q1) break
                    else if (32 exist Q1) {
                              open Q1
                              StartFile
                              break
                              }
                    else if (message "\nCreate new file " message Q1 ask "? ") {
                              if !stopped {open Q1 DefaultRuler} {
                                        break
                                        }
                              }}
          }
     set Q1 Q0            ; preserve mask for next time
     mark{
          r bufswitch
          if (!modf && IsUnnamed && IsOnlyRuler) close
          }
```

Figure 5.5
The OpenFile macro.

We Were Stumped

When we started to develop this hypertext macro, we were clueless. We were so uninformed about it that we just went to the Core.spm code and used the **F7** search key to look for the word, "open". We found 43 references. One was the long, deeply nested example shown in Figure 5.5.

This coded macro is 51 lines and involves dozens of commands. We decided to edit the *OpenFile* routine and to substitute macro primitives where they might accomplish our purpose. In programming books you will see neatly drawn examples of routines that run efficiently the first time. When we started experimenting with this code, we produced a horrendous mess with little difficulty. That's because we broke an elementary programming rule:

When you are first modifying OPC (other people's code), start by cutting the code to a kernel that will run, and then enlarge that kernel.

We also got off to a slow start because it just takes time to get used to the rhythms of any language. We're going to toss embarrassment aside and show you the mistakes we made. We hope this will help you avoid these same goofs in your own work.

Watching the Modifiers and the Registers

Our first mistake was misreading the *OpenFile* macro shown in Figure 5.5. We thought the 1 CheckWild expression on the second line meant, If CheckWild is True (nonzero). We also thought the expression 0 Allcaps meant that *Allcaps* should be set False (the string should be converted to lowercase). We also thought *mark* applied only to registers. Wrong. Wrong. Wrong.

0 Allcaps means capitalize the text that is in register Q0. (3 Allcaps would mean to capitalize the text in register Q3.) The 1 CheckWild command means to check to see if the string in register Q1 contains wildcards.

Another thing—although it is explained in some detail in the documentation—we didn't fully realize that *mark* and its kindred macros often mark locations in the current text as well as in any register. We could have set up simple tests and looked into registers. But we didn't. Instead, we lurched into deeply nested code.

An interesting part of the *OpenFile* coded macro is shown in Figure 5.6. We thought that "if (current = '\\'..." referred to some arcane subdirectory, like the expressions current = '/' and current = ':'. We couldn't understand why a mark was set. It took some work before we realized that this code merely detects *symbols* of a directory path in a filename, so it can produce the relevant directory. Eventually we also realized why we must set a mark while checking for a directory of a filename; the reason is because checking a path occurs in a specific

```
                    ; a hack to allow '/foo/', and 'a:' to pop a directory up
                    mark {
                        to Q0
                        toend r c
                        if (current = '\\' || current = '/' || current = ':') {
                            c insert "*.SPR"   ; add default mask
                        }
                    } ; end of hack
```

Figure 5.6
Interesting part of OpenFile macro.

register, while other operations happen in several different registers, on the status line, or on disk.

We wasted a lot of time on the last paragraph of *OpenFile*, which reads

```
set Q1 Q0; preserve mask for next time

mark{

    r bufswitch

    if (!modf && IsUnnamed && IsOnlyRuler) close

}
```

It merely closes a file that had been opened, but had not been used. We finally threw the paragraph away, thinking that it added some error checking that we didn't need.

We were stuck for a while on expressions such as:

```
else set Q0 " "
```

It merely clears the Q0 register; it sets it to . . . nothing. It's important to clear a register before you use it, lest you get an unexpected result.

A lot of our confusion came from deciphering lines that contained multiple commands. We were puzzled by the line:

```
message "\nFile to open: " set Q0
```

The *message* macro just displays a message on the status line. The set

Q0 expression is really a separate command. Normally *set* takes two arguments. But if the second argument is missing, Sprint will wait for the user to enter it from the keyboard. So this line puts a message on the status line, prompts for input, and then takes the input and sets the Q0 register to the string entered by the user.

You can try these expressions interactively if you like. For example, press **Shift-Alt-X** and then enter **message "\nFile to open: " set Q0**. Sprint will display the message "File to open:" and wait for you to enter some text. If you try this, you will notice that Sprint also displays the current contents of Q0.

Reading a Word from the Screen

The dialect may seem clear to those who write and work in Sprint macros, but we remember it as slow going at first. So, lost in this thicket of register semantics, we finally surrendered. We just tried to get Sprint to read a word on the screen and then plug it in, somehow, to the *OpenFile* coded macro. The result was an unqualified disaster.

First, we tried to use the Q0 and Q1 registers, like the Borland programmers do, but we discovered that in the process of writing and executing our test macro we were unintentionally loading and unloading those registers. Every time we thought we had successfully passed a filename to register Q0 we would try to dump the register and find it empty. We tried to use Q1 and pass the filename back and forth with Q0, like a shell game. We were hoping to trap our target in one of the registers, and then somehow backtrack into the desired code. No go.

We also had a rough time getting Sprint to read a word from the screen. We wrote several variations of a one-line macro that got the cursor to

- Find a letter string that actually is a word.
- Reverse to the beginning of the word.
- Move forward through the word.
- Write the word to memory.

One day, on a search-and-destroy mission through Core.spm, we discovered *SelectWord*, a coded macro that has two more coded macros nested in it. At the lowest level is *WordFwd*, a coded macro that just advances the cursor to the end of a word. At the next level is *MaybeSet*, which repeats *WordFwd* but trims trailing and leading spaces from a word. The entire routine also tests for end-of-file.

In the first few versions of *FindFile*, *SelectWord* seemed to serve well as a subroutine. But later we ran into a boobytrap when we enhanced the macro so that it could handle wildcards or drive specifications. When we pointed to the expression C: and fired up *Find-File*, instead of providing a dialog box with a list of filenames from the root directory, Sprint asked if we wanted to open a file with the name C.

We dumped *SelectWord* and chopped the code for picking up the filename to these lines:

```
1.       KopyWord:

2.               set Q4 " " set Q7 " "

3.               r

4.               to isgray

5.               setmark

6.               to isgray

7.               copy tomark Q4
```

The first line is a label that defines the *KopyWord* macro. *KopyWord* is actually a macro in its own right, but we use it as a subroutine or submacro. The second and third lines clear the registers and change the direction of cursor movement, respectively. The fourth line (to isgray) moves the point back to the character in front of the word. That's because the character in front of a word is a gray character. (It's difficult to explain simply what a gray character is. It may be a space, but it may be another invisible character such as a line delimiter, or a tab, etc.) So this is the situation:

```
WORD

  ↑

  ↑

point
```

The fifth line (setmark) moves the mark to the point. You can think of it like this:

```
WORD

 ↑

 ↑

mark
```

Now the mark stays where it is. But the sixth line (to isgray) moves the point forward up to the next gray character — the character after the end of the word:

```
WORD

 ↑      ↑

 ↑      ↑

mark   point
```

Now we've got the word surrounded! The area between the point and a mark is known as the region. The last line (to mark Q4) copies the region between the mark and the point into a memory location, namely the Q4 register. Line-by-line commenting of the complete *Find-File* macro appears in Figure 5.7. You might want to study the *Kopy-Word* submacro and execute this code line-by-line using **Shift-Alt-X** and see for yourself what happens. You can watch the cursor move along with the point as each command is executed. (Remember, the cursor is always to the right of the point, and the point is always between two characters.)

We set up a test file with a simple line of text, pointed with our cursor at a filename in the text, executed the *KopyWord* submacro, and then peered into register Q4. Voila! The word was there. We were on our way! Figure 5.8 shows how the status line revealed the contents of Q4 during this test of *KopyWord*.

Things rapidly improved. We shifted the filename into register Q7. That way, while debugging, we could use **Shift-Alt-X Q4** to see if the filename was copied into register Q4.

We noticed that if we pointed to a word that was styled in boldface, our macro might pick up the boldface code, **^B**, along with the filename. We developed a routine to strip control codes from any filename we might point to. We also switched operations to another memory register, Q7. We then could press **Shift-Alt-X Q7** to verify that the filename was copied from memory register Q4 to Q7, and that while in memory register Q7 the string was edited to a legal filename. See Figure 5.9.

We tested; it worked. But our macro still didn't account for all possibilities. If the legal filename included wildcard characters, we wanted to open a dialog box of filenames from which we could choose. It is possible to point to a word on screen that names an open file. In

```
; FILENAME: FINDFILE.SPM

; DATE: November 19, 1989

; The main macro in this listing is FindFile, which allows a user to
; begin editing a file by putting the cursor on a filename and pressing
; a hotke, if one has been assigned.  The filename can include wildcards
; or just the name of a drive; if so we throw up a menu of files
; to choose from.
; Forward Declarations:  We need to declare all the macros that
; Findfile will be using, since they appear later in the file.

KopyWord :
MyDelChars :
AddStars :
EditTheFile :

;*************************** FindFile ****************************

;USE:  switch editor into file pointed to by cursor

FindFile :

    KopyWord       ; Copy filename from screen into Q7 register
    MyDelChars     ; Delete any control characters from filename.
    AddStars       ; Add *.* if user gave only drive or pathname
    EditTheFile    ; Edit the file specified in Q7 register

;*************************** KopyWord ****************************

; USE: copy a word from the screen into Q4 register.

KopyWord:
                            ; Assumption: cursor is on word.
    set Q4 "" set Q7 ""     ; Clear registers,
    r                       ; Reverse direction of cursor movement
    to isgray               ; Move back to "gray" char.
    setmark                 ; Set a mark at the current point.
    to isgray               ; Move point (forward)
                            ; up to gray character,
                            ; Mark is now on left side of word,
                            ; point, on right side.

    copy tomark Q4          ; Copy the region between the point
                            ; and the mark to the Q4 register.
```

Figure 5.7
Completed hypertext macro.

```
;************************* MyDelChars ****************************

; USE Delete any control characters from filename

MyDelChars:
        4 AllCaps         ; Put filename in capitals.
        set Q7 Q4         ; Copy register Q4 to Q7
                mark
                (         ; Set a mark to work in registers

                ; In register Q7, look for Typestyle
                ; characters and delete them from the filename
                to Q7     ; move point into Q7 register.
                        if (current = '^B'|| current = '^E'||
                            current =  '^U'
                            )
                            del
                        toend if (previous = '^N') r del
                )

;***************************** AddStars ****************************

;USE: add *.* to filename if user entered only a drive or
;     pathname such as c:\sprint\

AddStars:

        mark      ; don't move cursor while doing following commands
                (
                to Q7   ;move point into Q7 register
                toend   ;go to binary zero at end of Q7 register
                r c     ;move back one cursor position

                ; If cursor is on a backward or forward slash, or
                ; a colon, insert "*.*"

                if (current = '\\' || current = '/' || current = ':')
                    (
                    c           ; go forward
                    insert "*.*" ; insert "*.*" into Q7 register
                    )

                )
; ***************************** EditTheFile **************************

; USE: edit the file whose name appears in the Q7 register.

;    NOTE: The buffind macro, which we use here will search through
;    all open buffers for the filename specified after buffind.
;    Buffind returns True if it finds the filename and the editor
;    "automatically" switches to the open file


EditTheFile:

    ;If filename contains a wildcard we just give open command
    ;This will throw up a menu of files and then switch to the
    ;file that the user picks. We use abort to bail out so the
    ;rest of this macro will not execute. Note that 7 checkwild
    ;checks for a wildcard in Q7

    if (7 checkwild) (open Q7 abort)

    if (buffind Q7) ; if file is in an open buffer, switch to it
;       no need for statement here since buffind automatically
;       switches into file if it is found in buffer
    else
        (
        ; if file exists on disk, open it and switch to it
        if (exist Q7)    ; if file exists on disk
            open Q7            ;open the file,
        else
            (
            ; ask user if she wants to create file.
            if (message "\nCreate new file " message Q7 ask "? ")
                (
                open Q7                ;open the file
                DefaultRuler           ;insert default ruler line
                )
            )
        )
```

Figure 5.7–*Continued.*

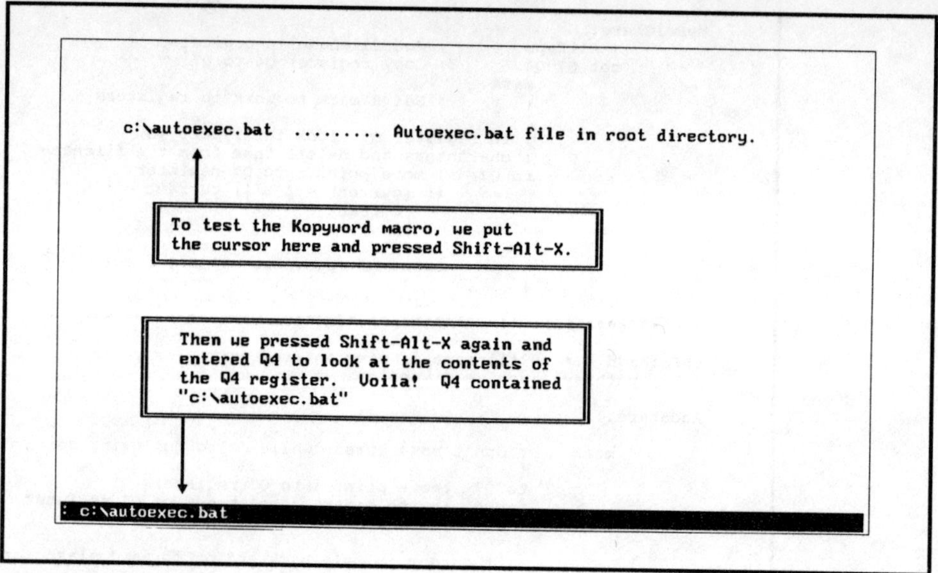

Figure 5.8

Testing of *KopyWord* macro.

```
MyDelChars:
        4 AllCaps          ; Put filename in capitals.
        set Q7 Q4          ; Copy register Q4 to Q7
             mark
             (             ; Set a mark to work in registers

        ; In register Q7, look for Typestyle
        ; characters and delete them from the filename
        to Q7     ; move point into Q7 register.
             if (current = '^B'|| current = '^E'||
                 current =  '^U'
                 )
                 del
             toend if (previous = '^N') r del
             )
```

Figure 5.9

The second subroutine of working hypertext code.

such a case we didn't want our macro to read the file on the disk, but to switch to the open file. We found we could handle this with one statement:

```
if (buffind Q7)
```

Here the *buffind* macro searches all of the open buffers, and if it finds the file named in Q7, it immediately switches the editor into that file. We put all of the commands related to opening the file into one sub-macro called *EditTheFile*:

```
EditTheFile:
    if (7 checkwild) (open Q7 abort)
    if (buffind Q7)
    else
        (
        if (exist Q7)
        open Q7
            else
                (
                if (message "\nCreate new file " message
                Q7 ask "? ")
                    { }
                    open Q7
                    DefaultRuler
                    }
                )
        )
```

In *EditTheFile*, if the filename contains a wildcard, we just give the *open* command. Whenever we pass a string containing wildcards to *open*, a menu of files appears and then switches to the file picked by the user. We use *abort* to bail out so the rest of the macro doesn't execute. Note that "*7 checkwild*" passes 7 to *checkwild* so that checkwild looks for a wildcard in Q7, where the filename resides.

If the file is already open, in a buffer, as Sprint likes to call its active files, we'd just like Sprint to switch to that active file, to that buffer. The function is achieved with if "*buffind* Q7", which means that if you find the filename in a buffer, switch to it. There is no need for any additional statement after "if" here because *buffind* automatically switches into the target file.

A third possibility in the procedure is that the file exists, but is on disk. Sprint uses the *exist* macro to check that, and we need only say, if (*exist* Q7) *open* Q7. If Sprint finds the file on disk and opens it, that automatically switches the editor into that active file, into that buffer, and ends the macro.

A final possibility in the procedure is that the file does not exist. Here we want an option to end the routine or to open a new file. If the file is not on disk, this code will execute: (*message* "\nCreate new file" *message* Q7 *ask* "? ").

That's the syntax for user input that we mentioned earlier. The *message* macro sends a string to the user. The \n in the string argument clears the status line for the message, which follows. Next we repeat the *message* macro with the contents of Q7. Q7, remember, contains the filename. Next the *ask* macro awaits a **Y** or **N** input from the user.

If the user enters **Y**, lines 13 and 14 execute. They create a new file and insert a ruler using the handy *DefaultRuler* coded macro, which we found somewhere in Sp.spm or Core.spm.

Using Forward Declarations

If you refer back to Figure 5.7, you will see that we begin with a series of forward declarations. Here, these declarations are names of macros used in the program. We sometimes refer to them as submacros because the main macro, *FindFile*, calls them as subroutines. We must declare these submacros at the beginning of the file. Otherwise, Sprint, acting as a compiler, will give an error message when it encounters a call to a macro that has not yet been defined. The format for forward declarations is strict. Each one must be on a separate line, flush left, and each must end with a colon.

Notice that in Figure 5.7 the *FindFile* macro comes immediately after the forward declarations. This macro shows the structure of the program because it calls each of the submacros:

```
FindFile :


    KopyWord      ; Copy filename from screen into Q7 register
    MyDelChars    ; Delete any control characters from filename
    AddStars      ; Add *.* if user gave only drive or pathname
    EditTheFile   ; Edit the file specified in Q7 register
```

Notice that we observe the Sprint convention of using capitals for coded macros; one glance at our program tells us that *FindFile* is a coded macro comprised of four other coded macros.

We learned, in this first experience customizing a large macro, to throw away code and macros until we had the minimum needed to get a running kernel. We built in the convenient features later.

We suggest you load the *FindFile* and assign it to a hotkey such as **Alt-H** (for hypertext). Figure 5.10 shows an example of how you might use *FindFile* along with an Office Procedures Control File called Office.ctr.

By loading the Office.ctr file into memory, a worker could quickly scan all the office procedures and then jump into a selected file by pointing at the file with the cursor and pressing a hotkey. For example, in Figure 5.10, the cursor is on the filename Ship.pro. So the user could jump into that file simply by pressing **Alt-H** (if that is the hotkey assigned to *FindFile*). When the user closes the Ship.pro file, Sprint automatically returns to Office.ctr, with the cursor still in the same position.

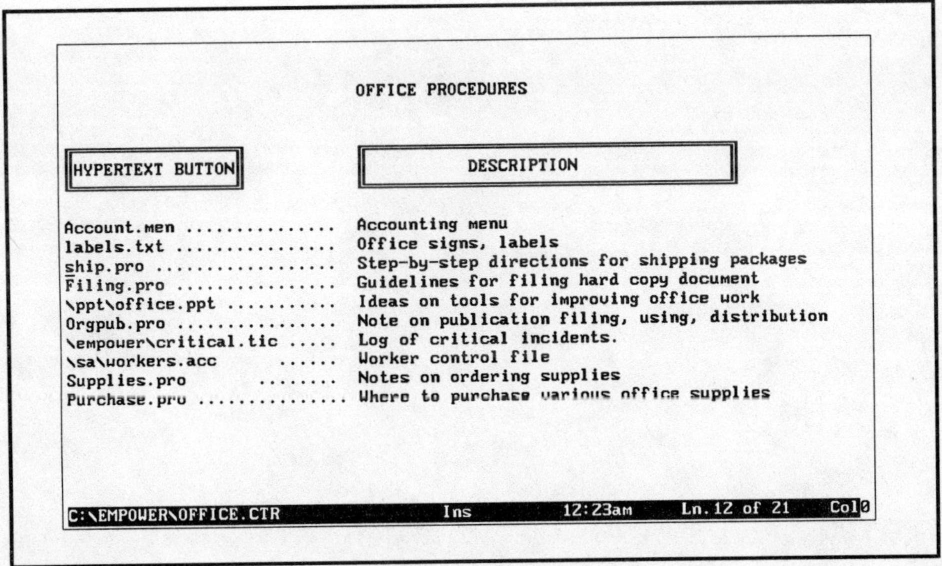

Figure 5.10
Using the FindFile Macro to access hypertext.

> **Where We've Been, Where We're Going**
>
> In this chapter you've learned to control the cursor, select appropriate Q registers, and distinguish Coded Macros from primitive ones. You've also seen how it's possible to develop a macro that gives Sprint hypertext capability.
>
> In Chapter 6 we will build on the hypertext code developed in this chapter. Hypertext tools and Sprint coding will give us system-wide access to routines and files. Small variations in the code will allow us to run programs outside Sprint, even to open files in those other programs, work on the files, and then return to Sprint with modified, updated files.

Chapter 6

Creating Hypertext Command Buttons

In this chapter, we're going to augment the macro that finds files, presented in Chapter 5. We will develop a macro that can decide whether a word or phrase on screen is an executable program and either run the program or launch the *FindFile* macro. In hypertext terminology, we will be creating what is called a command button. A button is a special icon or highlighted word or phrase that shows that hypertext is available if you want it. When you press a command button (by pointing to it with the cursor and pressing a hotkey), the system carries out the command.

HOW TO CALL A PROGRAM

FindFile from Chapter 5 couldn't run an executable file—it could only open the file and show us its contents. But Sprint offers us *call*, a handy macro for calling external programs. To execute a program, all we need to do is pass its name to the *call* macro. We did this in a new macro, *RunProg*, which appears in Figure 6.1.

```
;  *************************** RunProg ***************************

;  USE: Execute boldfaced DOS command or jump into text file.
;  First we get a buffer to hold the string.  Then we look
;  for a delimiter that shows whether the string is executable.
;  If we find the delimiter,  we run the program; otherwise,
;  we return to the previous cursor position and launch the
;  FindFile macro.

RunProg:

  set QN ""                        ;clear an unused register
  set marknumber 9                 ;save cursor position

  if istoken                       ;if cursor is on a word
    r to isgray                    ;move point backwards to
                                   ;gray character--this moves
                                   ;cursor to first character of word

  ;If first character is boldfaced
  if (current = '^B')
     (
     to istoken                    ;go to first letter
     MaybeSet                      ;turn on highlighting
     '^N' csearch                  ;move cursor to ending delimiter
     copy tomark Qn                ;copy region to QN register
     0 -> select                   ;turn off highlighting
     16 call "command /c" QN       ;run the program
     return                        ;end this macro
     )
  else
     (
     to marknumber 9               ;go back to where we were
     FindFile                      ;run the FindFile macro
     )

  ^R: RunProg        ;bind Alt-B to RunProg macro
```

Figure 6.1
The RunProg macro.

As you examine Runprog.spm, notice that it can call the Find-File.spm code from Chapter 5. We developed *FindFile* in tandem with *Runprog*. A special calling routine appears in Runprog.spm—one that can work in almost any Sprint context to call almost any program or DOS command.

We offer two cautions. First, the Sprint schedule of buffers says that buffer Q5 is reserved for DOS commands. For our own reasons—mostly to audit coding in progress—we decided to use buffer QN (buffer 23). Throughout this macro and in several others, you could substitute Q5 for QN.

Second, our coding presumes that a path command exists in the root directory, pointing DOS to the correct subdirectory for each program name. Without a path command, we had to set and reset directories in the code with the *cd* command. That cluttered the code. To tidy things up, we put all our external DOS commands in a subdirectory and we inserted a path command in our Autoexec.bat file. *Runprog* can find a program anywhere on our hard disk because it works through DOS and refers to the path command to find a program if it is not in the current directory.

We help *Runprog* distinguish between text files and programs by boldfacing program names and DOS commands. If a string is a DOS command or a program name—that is anything you would type at the DOS prompt, *Runprog* will execute it only if it is in boldface. Then we can execute commands and programs from within Sprint just by pointing with the cursor and pressing a hypertext hotkey. (Keep in mind that in a larger sense, commands to run other external programs, such as PARADOX or QUATTRO, are also DOS commands).

Runprog instantly turns Sprint into an impressive, virtually unlimited automenu system. You can write notes about each DOS program to your heart's content. Any Sprint document file can link to other programs or other text files.

When you put text in boldface, Sprint inserts Ctrl-B (^B) at the beginning of the highlighted area and Ctrl-N (^N) at the end. Our macro tests for the codes. If it finds them, it stores the program name in a buffer, and then starts the program.

But if we point to a word in plain text with the cursor and press our hypertext hotkey, the system will open a file with that name, or create one. Because of the power of Sprint's macro language, this increased flexibility added just a few more lines of code to our user interface.

Examining the *Runprog* Code

Before continuing, we suggest you try the new macro. Type it in and save it to your Sprint subdirectory. In another file, boldface a few DOS commands—then one-by-one put the cursor on each of the boldfaced commands and press a hypertext hotkey. See if you can make Sprint run some of your favorite programs. Then put the cursor on a filename (which is not boldfaced) and see if Sprint will open that file.

The *Runprog* listing is well commented. We'd like to review the operations. As mentioned in Chapter 5, we moved operations to the QN memory register because it is used even less than the Q4, Q7, and Q9 registers. Here's how:

```
set QN ""

set marknumber 9

if istoken

  r to isgray
```

The first two lines clear the memory register QN, and put a mark, numbered 9, in the file (on the screen) where we point with the cursor. We had trouble with the *marknumber* primitive at first because we wrote it as *mark number*, and Sprint didn't evaluate the command. The words must be run in together. The remaining code tells Sprint that if the cursor is on a token (a character that is part of a word), it should reverse to a gray character. This puts the cursor on the beginning of the word.

Although the code looks elementary, it disguises a potential minefield. Our code kept blowing up when we assumed that any string was alone on a line or was surrounded by whitespace. Strings frequently begin or end with capitals, indents, linefeeds, carriage returns, and control codes—characters that seem transparent to us when we are writing code but that mangle the macro during execution. Watch out for them.

We could have expressed the previous lines like this:

```
set QN ""  set marknumber 9 r to isgray
```

The same result would be achieved most of the time. The styling of the code tells you something about the way it evolved. By expressing the functions as four lines rather than one, we could debug line-by-line. We need not have used If statements, but they indicate that we are aware the cursor may not always be beneath a word.

We styled the code so program control drops through the code one statement at a time. If we mistakenly put the cursor on a blank line and execute *Runprog*, control drops all the way to the bottom of *FindFile* and asks if we want to open a file with no name. We think the approach is easier than filling the code with error routines.

You can check if *marknumber* is properly set by pressing **Alt-G** and giving the number of the mark. Marks can be set with **Alt-M**, if you haven't assigned it to a personalized menu system, as we did in Chapter 4.

The next code group should look rather familiar:

```
if (current = '^B')

    {

    to istoken

    MaybeSet

    '^N' csearch

    copy tomark QN

    0 -> select
```

The first line was discussed in Chapter 4; it looks for the boldface control code. If it is found, the cursor is advanced to the first letter, istoken. *MaybeSet* is the coded macro that didn't work for us in FindFile.spm in Chapter 5, but works well here; it begins highlighting a word. The word is highlighted until Sprint encounters the Ctrl-N code that indicates that the boldface ends.

There is an implicit assumption that we correctly boldfaced the program's name on the screen before we invoked *Runprog*. What if we didn't? If we boldface an entire paragraph of text and call the macro, we get the DOS error message, "Bad command or file name." This is an example of letting the operating system produce our error message. Why should we redundantly code an error message if we can pass a bad string to DOS and DOS does the job? You might argue that DOS may require a few seconds to search for a program and that users may lose time waiting for DOS to return an error message. The choice is yours. You may (or may not) want to spruce up the code with more error checking.

The next line of code:

```
copy tomark QN
```

copies from ^N (at the end of the word), where the point is, to the mark that *MaybeSet* put when it turned on highlighting. We know that because we looked at the coding for the *MaybeSet*.

Because *MaybeSet* turned on highlighting, we have to turn it off:

```
0 -> select
```

Select is one of the global variables, listed in Appendix F, that can take a value of 1, for on, or 0, for off. We turned it off just by assigning zero to the variable.

The next line in the code is

```
16 call "command /c" QN
```

Call is a powerful macro that exits to DOS and calls an external program. The syntax is

```
  # call "string"
  ↑         ↑
argument  name of program
```

The # symbol represents a number—an argument we pass to *call*, and "string" is the name of the program.

We'll skip over the meaning of 16 for now and come back to it later. The "string" in our macro consists of "command /c" plus the contents of the QN register. Sprint automatically concatenates this into one string for us. Notice that the first program name is command. By convention, when you use the program name "command" here, Sprint looks at the DOS *Comspec* environment variable and substitutes the name that *Comspec* is set to. If you're not familiar with the DOS *Comspec* variable (or need to refresh your memory), just enter **Set** at the DOS prompt. You will see something like that shown in Figure 6.2.

Notice the line in the figure that says Comspec = C:\command.com. The DOS *Comspec* variable is set to C:\command.com. Unless you are some DOS wizard who is using a different command processor, *Comspec* will be set to command.com on your system, too. In short, then, whenever you refer to command as a program, Sprint first looks at the *Comspec* variable to see which command processor it should use. Usually, it will be command.com. If you want to use command.com directly, you also can write "command.com" instead of "command."

The /c switch in the macro tells DOS to execute the following

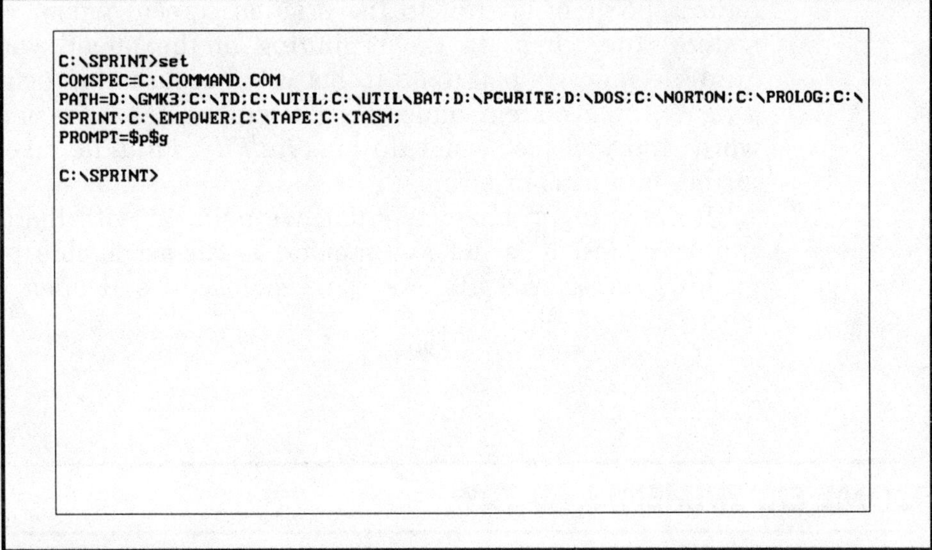

Figure 6.2
Examining DOS Environment with Set.

string (QN) and then to return automatically to Command.com. Earlier, remember, we moved the boldfaced program name into the QN variable.

Sprint doesn't always follow the expected language syntax. For example, you expect an argument to be some expression that follows a command, and a switch to be some character that might modify an argument. In Sprint syntax, an argument can, like a modifier in English, come before the verb. We call the /c in the preceding example a switch because it modifies the way Sprint starts Command.com. When you encounter argument or switch in discussions of Sprint macros, just look for a modifier to the macro, either before the word or after it.

The remainder of the macro:

```
return
else
    {
    to marknumber 9
    FindFile
    }
```

returns program control to the original screen, where we started, or restores the cursor to the beginning of the target word and starts FindFile.spm. We had to do it that way because at the end of the *Runprog* routine, you may remember, the cursor was at the end of the target word, and that just won't do for *FindFile*. *FindFile* takes care of any further problems or errors.

If the string of characters that we point to with the cursor has no control codes, it is not a command or an executable program. That means it must be a file. We can just load it and open it, or offer to create it.

SOME EXPERIMENTS TO TRY

Passing Arguments to *call*

Now let's take a closer look at the 16 that we passed to the *call* macro in the first part of the code. Use the line:

```
16 call "command /c" QN
```

It provides an opportunity to play with an interesting macro. To do this experiment, first set up a tiny test macro like this:

```
Callit :

    16 call "command /c time"
```

Save the code to Callit.spm in your Sprint subdirectory. Use the **Shift-Alt-R** technique to compile the macro. And then run it by pressing **Shift-Alt-X** and entering **Callit**.

After you test Callit.spm, point to time and start *Runprog* by pressing your hypertext hotkey. Notice that the tiny test file and *Runprog* do the same thing. As we mentioned earlier, the 16 in front of the call is an argument:

```
16 call "command /c time" QN

  ↑


argument.
```

When 16 is passed as an argument to call, Sprint overlays the called program on top of itself. That way you can execute even large, memory-consuming programs from Sprint. We found that Sprint freed up all but 3K of available memory when we used 16 as an argument to call! When you use 16 as an argument, Sprint will re-execute itself after the external program terminates.

Passing 1 to *call*

Now let's try a different experiment. Let's change the argument in *Callit* to 1 so it reads like this:

```
Callit:

    1 call "command /c time"
```

Recompile and run the macro again. What happens? Figure 6.3 shows the result we got.

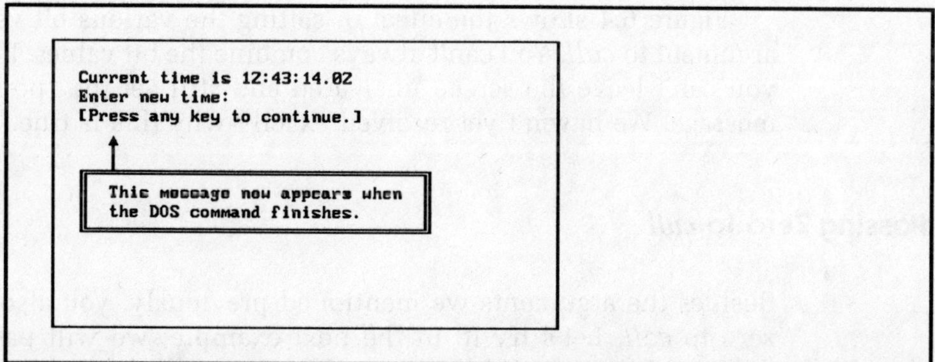

Figure 6.3
Passing 1 to the *call* macro.

When you pass *call* a 1, it will display the "Press any key to continue" message after the external program executes. But now, Sprint will stay in memory and will not overlay the external program on itself.

Actually, when the number you pass to *call* has its first bit set, the "Press any key to continue" message will be displayed. Using the argument 1 sets the 1 bit.

Passing 17 to *call*

To prove the "Press any key . . . " message appears when the 1 bit is set, try passing the number 17 to *call*:

```
Call :


    17 call "command /c time"
```

Sprint does two things: It overlays the external program on itself, and it also displays the "Press any key to continue" message. To get whatever effects you want, add together the bit values associated with effects you want. You could also let Sprint do the addition for you, like this:

```
Test :


    1+16 call "command /c time"
```

That clarifies exactly which bits you are turning on in the argument.

Figure 6.4 shows the effect of setting the various bit values in the argument to *call*. You can't always combine the bit values. For example, you can't leave the screen uncleared and still get the "press any key" message. We haven't yet resolved exactly why this is true.

Passing Zero to *call*

Besides the arguments we mentioned previously, you also can pass a zero to *call*. Let's try it. In the next example, we will pass zero and drop the /c switch and the string that goes with it. (A string or variable must always follow the /c switch.) In addition to these changes, we will display a message to the user with the *exitmessage* primitive:

```
BIT           Instructions to call when this bit is set:
VALUE
--------      -------------------------------------------------------
1             Display "Press any key to continue" after the external
              program executes.

2             Unresolved.

4             Reserved.

8             When restarting Sprint, run the "restart macro."

16            Overlay Sprint with the called program.

32            Don't clear the screen; put the cursor in the lower
              corner before starting the external program.
```

Figure 6.4
Setting various bits in call argument.


```
GotoDOS :


    exitmessage "Be sure to type EXIT to come back to Sprint!"


    0 call "command"
```

What do you think this macro will do? Figure 6.5 shows what happens.

Sprint gives the DOS prompt back to the user. Sprint also displays our message: "Be sure to type EXIT to return to Sprint!" You also can get to the DOS prompt using the existing Sprint menu system, but it is not so easy. For example, you can press **Alt-U** and select DOS Command. Then when Sprint prompts for the DOS command, enter nothing. That is, just press **Return** with nothing on the status line after the DOS command prompt. The problem with this is that you may have to backspace to erase your previous DOS command before pressing **Return**. With the *GotoDOS* macro you can drop out to the DOS prompt with a single keystroke. We like to use *Alt-D* as a hotkey to kickstart this macro.

Dropping "Command"

It's also possible to drop the "command" from the string that we pass to *call*. We can pass the name of an executable program or external DOS command to *call*, like this:

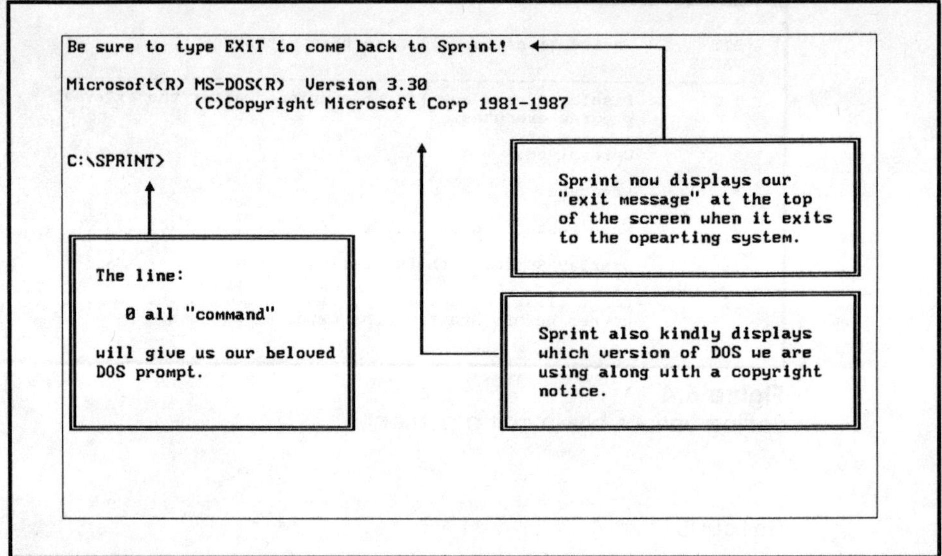

Figure 6.5
Launching command.com.

```
Test :

    0 call "progname"
```

This approach will work with external DOS commands, that is, those commands that exist as executable files. But it won't work with internal DOS commands such dir, type, and so on, as you can see in Figure 6.6.

Before we leave this chapter, we thought you might like to see some examples of how one user is employing this hypertext macro in his work. He assigned the macro to **Alt-F10**, which in Sprint normally does nothing but pop up the Main Sprint menu. Because **F10** already does this, he can adopt **Alt-F10** for his own use. He created a file called Menu.spr and stored it in the Sprint subdirectory. When working in Sprint, he opens a secondary window and loads Menu.spr into that window. When he needs to execute some other program or view a related file, he flips to the menu by pressing **Shift-F6**. Then, to zoom off to a node in the network, "hyperland," he points to the program or file on the menu and presses **Alt-F10**—the hypertext hotkey. Figure 6.7 illustrates the hypertext menu system in action. The top window

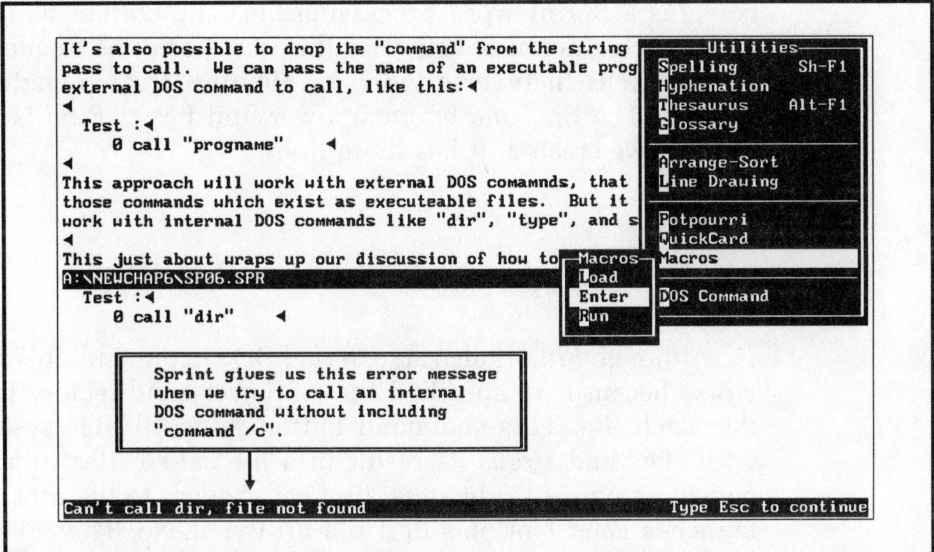

Figure 6.6

When you don't use "command /c".

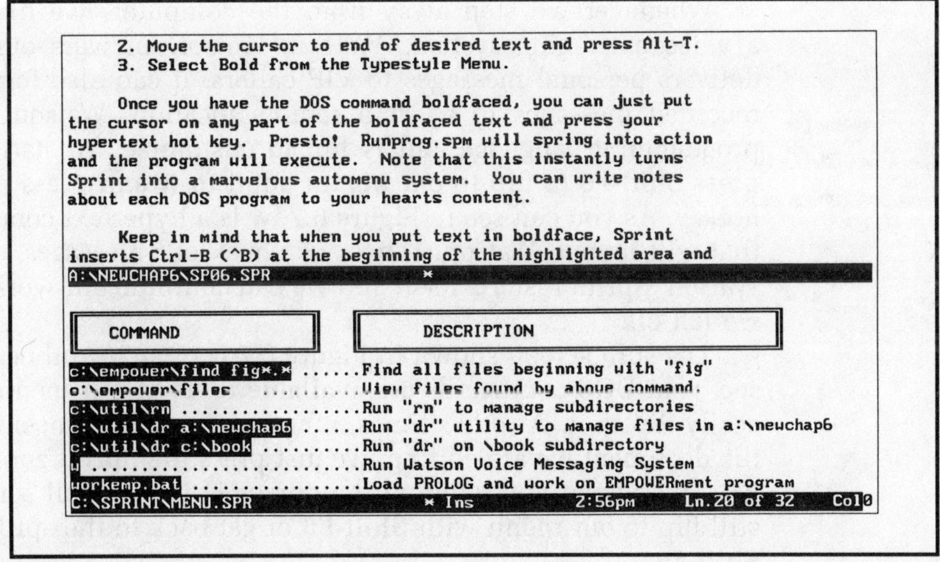

Figure 6.7

Using a Hypertext Menu while editing with Sprint.

contains a Sprint word processing file. The bottom window contains Menu.spr—a menu of activities this user performs frequently.

The lines in inverse video in Figure 6.7 are hypertext command buttons. The first one is c:\empower\find fig*.*. *Find* is a DOS batch file that we created. It has these lines:

```
cd \

ff %1 > \empower\files
```

Although *Find* is also an external DOS command, this hypertext call works because we specified the empower subdirectory in referring to the batch file. This command button finds all files system that start with "fig" and stores its result in a file called files in a subdirectory named empower. Notice that find.bat changes to the root directory and launches Peter Norton's find file utility: ff.exe. The %1 is a standard DOS .bat file argument symbol. When we call find.bat with an argument, that argument gets substituted for the %1. The > \empower\files redirects the output of ff to \empower\files. To see the names of all these files and perhaps view them, we just point to the next line, C:\empower\files, and press our hypertext hotkey.

Whenever we step away from the computer, we like to activate a voice messaging system: Watson. Watson answers our phone and delivers personal messages to VIP callers. It can also forward callers' recorded messages to us at a remote location. Watson has its own programming language and is fun to customize. To start Watson, we press **Shift-F6** to flip to our Menu, point to w and press our hypertext hotkey. As you can see in Figure 6.7, w is a hypertext command button that will launch Watson. When we check our messages and exit from Watson, Sprint restarts itself and we can continue our work right where we left off.

The split screen shown in Figure 6.7 is often useful because we can see what DOS commands are available to us in our menu and we can easily flip to it. At other times, when we want to concentrate only on the document we are editing, we just press the Sprint zoom key, **Shift-F5**. This zooms the window the cursor is in to a full screen. We can still flip to our menu with **Shift-F6** or get back to the split screen with **Shift-F5**.

WHERE WE'VE BEEN, WHERE WE'RE GOING

In this chapter we used coded macros and primitives to develop a program that calls other programs or calls another macro. We used the *call* macro in different ways by passing it an argument in the form of a number. We learned how to launch another program in such a way that Sprint releases all but 3K of its memory to the external application program or DOS command. We created a DOS menu file to keep in a handy window while editing a Sprint file.

In Chapter 7 we will continue to explore hypertext. We will develop what is called a hypertext reference button—a button that links to another point in the same node (file).

Chapter 7
Programming Style and Hypertext Reference Buttons

In this chapter we will pull together some important programming practices we have implied in previous chapters. These are styles and habits we've learned through trial and error. They are our personal guidelines developed from writing a few hundred macros, small and large.

While we explain these ideas, we'll continue to build on the hypertext macros discussed earlier. Before we get to the programming details, let's consider why hypertext is useful.

WHY HYPERTEXT IS USEFUL

Why do we need hypertext? After all, we can use the **F7** key to search for an expression, and Sprint provides an entire menu of powerful search-and-replace tools. One important reason is that with traditional search procedures *you have to know what to search for*. You can search for a key word, but that key word may not occur in the text exactly the way you think it might. On the flip side, the word or phrase may appear too many times, and you may have to wade through scores of references to a word until you find what you want. We experienced this when we tried a traditional search through a file containing documentation on Sprint macros. We wanted to find the macro that would give us the current cursor position. We searched for various words: "position," "byte," "cursor," and so on. We found many occurrences of these words before we finally came upon the *offset* macro (which returns the character offset from the beginning of the file).

With a well-designed hypertext network, you don't have to think of a keyword to search for. You have a starting place—a table of contents at the beginning of the file. This table of contents is in the form of an organized set of hypertext buttons. It acts as a control node—a node from which you can control your movement through the hypertext network. (A node, remember, is a chunk of data usually related to a single topic or idea. A node may be an entire file or part of a file.)

Another advantage of hypertext is that while you are reading about a certain topic, you can take a quick detour to investigate a related topic just by putting the cursor on a key word or phrase and pressing a hotkey. Then when you are ready, you can instantly pop back to where you were to continue your reading of the primary node.

To enable this kind of research in Sprint, we created a hypertext reference button. Here, a reference button is highlighted text that can transport you to a specific destination within the current node.

We call our hypertext reference button macro *refer*. It works like this. When you put the cursor on an underlined word or phrase and press a hotkey, Sprint immediately begins a search for the same string only marked as an italic font. When the macro finds the line containing the target, it scrolls that line to the top of the window and returns control to you which enables you to immediately start editing or reading the reference text. The macro also displays a message on the status line explaining that you can return to the previous position by pressing **Alt-B**.

This macro illustrates several macro programming techniques and concepts. We'll present the *refer* macro at the end of this chapter, after we've worked our way through some important terms and concepts.

- How Sprint loads
- How Sprint quits
- Coding small macros
- Documenting code
- Decision-making commands and branching
- Controlling repetition
- Using variables and labels
- Talking back to the program
- Exiting routines
- Debugging a macro that doesn't run

HOW SPRINT LOADS

On start-up Sprint loads Sp.ovl, which always contains the user interface you were previously using. (Note that you load and save interfaces from the User Interface menu, which you can access from the Customize menu.) Sprint keeps user interfaces in files with an extension of .ui. When you load a different interface, Sprint copies that file to Sp.ovl. That way the next time you start Sprint, the interface you last selected will still be active.

Each time you open a file, Sprint reads it and also saves it to a backup file, Sp.swp. Sprint saves changes to Sp.swp if the background save switch is set to a value between 1 and 60 seconds. You can turn off the background save operation by setting the switch to zero. (You can access this switch through the menus by pressing **Alt-C O B**.) The single backup file, Sp.swp, is a sort of flat-file database that contains as many separate files as you have open.

If Preserve Editing Session on the Customize menu is set to Yes, the default, Sprint keeps the contents of the backup file on disk when you quit. You automatically open the backup file when you restart. Files that were open when you quit are automatically open again when you restart. If Preserve Editing Session is set to **No**, the backup file is erased, and when you restart, a new, empty backup is created.

HOW SPRINT QUITS

Sprint uses Sprecove.com to recover the backup file, the swap file, if you lose power or turn off your system while working in Sprint. Note that the .com extension of the filename makes it recognizable by DOS as an executable file. While loading, if Sprint discovers that an abnormal end, an abend, occurred the last time it ran, Sprint calls Sprecove.com.

The program provides an error message:

```
Last session (C:\Sprint\Sp.swp) not finished

R  -  Recover last session

D  -  Discard last session

Q  -  Quit to DOS

Option: __
```

If you choose Recover last session, Sprecove.com begins reading Sp.swp. Sprint records sessions in blocks. Sprecove.com tells us how many blocks were available, then how many blocks were in use—how stressed memory was—and finally it produces a table. The table tells us how many characters and lines were in use in the clipboard (the memory location for copy-and-move routines), and how many characters and lines were in use for other files that had been opened. Sprecove.com then opens those files and returns to the Sprint loading sequence.

If you had assigned a shortcut to a key, but discover it's gone, that's because Sp.ovl has changed. Maybe someone reinstalled Sprint or loaded a different user interface. Remember, when you compile a macro and assign it to a hotkey, upon exiting to DOS, Sprint will save the compiled macro and the key binding information to Sp.ovl. (See the discussion of *ovlread* and *ovlwrite* in Appendix E.) Sometimes Sprint may take it upon itself to start recompiling sp.spm! This may happen if you don't have enough free memory to load Sprint. If this happens you may lose your custom user interface.

> **Tip**
>
> Whenever you refine your current interface, save it immediately with the User Interface menu. You can do this by pressing **Alt-C U S** and entering a unique name. Later if anything goes wrong, you can easily reload by pressing **Alt-C U L** and choosing your interface from a menu.
>
> Note that when you save your interface, Sprint will create a file with the name you specify. It's extension will always be .ui.
>
> **Note:** Sprint does not store Glossary items in the Sp.ovl file, but in the file you have defined as the current Glossary file. Glossary files always have the .Spg extension. Sprint stores Glossary items in the .Spg file when you quit Sprint.

But Sprint stores all key binding information in Sp.ovl.

So if you defined a Glossary item and assigned it to, say, **Shift-Alt-M**, Sprint stores the Shift-Alt-M and the Glossary item name in *Sp.ovl*, but not the Glossary item itself. So if you move to another computer and you want to take your complete customized interface with you, be sure to bring along both your .ui and .Spg files.

CODING SMALL MACROS

Now to some coding practices. The best advice we can give you is to code small macros. Break a task into the functional parts. Each part can become a small macro or paragraph of code. You can precede each paragraph with a descriptive comment that will help later if you have to separate apples from oranges. Macro names can be descriptive, too. You can use both upper and lowercase letters in macro names if you want, like in the macro *ToUpperCase*.

An advantage of using a macro for each functional element of a task is that you can usually reduce the main logic of a program to a small macro that contains just a screenful of commands. And you can test each macro independently to make sure it carries out its specific function correctly.

As a rule of thumb, if a macro takes more than 25 lines of code, consider breaking it into smaller segments. Make each segment into a separate macro with a unique name.

CHOOSE UNIQUE MACRO NAMES

When we first started developing the hypertext macro in this chapter, we decided to borrow code from *core.spm*. We borrowed the macro *Locate* and modified it to suit our purposes. We tried using the Locate label on a paragraph of our new, altered code, but our variation corrupted the original *Locate* macro! When we hit the **F7** key to find an expression, the Sprint program did strange things—it repeated what we had been experimenting with.

So even if your coding copies some other macro, give the paragraph a unique macro label. This strategy prevents you from corrupting a paragraph of existing code with a slightly changed paragraph of code assigned the same name.

Tip

Be sure to use macro names that do not conflict with existing code!

DOCUMENTING CODE

Inventive labeling of code goes hand-in-hand with documenting code as you write it. The original Sprint code does not contain many comments. When studying Sprint code, you can find yourself in a deeply nested routine without the slightest idea what the author is trying to do.

A good way to learn how undocumented code works is to move a paragraph you are studying into a temporary file, relabel it, and then compile it under the new label by pressing **Shift-Alt-R**. Then test the macro by pressing **Shift-Alt-X** and entering the new label. In doing this, you may want to insert statements that display the value of numeric variables or values returned by macros. *put* is a useful macro that will display whatever numeric value is passed to it. You can also include a string following *put* to specify the desired numeric format. (It works like the format string in C.) You can include comments and a carriage return specification in this string, too. Here's an example:

```
testoffset :

  offset

  put "\nCursor is %d characters from beginning of file."
```

To test this routine yourself, follow these steps:

1. Save your current Sprint User Interface. (Press **Alt-C U S** and enter a unique name.)
2. Type the *testoffset* macro into a file called, say, *offset.spm*. While you are still in this file, press **Shift-Alt-R**. This compiles the macro and adds it to your current interface.
3. Move the cursor to some convenient location in a file. Keep in mind that the *testoffset* macro will insert a message directly into the file.
4. Press **Shift-Alt-X** and enter **testoffset**.
5. When you are done testing, restore your User Interface. (Press **Alt-C U L** and enter the name of your user interface.)

After you complete Step 4, the *testoffset* macro will execute immediately and display a message such as this line: "Cursor is 798 characters from beginning of file." Of course, it probably won't say 798 unless you happen to position the cursor exactly 798 characters from the top of your file.

In this example, it is the *offset* macro that returns the character offset from the beginning of the file. The *put* statement inserts a carriage return before printing the message. The \n is the newline character. It causes the carriage return. The %d asks Sprint to print the incoming numeric value as a decimal number. Sprint will print the number exactly where the %d appears in the string.

> **Tip**
>
> After you have finished testing, be sure to reload your user interface. If you don't, Sp.ovl will end up carrying around excess baggage—namely all of the test macros you have compiled.

Alternatively, as mentioned earlier, you could set the variable *ovlmodf* to zero and trick Sprint into thinking that you have not added any new macros to the system. Sprint will only save new macros if *ovlmodf* is set to 1. To set *ovlmodf* to zero, press **Shift-Alt-X** and enter **0->ovlmodf**.

Suppose you have already compiled a macro or you want to test a standard Sprint macro. In that case, you can just press **Shift-Alt-X** and enter the macro name and an equal sign. For example, you could enter **Shift-Alt-X** and then **offset =**. The = means to display the returned value on the status line.

After you learn what a macro does, take time to document it. Tomorrow you may forget what today seems clear and unforgettable. We recommend you put comments on separate lines above the code. Add a couple of carriage returns between the paragraphs. Use the semi-colon, ;, to indicate that a comment follows and place a comment before each paragraph to describe its function. Also, if space allows, add a comment at the end of each line—always start each comment with a semicolon. If space is not available, put the comment on a separate line directly above the code. When Sprint compiles code and writes it to the *Sp.ovl file*, it just ignores the ";" lines, so commenting does not slow compile or execution times.

DECISION-MAKING COMMANDS AND BRANCHING

The Sprint macro vocabulary has some interesting decision-making commands and many variations. Let's review those macros that can make decisions or cause branching.

If-Else

If-else is the decision-making command we use most frequently. For best results, we suggest that you use indentation to help the reader identify the if conditional and the *else* alternative.

The listing in Figure 7.1 provides an example of deeply nested *if-else* statements from *InitArg*, one of the start-up macros. The code is styled so you can clearly see the conditionals and count the True-False outcomes. There is an *else* alternative for the first *if*, easily identified by the indentation.

You can have multiple statements execute if the expression following an *if* is True. Also, you can have multiple statements that execute when control falls to the *else* part of the an *if-else* construct. A good coding practice is to surround the commands that belong together with delimiters so Sprint will consider them a single statement. Here's an example:

```
if (!giveup) {
    if (buffind Q0) {           ; in buffer
        if ((modf && ask "File already open, read over it? ")||
            (!modf && (datecheck Q0 > 0))) {        ; newer file
            clear
            read fname
            r toend
            StartFile
            }
        }
    else if (exist Q0) {
        open Q0  ; not in buffer, but exists
        StartFile
        }
    else    {               ; try fname.spr
        0 SetSPRExt         ; force default extension
        if (exist Q0) {             ; if file exists, open it.
            if !buffind Q0 (open Q0)
            StartFile
            }
        else {
            message "\nCreate new file "
            message Q0
            if (ask "? ") {
                if !(open Q0) DefaultRuler
                }
            }
        }
    }
```

Figure 7.1
Nested "if" statements.

```
IF (expression)

    {

    command 1

    command 2

    }

ELSE

    {

    command 3

    command 4

    }
```

If the expression is True (nonzero), commands 1 and 2 will execute. If it is False (zero), commands 3 and 4 will execute. If only one command follows an if expression, then you can drop the braces. But if you want multiple commands to execute only if a condition is True, be sure to surround them with delimiters.

Here's an example from *refer*, the hypertext macro that appears at the end of this chapter:

```
if (current != '^U')

    {

    '^U' r csearch

    }
```

To understand this code, it helps to know that *current* returns the ASCII value of the character that the cursor is currently on. The expression != means does not equal, and the line '^U' r csearch means to search backward for an underline character. The whole code means that if the cursor is not currently on an underline character, search backwards for this character. Notice the braces that surround the line following the if statement. The braces are required here. That's because '^U' r csearch really consists of three commands. To bind these commands together into a single statement, we need to surround them with delimiters.

If without *Else*

If can occur without *else* as you can see from this example:

```
if AutoCorrect LoadSpeller
```

If *AutoCorrect* returns True (non-zero), then *LoadSpeller* will execute. But if *AutoCorrect* returns False (0), the program skips over *LoadSpeller* and carries the argument zero or False to the next statement.

? Used as If

After some hesitation, we finally got comfortable with an *if-else* variant, the Sprint question mark, *?*. You can use the *?* character in an *if-else* structure to execute one of two commands; it tests whether a condition is True or False. The syntax is

```
expression ? command1 {:command2}
```

If the expression returns True (non-zero), the first command executes. If the expression is False (zero), control jumps to the command following the colon. Consider this example:

```
CharToUpper : int z

    z >= 'a' && z <= 'z' ? z - 20h : z
```

This macro (already in *Sp.ovl*) returns an uppercase letter if the incoming variable is a lowercase letter. The variable z takes on the value of the incoming argument. The *?* fires the z−20h instruction only if z is between lowercase a and lowercase z. Whenever you subtract 20h from a lowercase character, you change it to uppercase. For example, a lowercase c (63h) become an uppercase C (43h). If the character isn't a lowercase letter, control jumps to the expression following the colon, which is just a z. The effect, here, is that *CharToUpper* will return the incoming uppercase character unchanged. To try this macro, press **Shift-Alt-X** and enter

```
'c'chartoupper = "%x"
```

This command passes a lowercase c to the *CharToUpper* macro and asks Sprint to display the returned value in hexadecimal format on the status line. (The equal sign means to display the returned value on the status line.) So when you execute this command, you will see that the macro returns 43, the hex value for an uppercase C. You might want to repeat the **Shift-Alt-X**. Your previous command will still be on the status line and you can edit it. Change the c to, say, a. You'll get 41, the hex value for an uppercase A.

The *?* command can be a little tricky. As you may know, the *:* character alone and flush left in a macro means to execute the following commands immediately after compiling them. But in combination with the query character, Sprint recognizes the colon as the else part of an *if-else* structure.

Case

After you've got the hang of the query symbol, *case* is a snap. *Case* and its variants appear in several languages. Here is a paragraph from one of the Sprint search-and-replace routines:

```
StrFound case {

        0 message "Not found." 1 Bell,

        1 x message "%d replaced.",

        2 message "Canceled."

        }
```

StrFound, here, is a variable. An earlier routine previously set *Str-Found* to either 0, 1, or 2. If *StrFound* contains zero, then the "Not found" message will execute. If *StrFound* is set to 1, then a message will appear showing how many items were replaced. Note that an earlier routine must have set the variable x to an appropriate value. If x was set to, say, 9, then the routine will display this message: "9 replaced." If *StrFound* is 2, then the "Canceled" message appears.

In this example, notice that each line following case { begins with a number. But each such line need not begin with a hard-coded number. A line (within the case delimiters) may begin with an expression, a variable, or a macro that returns a number. Also, the beginning of such a line may contain multiple values separated by commas. The commands on that line will execute if the incoming value matches any of the numbers at the beginning of the line.

A $ symbol at the beginning of a line means that if no other commands have executed, then execute the following command(s) by default.

Tip

When writing a case statement, be sure that each alternative command line (except the last) ends with a comma.

The *TestCase* macro illustrates these points. We suggest you create a file called test.spm. Type it in, and then compile it with **Shift-Alt-R**. (This example also shows how a macro can insert a string into the current file just by putting the string in quotation marks.)

```
TestCase: int n

  n case

    {

    0     "You passed me a zero—adding 10 to it" n+10,

    1     "You passed me a 1—adding 99 to it." n+99,

    1+1   "You passed me a 2—multiplying it by 3." n*3,

    3,4   "You passed 3 or 4—multiplying it by 4." n*4,

    $     "Number > 4—returning same number" n

    }
```

After compiling this macro with **Shift-Alt-R**, test it by entering **Shift-Alt-X** and then a command like **2 TestCase** =. Sprint will insert text into the current file and also display the value that the macro returns on the status line.

Notice that the variable n takes on the value you pass to *TestCase*. Suppose you give the command 3 TestCase=. Then you would be passing 3 to *TestCase* and Sprint would set n to 3 at the beginning of the macro. But what value would TestCase return? Try it yourself and see if the result matches your prediction. What if you gave the command 33 TestCase =? After experimenting on your own, you can check your work with the result shown in Figures 7.2 and 7.3. Notice that *TestCase* returns 12 if you pass it 3 because the program multiplies the incoming argument by 4. Figure 7.3 shows what happens when you pass 33. Because 33 does not match any of the initial cases, the line that begins with $ executes, and the macro returns n unchanged. That is, the macro returns 33.

Case is useful in those situations where you have several possible outcomes for one situation. We nearly used it in *refer*, but we were able to do just fine with *if-else* commands.

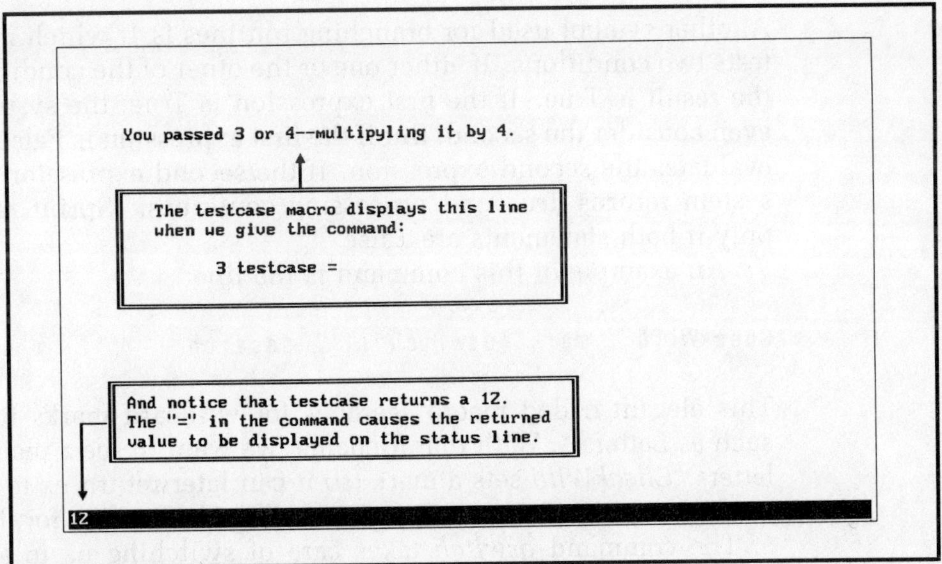

Figure 7.2
Passing 3 to testcase.

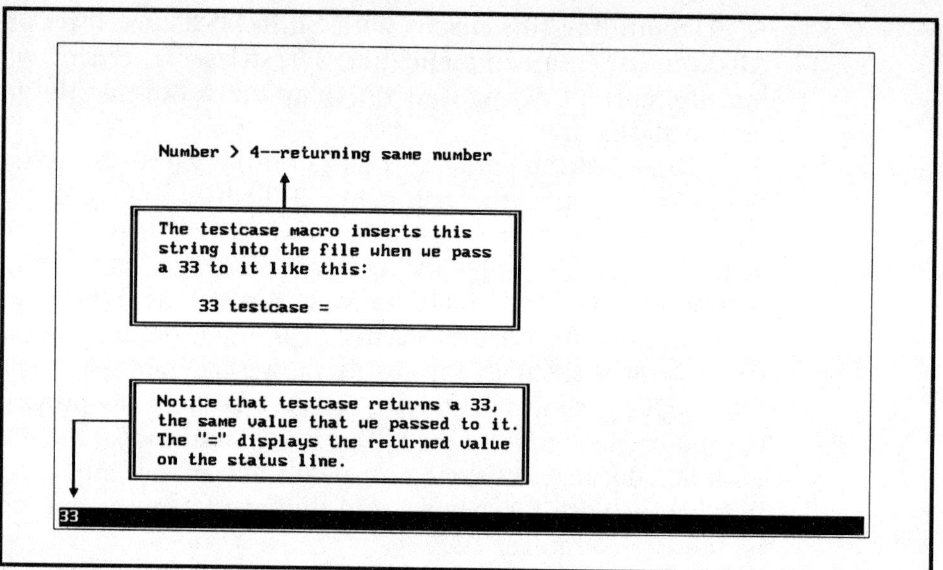

Figure 7.3
Passing 33 to testcase.

Using ||(OR)

Another symbol used for branching routines is || which means OR. It tests two conditions. If either one or the other of the conditions is True, the result is True. If the first expression is True, the system does not even consider the second. But if the first expression is False, the system evaluates the second expression. If the second expression is True, the system returns True and processing continues. Sprint returns False only if both statements are False.

An example of this command is the line:

```
CheckWild : mark (qswitch ('*' csearch || ('?' r csearch)))
```

This elegant coded macro searches for wildcard marks in filenames, such as Letters.*. With that filename, we want to see a menu of all our letters. *CheckWild* sets a mark (so it can later return us to our current work), then switches to a Q-register, where it searches for the character *. The command *qswitch* takes care of switching us to a Q-register. (The register we switch to depends on the incoming argument.) The command '*' *csearch* means to search for an asterisk.

If *csearch* finds an asterisk, it returns True and *CheckWild* immediately returns True without bothering with the rest of the command line. But what if *csearch* fails to find an asterisk? It will keep checking for an asterisk until it reaches the end of the Q-register that we have switched to. If *csearch* fails to find an asterisk, it returns False. But because of the || symbol, *CheckWild* will continue and evaluate the next expression to see if it is True. So *CheckWild* will reverse direction and search toward the beginning of the Q-register for ?. If the result is True, there still is a wildcard character in the filename list, so *CheckWild* returns True (1). Otherwise, *CheckWild* returns False (0). In one line of code, Sprint can check one or two conditions, as necessary, and return one of two answers.

The || symbol is used in branching because if the first condition is False, the second condition can be evaluated. The symbol can help create an intricate command, with several conditionals. Experts like to use || and it often appears in long command lines.

Using ! for NOT

The ! symbol means NOT as in the C language. You saw it earlier in the example that began

```
IF (current != '^U')
```

Here is a simple example to show how it might be used:

```
testnot: int x

   IF ! x

   "You passed me a zero."

   ELSE

   "You passed a non-zero value"
```

The variable *x* declared after the macro name is local to this macro. That is, it is not known to any other macros. Here, *x* takes on whatever value is passed to *testnot*. The IF ! x statement means: if the variable

x is NOT True (greater than zero). So the expression ! x will be true whenever x is zero. To test this macro, pass it the number 3 like this:

```
3 testnot
```

You will see "You passed a nonzero value" displayed on the screen. In working with !, just remember that it flips the truth of the expression that follows it. A True value (greater than zero) becomes False (valued as zero).

Controlling Repetition

Sprint's macros for controlling repetition include the *do*, *while*, and *do . . . while* macros. They vary in the way they are implemented, but they recall the *do* and the *do . . . while* commands from the language C.

With the *do* macro, a command executes indefinitely until Sprint encounters the *break* macro or you press an abortkey, such as **Esc**. We avoid some algorithms that could use *do* loops to avoid as well the *break* macro, when that is possible.

The *do . . . while* pair sometimes seems more appropriate. A command repeatedly executes until the *while* condition returns False. But the test is after the *do . . . while* command, so the loop runs at least once.

The *while* macro tests some statement first, and only if it is True does the macro execute the command, so a command may not be executed at all.

These three related commands control repetition, each in their own way: The *do* macro executes until interrupted; the *do . . . while* macro executes and then tests; and the *while* macro tests before it executes. All of them respond to the *break* macro.

There's one caution. The *break* macro may break you only out of the nearest enclosing loop. If *do* loops or the variants of *do* are nested, you may be broken out of a loop without exiting the entire macro. Poor placement of *break* will abort the macro when you may have wanted only to exit one of its loops. Figure 7.4, a listing for the macro *MenuBind*, displays a *break* command that appears to exit only an *if-else* statement but that actually aborts the *do* loop.

The example, from the *Sp.spm* code, uses *break* nested in the third

```
MenuBind:
    do {
        status "\nShortcut for menu item: " GetKey->x
        if x = '^[' (0 return)         ;Escape key aborts
        if (x CanAssign) {
            x keypushback
            if (x > 255) (0 keypushback)
            break
            }
        else AssignError
        }
        '^J' return
```

Figure 7.4
The MenuBind macro.

level of the macro to break out of a *do* loop. If a key assigned
to a shortcut is legal, it is accepted and the user breaks out of the key
assignment routine; otherwise, an error message is given, a hard return
(^J) is issued, and the program returns to the calling macro.

Repeat is a good macro for repetition because it can take a value,
an argument, that continues the action for some definite time. Sprint's
repeat is similar to the repeat/until pair in Pascal. Repeat takes an
argument of #, a number, and repeats a command # times.

Even if the argument for *repeat* is set to zero, it does the related
command at least once, as in the *do ... while* pair, because the test is
made after the *repeat* macro executes.

Using Variables and Macro Names

In the reference button macro at the end of this chapter, we use a
variable called *SearchDirection* to control branching. If *SearchDirection*
is set to 1, we search forward; if *SearchDirection* is zero, we search
backward. Here is the code we used:

```
if SearchDirection

        (SearchOpt f search qd) ; search forward

    else

        (SearchOpt r search qd) ; do a reverse search
```

The statement if SearchDirection is the same as If (SearchDirection <>0).
But we don't need a full comparison between two variables after an

If statement. A simple variable (or even a macro) is enough. If the variable or macro returns nonzero, it is considered a True expression.

SearchOpt is also a variable. We set it to 1 earlier. So we are simply using *SearchOpt* to pass a 1 to the *search* macro. When we pass a 1 to the *search* macro, we are specifying that we want lowercase letters in the search string to match with either upper or lowercase letters in the search text. See Figure 7.5 for a list of search options.

The f before search specifies that we want Sprint to search in a forward direction. The r specifies that we want a reverse search. The qd after search specifies what we want to search for. The name of a register, which *contains* the string we want to find, is specified here by qd.

The value a variable contains is critical, because it often decides the destiny of a macro—what path it will follow. Earlier we discussed how variables take on their values. Let's review some important points:

1. A variable that you declare with int after a macro name, takes on the value of the current argument. Such a variable is local to

Figure 7.5
search Options

If You Want:	Then Pass This Argument To The *search* Macro
exact search	0
lowercase to match upper	1
wildcards	2
word only matching	4

If you want to combine *search* options then add the numbers. For example, to match uppercase letters with lowercase but limit matching to words only, you would pass 5(1+4).

The Sprint wildcard options are extensive; for details on the many different kinds of wildcards including sets, just press **Alt-E S U F1.** Then press **PgDn** for more details.

the macro in which it appears. Other macros do not have access to the contents of this variable. The *n* variable we used in the *TestCase* macro is a local variable because we defined it after the macro label.

2. You cannot use an equal sign to initialize a local variable. A variable you declare at the top of a file—before any macro names have been declared—takes on the value specified after the equal sign, as in the expression int SearchOption = 2. Such a variable is global; it is known to all macros.

3. You can set either a local or global variable to a new value with the −> operator. For example, to set SearchOpt to 3, you would code: 3 −> SearchOpt.

See Appendix E for a list of the global Sprint variables along with a description of what you can use them for.

Macro Labels

Macro labels help to identify the purpose of a piece of code. But they also enable you to control program execution. You can have one macro call another simply by naming the other macro. An example from our *refer* macro is

```
Refer:

    SetSearch                ; move string into qd register

    if FindString            ; if findstring routine succeeds

    {

    wlines scroll            ; scroll so target is at top of screen

    message "Press Alt—B to return to previous position."

    return                   ; and return so user can edit

    }
```

In this example, these commands are actually macros: *SetSearch, Find-*

String, *wlines*, *scroll*, *message*, and *return*. The *Setsearch* and *Find-string* macros we coded. The others (in all lowercase) are Sprint macro primitives.

I/O OPERATIONS

There are several message commands that can aid communication with the user. The main ones are *message*, *mode*, *ask*, *status*, *error*, *exitmessage*, and *set*. Each of these is discussed in detail.

The *message* Macro

The *message* macro displays a message on the status line. Here's an example:

```
message "Hello world."
```

The message will stay on the screen until either the user presses a key, or another message (or status) command clears the status line by embedding \n in its message string.

The general syntax for the *message* macro is

```
# message "string"
```

represents an optional numeric argument, and "string" represents the text you want displayed on the status line. You can use the % character to show where you want the numeric argument displayed in the message.

We use *message* in debugging to send messages to ourselves about program failure. One of our favorites, used only for development when no one else is watching and activated when a program abends, is

```
message "\nThink you're so smart, don't you?"
```

Notice how we used \n to do a carriage return. This has the effect of clearing the status line before displaying the "Think you're so smart" message.

Wherever a string is called for, you can always substitute a Q-register. So you can use a Q-register as the argument for the *message* macro. The expression message Q0 takes the contents of the Q0 register and puts it on the status line. Often Q0 contains a program name.

Sprint uses *message* in its search and replace routine, which we discussed earlier on page 125. In this routine Sprint reports how many strings have been replaced, if any. Message 1 uses the macro format sign to tell us how many expressions were replaced:

```
StrFound case {

        0    message "Not found." 1 Bell,

        1    x message "%d replaced.",

        2    message "Canceled."

        {
```

Previously the variable *StrFound* was set to either 0, 1, 2, or 3. The variable x was set to the number of replacements that were carried out. So if *StrFound* is 1, and x is, say, 12, the routine will display this message on the status line:

```
"12 replaced"
```

The *mode* Macro

The *mode* macro pushes the usual status line 25 to line 24 and then adds a second message line for a modal instruction, such as "Keyboard recording on . . . ". The message remains on throughout the macro. *Mode* uses the *statline* macro variable to adjust the screen display.

The *ask* Macro

The *ask* macro displays a string on the status line and waits for a response of **Y** or **N** from the user. If the user presses anything else,

ask beeps the speaker. Try the *ask* macro yourself. Give the command
Shift-Alt-X and enter

```
ask "Want to continue?" =
```

What value does *ask* return when you enter *Y* and when you enter *N*?
Here's a practical example that uses *ask*:

```
message "\nCreate new file "

    message Q0

    if (ask "?")
```

This example comes from one of the start-up macros. First the program
puts a message on the status line. Then the program adds a filename
to the message (from the Q0 register). Then a question mark appears,
to which we can answer *Y* or *N*. The message can use any filename in
Q0 and then allows the user to decide if the filename is appropriate.
(**Note:** Besides **Y** and **N** the user can press **Esc** or the key that you have
defined as the abort key. **Esc** (or the abort key) returns zero. You can
define the abort key by setting the *abortkey* variable. For example, the
code for **Shift-F10** is 11Ah (hex 11A). So to make **Shift-F10** the abort
key, you would code

```
11Ah -> abortkey
```

The *status* Macro

The *status* macro puts a temporary message on the status line. When
a subsequent *message*, *status*, or *ask* command is given, the message
disappears. You may want to use *status* to tell the user what is hap-
pening while your program carries out a time-consuming operation.

The *error* Macro

The *error* macro shares with the *message* macro the ability to dump
a memory buffer into a message as well as the ability to use **%d**. But
error also waits for the user to press **Esc** (an *abortkey*), and then aborts
the current macro.

The *exitmessage* Macro

We used the *exitmessage* macro in an earlier chapter. It puts a message on the screen when the screen is reset. Sprint resets the screen when a user exits to DOS or calls another program.

The *set* Macro

Usually *set* just copies a string into a Q-register. For example, to set QD to "Kumiko's Boutique" you might write

```
set QD "Kumiko's Boutique"
```

Sprint will wait for the user to enter a string from the keyboard if you just say

```
set QD
```

You can combine *message* with *set* to prompt the user and then input a string:

```
message "\nPlease enter name of project: " set QD
```

EXITING ROUTINES

Just as there are several message macros, there are several macros for exiting macros, routines, or entire programs. Because of their lack of ambiguity, our favorites are *break* and *return*. With *return*, we're reminded of similar commands in other languages—it's a sort of generic "go back to the calling macro." *return* also carries the current argument—True, False, or null—to the calling routine or program. *Break* also is a command familiar from DOS, Basic, and other languages, but in Sprint it merely breaks us out of a *do* loop or the closest enclosing loop. *break* quits a routine within a macro; *return* quits the macro.

Two exit commands that can be more subtle are *abort* and *stopped*. Like some other Sprint macros, *stopped* is followed by a command,

and the command executes before *stopped* executes. That prevents interruptions of processes that are best allowed to finish, such as a cycle of a *do* loop. If the user presses an *abortkey* such as **Esc**, the *do* loop finishes and then *stopped* returns True.

Often the programmer makes arrangements for a True result from *stopped*, such as a graceful exit. The editor also can cause a True result for *stopped* when it encounters an error or an *abort* macro linked to a *stopped* macro. The program really perceives *stopped* as:

```
If you get stopped, finish your current task and

then report to me for some other duty.
```

When you have three or four menus on your screen, one a submenu of the other, you are using the macro *abort* if you repeatedly press the **Esc** key and one menu after another disappears. *abort* exits to the closest enclosing menu macro. If it is within a macro standing alone, *abort* exits the macro. If the programmer links *abort* to an *exitmenus* macro, *abort* exits and wipes out all the menus.

TOSSING AN ARGUMENT AWAY

Remember, whenever you call a macro, it will return an argument and pass it along to the next command. Sometimes you may not want this to happen because the value passed on may corrupt the action of the succeeding macro. To throw away the current argument, just put $ on a line by itself. To test this, try:

```
testdollar:

    3 ; create the argument 3

    $ ; toss away current argument

    message "%d" ; display the argument
```

Notice that this macro does not display a 3, but a zero. If you delete or comment out the line with the $, the routine will display the number 3.

DEBUGGING A MACRO THAT DOESN'T RUN

When you begin writing macros, they may not run perfectly on the first attempt. If you get a lot of experience and you are writing multi-paragraph macros with involved branching and menus, they won't run too well either. (That's why it's best to stay with short macros, each of which you can easily debug.)

Still, the more experienced you get, the more adventurous you become and the more debugging you will do. We have developed a debugging routine that incorporates seven questions:

1. Did I label the macro poorly? Was it overwritten?
   We do this regularly, so don't feel badly if it happens to you. You can give the most innocent label to a paragraph within a macro, only to discover that the label is used in some obscure routine and you have either overwritten the existing routine, or, on reload, your novel routine has been overwritten. So, devise a label and then use search keys to check working code for a hit; if you get none, the label probably is safe. If you think your macro may have been overwritten, just recompile it.

2. Did the macro simply exit to the editor?
   When you invoke the macro, see the screen blink, and see nothing else happen, the editor probably called your macro and then never started it or suffered an abend. You'll abend if the compiled version is missing labels, doesn't have executable code where it's expected, or simply can't cope with your whole scene. Major surgery is indicated.

3. Did I code in small macros?
   If you code small macros, you can more easily debug them and develop a library of useful working code. You can easily change the order of execution of the main code by referring to these small macros in different ways. You can test each macro to see what it is returning. You also can add comments above each macro to explain its use.

4. Did I send messages to myself?
   If you embed *status* and *message* macros within your program, you usually can identify a paragraph that the editor skipped or is running slowly, as well as places where the program hangs. You can also have a macro insert statements into a Q-register for later study. (See item 7.)

5. Did I check built-in macros for odd arguments, linked commands, or unexpected variables?

   Variable declarations made when Sprint loads can affect macros you may use. Check them; the listings are in each program macro in the Sprint loading sequence, which is described in the beginning of this chapter. The variable *GlobalSearch*, for example, affects almost everything done in the Search-and-Replace menu. Some macros, such as *stopped*, take arguments after the command. Those seem to function as adverbs. In the sentence, "He ran quickly," we remember quickly as a modifier, but the power and the action are in the command ran; that's what controls the entire expression. Modifiers also can precede Sprint commands.

6. Am I aggressively using the *menu* macro?

   You can get a customized menu up and running by writing it, isolating it in its own macro, and testing it. Then you can call your customized *menu* macro from the developing macro. If the menu pops up, you know that the macro executed at least to that point. As other paragraphs come on line, you can branch to them through the menu. If a macro is buggy, the system may hang when you invoke it through a menu, and you'll be able to spot the problem quickly.

7. Am I getting an abend because of aborts?

   There may be *break*, *abort*, or *return* commands in your code that are not performing the way you expect them to. If you are branching to or calling a routine with conditional exits, your macro may be ending abnormally, without doing all its work. To detect the problem, you might try tracing the execution by inserting statements into a specific Q-register. Here's an example:

```
mark (9 qswitch "\nMade it routine X")
```

This line will insert a carriage return and the string "Made it to routine X" into Q-register number 9. After running the program, you can go into Q-register 9 and see what it contains. Press **Shift-Alt-X** and enter **to Q9**.

Important

___

To get out of a Q-register that you enter in this way, press **Ctrl-F9** and select the file that you want to move into next.

OUR REFERENCE BUTTON MACRO: *REFER*

We developed the *Refer* macro to illustrate many of the concepts discussed in this chapter. By now you are acquainted with enough macros and syntax rules to read it. It appears in Figure 7.6. If you don't have the disk that is available, containing the code in this book, we suggest you put the contents of this figure into a file called Refer.spm. Notice that the listing contains several macros. The main controlling macro is *Refer*, which appears at the end of the file. We put it there because we did not include forward declarations. Once you have typed in the text, press **Shift-Alt-R** to compile all the macros in the file. When all goes well and you have no error messages, you are ready to roll!

To use the macro, first create a reference button— enter some text and underline it. Then move to another location in the same file and enter the same text, but italicize it. Now move the cursor onto any part of the underlined text and press **Alt-R**. You will find that Sprint immediately searches for and lands on the italicized text. To jump back to the underlined text (the reference button), press **Alt-B**.

We have found many uses for this macro including an index into a file that contains a description of all Sprint macros. Instead of having to page down manually or search through many occurrences of some term, we just move the cursor to the term in the index at the top of the file and press **Alt-spacebar**.

Consider, too, that you can include many references to a single point in the file. When you activate a reference button, Sprint bypasses all of the reference buttons and moves directly to the reference point.

This allows us to embed many cross references in our help system. So when we are reviewing, say, the *bell* macro, we can easily jump to a related macro such as *message*, *prompt*, *sound*, *sounddur*, or *soundfreq*. Then we can press **Alt-B** and instantly return to the reference button that we branched from.

The code follows. You will notice that we have commented it thoroughly for your reading pleasure.

We suggest you work with *Refer* and modify it. For example, you might want to combine it with the previous *Runprog* macro so the user need only press one hotkey. The macro could then decide whether to run a program or jump into another file or destination within the current file.

Another enhancement would be to extend the capability of the *go-*

```
;
; Filename: REFER.SPM
;
;NOTE:  the main macro in this file is "refer"..  It appears at
;       the end of this listing.

;*************************** SetSearch ******************************

SetSearch:

; Read the underlined expression from the screen and put
; it in the Q2 register.  NOTE: we assume user has put the
; cursor on an underlined word or phrase

    set QD ""  ;clear QD register before loading
    set marknumber 9 ;save cursor pos. in Mark No. 9

;  If we are not already on an underline character
    if  (current != '^U')
       ('^U' r csearch)    ;reverse search for underline character

;  If we are on an underline character...
    if (current = '^U')
       (
       Maybeset             ;set a mark & turn on highlighting
       '^N' csearch c      ;move to ^N (highlight entire line)
       )
       else
          (
          rawout "^G"
          message "Please put cursor on underlined text"
          to marknumber 9
          return
          )
;   Copy target string into QD register
;   Note that we are copying the area of text from the
;   point up to and including the mark into the QD register
    copy tomark QD
    Unselect                ;turn off highlighting
;

;
```

Figure 7.6
The Refer macro.

back macro. Currently, this macro only remembers the previous reference button. In a more developed hypertext system, a user can go exploring and branch among several different nodes, and then quickly back up to the original starting place by repeatedly pressing the *goback* hotkey.

```
; *************************** FindString2 ******************************
;
FindString2 :

;USE:   search forward or backward depending on value of SearchDirection
;       Note: SearchOpt we previously initialized to 2, meaning that
;       lowercase in search string can match uppercase in text.

  ;If the SearchDirection variable <> 0
  ;    search forward.
  ;If SearchDirection is 0
  ;   we search backwards.

  if SearchDirection              ;if SearchDirection <> 0
     (SearchOpt f search qd)      ;search forward to end-of-file
  else
     (SearchOpt r search qd)      ;search backward from the point

;*************************** Goback ********************************

;    USE: Return user to initial hypertext button--that is,
;         the underlined text.

Goback:
   to marknumber 9

;



;



; Replace underline character with italic character.
;---------------------------------------------------
   mark          ;mark our place in current file
      (
      to QD    ;go into Q2 register
      ('^U' csearch)    ;goto underline character
      ('^E' -> current) ;replace it with italic char.
      )

; Convert target string to lowercase to aid matching
;---------------------------------------------------

   mark                    ;save place in file
      (
      to QD                ;go into QD register
      mark                 ;set mark at beginning of reg.
         (
         toend             ;move point to end of register.
         RegionLower       ;change everything beween point
         )                 ;and mark to lowercase
      )

; initialize variables
;---------------------

   0 -> globalsearch    ;search from expression, not top of file
   1 -> searchdirection ;initialize search forward
   1 -> SearchOpt       ;Specify that lowercase in search string
                        ;can match uppercase in text.
;


;
```

Figure 7.6—*Continued.*

```
;***********************************************************************
;****************************** Refer **********************************
;***********************************************************************

    ; USE: this macro moves the underlined phrase that the cursor is on
    ; into the QD register.  Then it replaces the underline character
    ; with an italic character (^I). The SetSearch macro handles this.

    ; Next the FindString2 macro searches forward from the current
    ; position for the "target" phrase; if we don't find the
    ; target, we search backward.  If we fail to find string we, display
    ; "Sorry" message.  If we find the string, we scroll the line that it
    ; is on to the top of the screen and then return.  User can return
    ; to initial position by pressing Alt-B, which starts goback macro.

Refer:
   SetSearch  ; move string into qd register
   if FindString2 ; if FindString2 routine succeeds
      {
      wlines scroll     ;scroll so target is at top of screen
      message "Press Alt-B to return to previous position."
      return            ;and return so user can edit
      }
   else
      {
      0->searchdirection      ;set search direction to reverse
      to marknumber 9         ;go to original file position
      if FindString2          ;search again, but backwards
         {
         wlines scroll        ;scroll to top of screen
         message "Press Alt-B to return to previous position."
         return               ;and return so user can edit
         }
      else
         {
         to marknumber 9      ;go back to original position
         message "sorry could not find expression."
         }
      }

; hotkey assignments
; ----------------------
^R : Refer  ; assign Refer macro to Alt-R
^B : Goback ; assign Goback macro to Alt-B
;
;
```

Figure 7.6—*Continued.*

IN CONCLUSION

We've covered a lot in this book. Along the way we've developed a customized menu system and three kinds of hypertext macros: *Findfile*, *Runprog*, and *Refer*. But there is a lot more to learn about Sprint macro programming. The appendices are provided to give specific information that can help you continue your study. In addition, Appendix H explains how you can use CompuServe to download and examine other useful Sprint macro programs. Have fun. If you encounter a boobytrap or just get frustrated, you may want to go for a walk, take a cold shower, or, perhaps, go screaming into the woods. You'll come back re-invigorated and ready to start coding a new time-saving, productivity-boosting Sprint macro!

Appendix A

Sprint's
Unique Keyboard

We've seen programmable keyboards, but Sprint's is the most sophisticated. The Sprint keyboard is layered and can be customized to an unprecedented degree. If you like rearranging your keyboard, you can program Sprint 512 ways. A word processor that makes so many keystrokes programmable is awesome.

We will discuss keyboard hardware and the operating system in general, and we will cover the Sprint program in particular. After a brief comparison of the PC and the AT keyboards, we'll review the key assignments Sprint makes when it loads, how to customize a keyboard, and how to make it portable.

Sprint manages the keyboard in a distinctly different way than earlier word processors. The price paid for this convenience is more complexity. Many programs use no more than 384 keys and key combinations; Sprint uses 512. The electronics and the management of keyboards isn't difficult, but we reviewed keyboard design to understand some of Sprint's subtleties. This appendix attempts to save you that trouble.

We make distinctions among four classes of keys and characters because so much keyboard language is redundant or ambiguous. We refer to the first 256 keys, which are mostly letters and numbers on the keyboard, as the *ASCII* keys. Most keyboards handle these keys the same way. We refer to the next 256 characters as *special PC characters* because they're often used for PC operations. *Special PC characters* are subdivided into the *function keys*, characters 256 to 383, which include keys F1 to F10 on the PC keyboard (F1 to F12 on the AT keyboard), and the *meta keys*, characters 384 to 511, which are three-key combinations that include the **Alt** key.

HARDWARE DETAILS

Sprint is like a conventional keyboard in the value it assigns after an ASCII key is pressed. Programs evaluate two bytes of information for each ASCII key pressed. The first byte, called the *main byte*, tells software which key was pressed. The second byte, the *auxiliary byte*, holds the scan code (hardware value) of the key. Most programs, including DOS and Sprint, read only the first byte of an ASCII key code. Some programs, such as Framework, also read the second byte of ASCII keys.

It is with the next 256 keys—the upper reaches of the keyboard—that Sprint and other programs part company. For special PC characters, IBM keyboards and software use a hexadecimal keycode, such as 0000:003B, that translates in decimal to 0000:0059. The main byte is zero, indicating that we are out of the range of ASCII characters and are using special PC characters. As with ASCII keys, the auxiliary byte is the scan code for the key. If there was no translation through software, the zero first byte and 59 decimal in the auxiliary byte means key **F1** was pressed.

Sprint refers to the zero byte for special PC characters as a *null prefix code*. Others call it the zero main byte. Whatever the name, we're referring to an empty byte used as a placeholder to indicate a character above 255—for example, key **F9**, a mouse key, a cursor arrow, or **Ctrl-Space**. For simplicity, we'll continue this discussion using decimal codes, in base 10, rather than hexadecimal codes, in base 16.

Rather than subscribing to the two-byte label for keys above 255,

Sprint translates the key code into a single, four-digit number. The key **Ctrl-F8** might be 0000:0128 in decimal for IBM, and 0283 in decimal for Sprint. Sprint adds 255 to the value of the special PC character, 0028, to get a one-byte code of 0283. Sprint gives the key another name, too. If you want to refer to that key in a macro, you must use the code F40. You can find the names of all the keys in the Spring User's Guide in Table E.1. This Table lists each possible key stroke, the hexidecimal number the keystroke produces, and the special code required to refer to that keystroke in a macro. You need only remember that special PC characters above 255 are designated in Sprint with numbers of 0256 and greater—255 plus the scan code for the key(s) pressed. Also, some of those keys have another name.

The keys above 0383 are even more distinct. These meta keys use the **Alt** key in a three-key combination, and some of the keys also include the **Shift** key and the **Control** key. Although that complicates Sprint keyboard codes, it extends the keyboard to 512 characters. **Shift-Alt-G**, for example, is Sprint key 0487. **Alt**, used with **Shift**, *meta-keys* —adds 0384—to the value of the g key, changing its value from 0103 to 0487.

Sprint is able to extend the keyboard to 512 characters because it meta-keys characters above 0383. **Shift-Alt-G**, if it could appear on the screen, would just produce a g, because the **Shift** effect is canceled when it is made with the **Alt** key.

BIOS DIFFERENCES IN PC AND AT KEYBOARDS

Now the software is slightly ahead of the hardware. Personal computers can't produce or display some of the Sprint meta keys. The problem is in the hard-wired BIOS, the read-only, Basic Input-Output System that boots the machine and routes keyboard codes. Several of the meta-key codes are not even produced by the PC BIOS.

The AT keyboards, with newer BIOS circuits, can produce more of the meta keys, but still can't use all of them. The AT keyboard is slightly different in another way. It has a **System Request** key to switch among programming tasks when the machine is in multitasking mode. Some of the function keys are repositioned, and two are added.

Probably the next generation of keyboards and BIOS will enable keyboards for as many as 512 characters. Sprint will be ready.

THE ROLE OF SOFTWARE

The Sprint coding is so intricate that keycodes can be manipulated by macros between the ROM BIOS and the Central Processing Unit (CPU). Sprint can directly process keypresses.

The Sprint program maintains its own buffer of key-presses called a *queue*, which can hold 1,024 characters. Keypresses also are stored by hardware in a BIOS buffer and in another hardware buffer in the keyboard. Any of the buffers can be flushed at certain times or filled with characters at other times.

When Sprint's internal queue is empty, Sprint uses a *Getkey* macro to fetch a keycode from the next buffer in the pecking order, the ROM-BIOS hardware buffer. The user might have pressed a **Y** or **N** in response to a Sprint prompt, but if the Sprint queue is empty, Sprint can't continue until *Getkey* fetches the keypress.

The keyboard buffer can hold up to 20 characters. Scan codes go from that buffer to BIOS, which can hold 15 characters in very low memory. Most programs use a DOS service to get a keycode from BIOS for delivery to the CPU. The main byte is stored in the AL-register (the low byte of the accumulator) and the auxiliary byte is stored in the AH-register (the high byte of the accumulator).

Getkey can use that DOS service, called interrupt 33, function 11. But *Getkey* also can directly issue BIOS interrupt 22 to get a key away from BIOS, into the CPU, and to the program. Because the Sprint program uses only a one-byte keycode—the auxiliary byte—the main byte in the AL-register is meaningless and the keycode is in the AH-register.

Getkey is not the only macro that can circumvent the operating system. The *key* macro also can go directly to BIOS. In BIOS, scan codes may be stored without leading zeros—not as 0012, but simply as 12. To fill out a byte, the *key* macro will add leading zeros, to return a code of 0012.

The *Sprint Advanced User's Guide* says that "the returned values from the BIOS are falsified into a zero prefix byte stream so that *key* always returns (full) bytes. Because of this translation, the BIOS stream does not match what is returned from the BIOS, although the letters, control keys, and arrow keys return the same things." In other words, if you try reading internal data with Assembler routines to find bugs in the BIOS stream, you're on your own.

THE SP.SPM KEY TABLE

There are about 211 special PC characters listed in the key assignment table at the end of the *Sp.spm* macro. Those keys are in addition to the 256 ASCII keys. The key table in *Sp.spm* lists the original assignments for function keys—assignments that we can change. We can return to the table in the original *Sp.spm* code, if necessary, to check the original assignments. It's a baseline we often have used to restore our keyboard after we totally mucked it up in some misbegotten adventure.

When we discuss key reassignments, however, we do not include the ASCII keys. Although they can be reassigned, that is rare because most users do not want to lose access to English and Arabic characters.

THE QUICKCARD KEY TABLE

Of the 211 function keys, the Sprint program can recall and list only about half of them. When you issue the QuickCard command from the Utilities submenu, a special macro called *Refcard.spm* is compiled. The macro reads memory for the key assignments and writes the assignments for a subset of 115 function keys to a file that it creates and names QCard.spr, a text file.

The QuickCard schedule is convenient because initially it shows us most of the factory settings for function keys that can be reassigned from the keyboard. As we customize the keyboard, QuickCard reports the current key assignments. Saving the Qcard.spr file to disk is a way of documenting the evolution of the function keys assignable from the keyboard, if you can avoid confusion among filenames.

HOW TO ASSIGN KEYS

Through Sprint macros, programming of the operating system, or a hardware change, any key can be assigned to represent any character. We limit this explanation to assignment of function keys through the Sprint program. There are at least three ways to reassign keys.

Key Assignments Made through Macros

The key assignment table in the *Sp.spm* macro is an example of a key assignment made in a macro. The table is a list of the original function for each key, what we might call the default value of the key. It is part of the Borland Advanced User Interface. Through macros such as *Sp.spm*, you can assign or reassign all 211 function keys.

If you write a macro and embed a new key assignment in it, as we did in Chapter 6, the reassignment is effective when the macro is compiled into binary code. It is written to memory, and when you quit Sprint, it is written to the overlay file, *Sp.ovl*. On start-up, Sprint reads the *Sp.ovl* file with the new key function, making the new macro available.

You can restore the key to its original meaning if you use the Reset Shortcuts command on the User Interface submenu. That command deletes the key reassignment in memory and in the overlay file, and then returns to the original (default) key assignment. Usually you also can change a key reassignment made in a macro by using the Function Keys command on the User Interface submenu. That command will give you prompts to reassign the key to another function.

If the macro's key is reassigned, the macro once bound to that key can be run by using the Enter command on the Macros submenu, or by pressing **Shift-Alt-X** to get the "macro:" prompt.

If you want to again bind the key within the macro, you can recompile the macro. Then the key assignment embedded in the macro again will be read into the overlay file, and that assignment again will be on top of the default value of the key.

Key Assignments Made with Menu Commands

If you use the Function Keys command in the User Interface submenu of the Customize submenu, you can reassign the subset of about 115 keys. Dispatch keys explain the difference in the number of keys you can reassign through the menu, 115, and those you could directly program through macros, 211.

Sprint has so many functions and macros that not all of them can be called with one key, such as **F9**, or with two keys, such as **Ctrl-X**. A three-key combination seems to be required. Among three-key combinations are meta keys above 0383. But some of the meta keys, such as **Alt-Shift-"** (**Alt-Shift-quote** key) won't produce a keycode, because neither the PC BIOS nor the AT BIOS recognizes them.

Sprint can assign several functions to **Ctrl**-key combinations, which are recognized. After it exhausts two-key **Ctrl** combinations, such as **Ctrl-I** to insert a tab, Sprint uses three-key **Ctrl** combinations. The **Ctrl-K**, **Ctrl-O**, and **Ctrl-Q** keys are dispatchers to the three-key combinations. **Ctrl-K-P**, for example, prints an entire file.

Sprint calls the binding of a third key to a **Ctrl-K** key Ctrl-K commands or CtrlKDispatch. We detour into this little thicket merely to explain that **Ctrl-K** commands, **Ctrl-O** commands, and **Ctrl-Q** commands cannot be reassigned through the menus. The key dispatch tables do not appear when we summon the QuickCard of key shortcuts and functions.

The dispatch keys largely account for the difference in size between the Quickcard listing of assigned function keys, and the key schedule at the end of *Sp.spm*. The dispatch keys could be reassigned, if anyone really cared, only by compiling a macro.

The Function Keys command on the User Interface submenu allows you to redefine only the meaning of **F1** through **F10** function keys, and any **Ctrl-Alt** or **Shift** versions of them, and any two-key **Ctrl**-letter or **Alt**-letter shortcut. The key reassignment commands from the menus can be used, then, only to shift commands from one **Function (1–12)**, **Alt**, or **Ctrl** key to another.

We discussed hardware, keycodes, function keys and meta keys to explain the apparent anomaly of the short QuickCard listing of function keys and the longer table of function keys at the end of *Sp.spm*.

To make and check changes, while reassigning function keys from the keyboard, you will be moving (inconveniently) between the Utilities submenu (to get to the QuickCard command) and the User Interface submenu (to get to the Function Keys command).

Key Assignments Made as Menu Shortcuts

The simplest way to assign a key is to use what Sprint calls a menu shortcut. If you are using some command from the menu frequently, you can highlight the command with the menu lightbar, then press **Ctrl-Enter**, and at the prompt enter a new key to call that menu item. If you have Menu Shortcuts turned on (it's on the Customize submenu), the new key assignment, the new shortcut, appears when its menu opens.

We reassigned **Alt-Q**, for example, to issue the QuickCard command, because we were checking QuickCard so often while preparing this appendix. **Alt-Q** then appeared beside the QuickCard command when we opened the Utilities submenu. When we quit Sprint, the new key assignment, the new menu shortcut, was written to the overlay file, so that when we started Sprint again, it was still there. It is permanently there until reset.

We could remove it by using the Reset Shortcuts command. That erases the new key assignment, the new menu shortcut, and restores the original meaning of the key.

Another way to deal with **Alt-Q** is to reassign it again. If we get tired of **Alt-Q** as a command to execute QuickCard, we can use the Function Keys command from the User Interface submenu to assign it, again, to some other duty.

A third way to change **Alt-Q** would be to highlight yet another menu item, and again press **Ctrl-Enter**, and again press **Alt-Q**. Then, through the Menu Shortcuts utility, **Alt-Q** could take on a fourth identity.

Here is the key table produced by QuickCard.

Key	Description
Ctrl-A	Edit/Cursor/Word-Previous
Ctrl-B	Misc/Screen Redraw (Reformat ASCII)
Ctrl-C	Edit/Cursor/Screen-Next
Ctrl-D	Edit/Cursor/Character-Next
Ctrl-E	Edit/Cursor/Line-Previous
Ctrl-F	Edit/Cursor/Word-Next

Ctrl-G	Edit/Delete/Character-Current
Backspace	Edit/Delete/Character-Previous
Tab	Insert/Tab
Ctrl-K	Ctrl-K Commands
Ctrl-L	Edit/Search/Find Next
Enter	Insert/Paragraph Mark
Ctrl-N	Insert/Break Line, But Stay on Line
Ctrl-O	Ctrl-O Commands
Ctrl-P	Menu/Typestyle
Ctrl-Q	Ctrl-Q Commands
Ctrl-R	Edit/Cursor/Screen-Previous
Ctrl-S	Edit/Cursor/Character-Previous
Ctrl-T	Edit/Delete/Word-Next
Ctrl-U	Edit/Block/Insert-Paste
Ctrl-V	Customize/Options/Insert Mode
Ctrl-W	Edit/Scroll-Down
Ctrl-X	Edit/Cursor/Line-Next
Ctrl-Y	Edit/Delete/Line
Ctrl-Z	Edit/Scroll-Up
Esc	Misc/Cancel
Ctrl-_	Insert/Special Hyphen
Ctrl-Backspace	Edit/Delete/Word-Left
Ctrl-Space	Insert/Non-Breaking Space
F1	Misc/Help
F2	Glossary/Recall
F3	Edit/Block/Toggle Select
F4	Edit/Block/Copy
F5	Edit/Block/Move-Cut
F6	Edit/Block/Insert-Paste
F7	Edit/Search/Find
F8	Edit/Search/Search and Replace
F9	Edit/Go to Line
F10	Menu/Main
F11	Menu/Main
F12	Menu/Main
Shift-F1	Menu/Spell
Shift-F2	Window/Resize
Shift-F3	Window/Open
Shift-F4	Window/Close

Shift-F5	Window/Zoom
Shift-F6	Window/Next
Shift-F7	Window/Scroll All Up
Shift-F8	Window/Scroll All Down
Shift-F9	Window/Close All
Shift-F10	Menu/Main
Shift-F11	Menu/Main
Shift-F12	Menu/Main
Ctrl-F1	Spell/Correct/Every Bad Word
Ctrl-F2	File/Save
Ctrl-F3	File/Open
Ctrl-F4	File/Close
Ctrl-F5	File/Pick List-Previous
Ctrl-F6	File/Pick List-Next
Ctrl-F7	Print/Paginate
Ctrl-F8	Print/Screen Preview
Ctrl-F9	File/Pick List
Ctrl-F10	Menu/Main
Ctrl-F11	Menu/Main
Ctrl-F12	Menu/Main
Alt-F1	Misc/Thesaurus
Alt-F10	Menu/Main
Home	Edit/Cursor/Line-Beginning
Up	Edit/Cursor/Line-Previous
PgUp	Edit/Cursor/Screen-Previous
Left	Edit/Cursor/Character-Previous
'5' on NumPad	Edit/Cursor/Line-Next
Right	Edit/Cursor/Character-Next
End	Edit/Cursor/Line-End
Down	Edit/Cursor/Line-Next
PgDn	Edit/Cursor/Screen-Next
Ins	Customize/Options/Insert Mode
Del	Edit/Block/Move-Cut
Shift-Tab	Insert/Indent
Ctrl-Home	Edit/Cursor/Screen-Top
Ctrl-PgUp	Edit/Cursor/Document-Top
Ctrl-Left	Edit/Cursor/Word-Previous
Ctrl-Right	Edit/Cursor/Word-Next
Ctrl-End	Edit/Cursor/Screen-Bottom

Ctrl-PgDn	Edit/Cursor/Document-Bottom
Ctrl-H	Edit/Delete/Character-Previous
Ctrl-I	Insert/Tab
Ctrl-J	Misc/Help
'Enter' on NumPad	Insert/Paragraph Mark
Ctrl-Alt [	Misc/Cancel
Alt-A	Layout/Ruler/Edit on Screen
Alt-B	Edit/Block/Reselect
Alt-C	Menu/Customize
Alt-D	Insert/Decimal Tab
Alt-E	Menu/Edit
Alt-F	Menu/Files
Alt-G	Edit/Place mark/Go to
Alt-I	Menu/Insert
Alt-K	Edit/Block/Toggle Column Select
Alt-L	Menu/Layout
Alt-M	Edit/Place mark/Set
Alt-N	Layout/Page Breaks/Insert
Alt-P	Menu/Print
Alt-Q	Menu/Quit
Alt-R	Layout/Ruler/Insert
Alt-S	Menu/Style
Alt-T	Menu/Typestyle
Alt-U	Menu/Utilities
Alt-W	Menu/Windows
Alt-X	Menu/Quit
Alt-Z	Customize/Screen/Codes
Shift-Alt-R	Macro/Run
Shift-Alt-U	Customize/User Interface/Load
Shift-Alt-V	Misc/Display Current Version
Shift-Alt-X	Macro/Enter

Appendix B

Special Control Characters

Any characters within the quotation marks in a Sprint macro are taken literally, except for these special character codes:

Character	Function
\a	Bell (also known as ASCII ^G)
\b	Backspace (^H)
\f	Form feed (^L)
\n	Hard return (^J)
\r	Carriage return (^M)
\t	Tab (^I)
\v	Vertical tab (ruler indicator, ^K)
\>	Wide space (spring, ^F)
\^	Caret
\\	Backslash
\'	Single quote
\"	Double quote
\NNN	A constant in octal notation
\xNN	A constant in hex notation
^X	Any control character (^A, ^B, etc.)

Appendix C
Sprint Symbols and Their Meanings

Sprint uses symbols and operators similar to those in languages such as C, Pascal, and Basic. The operators are evaluated in a similar order of precedence. But one exception is that the bitwise logical operators &, ~, ^, and | have a slightly higher priority in Sprint. The precedence of the operators is

```
Unary - and ~

*, /, %, &, and ^

<< and >>

=, -, and |

<, <=, = or ==, != or <>, >=, and >

Unary !
```

&&

|| and ->

All others, such as `if`, `while`, `attribute`

The Sprint editor processes only one expression at a time. For each expression, only one value is returned. That value is carried as an argument to the next expression. As explained in the Sprint documentation, some operators (such as +) take more than one argument. For those operators, the remaining arguments are supplied by words after the one being executed. The macro editor recursively calls itself to execute these post arguments and to evaluate things in order of precedence. For instance, the macro 1 + 2 first executes 1 (returning an argument of 1 if it is successful), then it executes +. The + operator saves the 1 argument, then executes the next word, 2, which returns an argument of 2. The + operator then checks the command after the 2 to see if it has higher precedence (if it does, it will be executed next). Then + adds the returned argument to the saved one, and returns a new argument of 3.

THE PRINTF % IDENTIFIERS

Also of some importance is the printf % convention carried over from the C language. Sprint borrows identifiers from the *printf* command. The identifiers use a percentage sign and a lowercase letter. This percentage sign should not be confused with the modulus operator %, which stands alone. In Sprint:

- %d means print a number as a signed decimal integer.
- %u means print a number as an unsigned integer.
- %c means print a number as a character.
- %x means print a number as an integer in hex format.

As in Basic, Pascal, and C, you can set the width of a printed field by placing a number between the % and the letter. For example, a decimal field width of 4 would be %4d.

If you need to print a percent sign when using a macro, you will have to enter %%.

An example of the printf % convention is this composite macro that finds a string. It reads in part:

```
StrFound case {

0    message "Not found." 1 Bell,

1    x message "%d replaced.",

2    message "Cancelled."

}
```

The %d is a placeholder that takes an integer telling how many matching strings were found and replaced.

MATHEMATICAL OPERATORS

+   The addition sign returns the sum of two values. In the following composite macro, a character in uppercase is converted to lowercase by adding 20Hex to it:

```
ToLower :

    if IsUpper (current + 20H->current) else c
```

++   Increments some variable by 1 and returns the result. This is an operator from C and C++. Some built-in variables that also can be Boolean expressions can be changed, returning 1 or 0 (True or False). But in general, this symbol just adds 1 to x. For example, the following composite macro increases the number of windows by 1 when it is called:

```
WindowOpen :

   if !zoom ++windows

   else {

      1 bell

      message "\nNo new windows may be opened while

zoomed."

         }
```

−	The minus sign. In (N − M), if N is null, M is returned. In the composite macro below, the routine counts the number of lines, then places the cursor on the next-to-last line:

```
BottomOfScreen : wlines − 1−>dline
```

−−	The opposite function and value of ++.
=	Returns True if the values are equal, and False if they are not.
==	The same as =.
N<>M N!=M	Both of these expressions return True if N is not equal to M.
>	Greater than. Returns True if the left value is greater than the right value. Otherwise returns False.
>=	Greater than or equal to. Returns True if the left value is greater than or equal to the right value. Otherwise returns False.
<	Less than. Returns True if the left value is less than the right value. Otherwise returns False.

<=   Less than or equal to. Returns True if the left value is less than or equal to the right value. Otherwise returns False.

<<   The shift left operator. Bits are shifted left the number of places indicated by the number following <<. For example, in binary, 1 is

```
0000 0001
```

If we shift the bits 4 places to the left, we get

```
0001 0000 (decimal 16)
```

So the expression (1<< 4) returns 16.

>>   The shift right operator. In the expression 203 >> 2, 203 decimal becomes 50 decimal. The number 203 in binary is

```
1100 1011
```

When we shift the bits right two places, the number becomes

```
0011 0010 (50 in decimal)
```

Notice that the two 1 bits on the right are lost, and two zero bits are added on the left.

~ (tilde)   The tilde does what is called a one's complement on a number. That is, it flips each of the bits. So if x = 10, then ~x will return −11. That is

```
0000 1010 (binary for decimal 10)
```

becomes

```
1111 0101 (binary for decimal −11)
```

Notice that ~ is a unary operator. That is, you put it in front of a single variable or delimited expression. You don't put it between two variables like a logical operator such as ||.

*   The multiplication sign. In the expression below, if x is greater than or equal to 0 *and* x is less than or equal to 9, a number is multiplied by 10 and x is added to it:

```
if (x >= '0' && x <= '9') (n * 10 + x - '0'->n)
```

N/M   N is divided by M, but an integer is returned. The value is rounded down to the nearest integer. To prevent crashes, division by zero is not undefined; when M=0, N/M=0. The following composite macro divides the number of lines on the screen by 2 to scroll the cursor to the center of the screen:

```
CenterScreen : (wlines/2) redraw
```

N\M   This division sign returns an unsigned integer, unlike the forward slash. Again, the value is rounded down to the nearest integer. The backslash also is used as an escape character—as with \n, a newline command—or as a symbol separating filenames from subdirectories in a DOS path. So observe the context of the \ symbol. For example, when sending an order to the print routine for a number of copies, an integer is required. The routine can't print a fraction of a copy, so $10\frac{1}{4}$ copies would be rounded down to 10. Here is an example from the program:

```
NumCopies "Number of Copies\>%d"

        PrintCopiesHelp 1 rangeget 9999 "Number of

        Copies" ->NumCopies,
```

%   The percentage symbol can be one of the most confusing symbols in Sprint. See the discussion at the beginning of this appendix about the use of % as a placeholder.

In macros, the sign also can mean, in effect, current. The

ovlread macro documentation suggests a command that reads

```
if ovlmodf ovlwrite "%"
```

It means that if ovlmodf is set to 1, save the changes to disk, using the name of the last overlay file read. (Note that Sprint sets ovlmodf to 1 whenever anything is changed that would require sp.ovl to be updated.)

% also functions as the strict mathematical symbol for modulus. In N % M, the value returned is N modulus M. The modulus is used in integer arithmetic to give the remainder when the integer on the left is divided by the integer on the right. In 13 modulus 5, the value is 3, because that is the remainder of 13 divided by 5. Much more often the % sign is used as the familiar printing symbol group and placeholder, such as %d in the language C.

–>   This is the assignment operator. You can use it to assign a numeric value to a variable as in

```
1079 -> x
```

This is like x = 1079 in BASIC.

LOGICAL OPERATORS

!   The not, or negation character. This has wide use in *core.spm* and *sp.spm* to shorten commands. For example, the *IsStartOfLine* composite macro, to test whether the pointer is at the start of the line, means if the cursor *cannot* be reversed from the point, or if it is at a new line, it must be at the start-of-line:

```
IsSol : mark (!(r c) || isnl)
```

|| This is the logical OR. This operator has the editor evaluate the expression on the left. If the expression is True, the value True is returned, the expression on the right is not even evaluated, and processing continues. If the expression on the left is False, the || symbol has the editor test the expression on the right. If that is True, the value True is returned, and processing continues. *False is returned only if both statements are false.* For example, the following composite macro tests whether a character is a letter. If the first condition is False, it is not lowercase, so the second condition is checked. If the second condition is False, it is not a capital either. If both conditions are False, it must not be a letter; then *IsAlpha* would return, False:

```
IsAlpha :

(current >= 'a' && current <= 'z') || (current >='A'

&& current <= 'Z')
```

&   The bitwise And. This operator forces evaluation of two values bit-for-bit, and returns 1 for a resulting bit only if the corresponding bits of the values are both 1. The classic example of the bitwise And is that $1 + 0 = 0$, and $0 + 0 = 0$, but $1 + 1 = 1$. In Boolean terms, a result is True only if *both* the first term and the second term are True. For Booleans, treated as 1 (True) or 0 (False), a value of 1 is returned only if both terms also evaluate to True. In the following example, if SearchOpt returns 1 (successful or True), the expression following it is executed:

```
if (SearchOpt & 1) (mark (to QD mark (toend

RegionLower)))
```

&&   This is the logical AND: An expression is True only if both elements of it are True, and it is False otherwise. In the following composite abbreviated macro, the *do* loop is triggered only if there is more than one window open and the zoom feature is *not* being used:

```
WindowResize :

    if (windows > 1 && !zoom) {

    do    {

        draw

        message "\nPlus (+) and minus (-) resize

        current window, ESC and ENTER exit."

        GetKey case {

        . . .
```

^　　The bitwise eXclusive (sometimes called XOR). In XOR, the value returned is 0 or False if two bits are the same, and 1 if two bits are different. In a Boolean True/False evaluation, if one expression is True and one expression is False, True is returned. This operator is rarely used.

^^　　This is like a logical exclusive OR. The ^^ operator means that one is True but not both. Here's an expression:

(A ^^ B)

If A is True and B is also True, the result will be False. If A is True and B is False, the result will be True. Also, if B is True and A is False, the result will be True. (We haven't yet used this operator, but someday it may come in handy.)

LITERALS

'X'　　When you type any legal keyboard character in quotes somewhere in a macro command, the macro will use the ASCII value of the character. Within a macro, for example, 'Z' is evaluated as 90 (or hexadecimal 5A). This process is relatively transparent to the user, however, because the output is converted back to English. You may be able to take advantage of this strict ASCII handling for long, complex sort routines.

To send a message to a user on the status line, you could the following form. Recall that \n is just an escape sequence that, in Sprint, clears the status line for the message:

```
message "\n This is a message to the user."
```

Q0 through QP
These are names of Q registers. The possibilities are from Q0 to Q9, and from QA to QP; 26 in all. An example: Set Q1 Q0 moves the string or value in Q0 to Q1; often the string is a filename.

^char
~char
~^char
These symbols, such as ^F2, ~A, and ~^I, just represent **Control**-key, **Alt**-key, and **Ctl-Alt**-key combinations used to call macros. The first command saves a file with the *Save* macro. The second command changes the ruler, and the third inserts a tab.

F1
The F keys with a number, 0 through 10, execute the macros bound to those keys. **F1**, for instance, calls the *HelpMenu* composite macro when it is invoked in another macro as 'F1'. **F0** is considered the spacebar; **F10** calls the Main menu. Sprint documentation refers to the function keys as "hyper" keys. They are listed at the end of the *sp.spm* macro. This is a five-page listing that can be subtle. But the program is generally faithful to the convention for such special keys—function keys, shifted function keys, cursor-control keys, and **Ctrl-Alt** combinations. On the hardware level, in the pair of bytes stored in the ROM-BIOS buffer for special keys, the low-order main byte typically is given the value 0 and the high-order auxiliary byte is given a value that represents the special key pressed. Sprint calls that, confusingly, number + 256. In the *sp.spm* key table, on the other hand, it says, more conventionally, "handle IBM function key 0 prefix." These keys are programmable and can be reassigned with macros. Before

you try invoking function keys or other special keys within macros, it's wise to be aware of the language of the documentation and to observe the assignments in the key tables. See also Appendix A on the Sprint keyboard.

$ This is frequently used in more complex macros. In Pascal, it is used as a compiler directive. In Sprint, it is used with *case* macros and it returns a value of 0, null, or False; or it selects the default option. The $ symbol thus is powerful for short, decision-making, branching routines.

?   The question mark character can be used in an if-then test to execute a command. It tests whether a condition is True or False. The syntax is expression ? command1 {:command2}. If the first expression is True, the first command (or series of commands) executes. If the expression is false, command2 (or a string of commands) executes. For example, in the following composite macro, the ? operates to fire the macro only if a chosen character is between lowercase a and lowercase z. If both conditions return True, the value 20 hex is subtracted from the character. A lowercase c (63H) would then become an uppercase C (43H). If the character isn't a lowercase letter, the character is unchanged (: z). Z is used here only as a variable name:

```
CharToUpper : int z
        z >= 'a' && z <= 'z' ? z - 20h : z
```

=   The equal sign is used only at the end of a macro. It echoes the number on the status line, the same as would the expression, message "%d". This is so you can quickly type macros such as 2 + 2 =, and see the answer 4 on the status line. It's also a good way to check the value returned by a macro. Here is an example:

```
testcube:  int x

    x*x*x        ;cube the incoming argument

    =            ;display argument on status line
```

If you give the command 3 testcube, Sprint will display 27 on the status line.

N = "string" The letter N, here, represents some numeric value. This expression will echo and format the string on the status line. For example, you can enter $2 + 2 =$ "%x" and see the answer in hex.

: When seen by the compiler in a macro command, **at flush left**, the colon alerts the editor to immediately execute the following command. It is used mostly with conversion files for different word processors.

It also is used with the ? operator, discussed earlier.

Appendix D

About Marks and Points

Points and marks seem simple at first glance, but the subject quickly becomes involved. Points and marks are crucial tools for navigation in Sprint. They can lead you astray or they can guide your macros and programs. You may want to make artful use of them.

The *mark* in Sprint can be considered a bookmark. It precisely locates a point in text between two characters, and marks the place you last visited in each file. When you have several files open and you are using several memory locations for things such as macros, glossary items, and routines that call other programs, you may have several marks spread about your system.

A *point* in Sprint is the position in the text where editing occurs. The point, like the mark, is always between two characters, or at the top of the file, or at the end of a file. When you copy text and insert it somewhere, you are inserting at the point. You should think of the point as an imaginary cursor, just to the left of the actual cursor.

Points and marks are abstractions, and we think they are unique to Sprint. It takes time to get comfortable with them. By the end of this appendix, we think you'll be setting marks and moving points fearlessly and artfully.

POINTS

We developed a macro called TestPoints. In TestPoints, a test mark and a test point are set up to display how the two can either help a program or jumble it. We experimented with this so we could watch it develop on the status line. Check it out:

```
TestPoints :

    Set Q7 ""

    message "\n" Q7

    2000 wait

    Set Q7 "Mary had a little lamb"

    message "\n" Q7

    2000 wait

    mark {7 qswitch

        insert "whose fleece was white as snow"}

    message "\n" Q7
```

We named this file Points.spm and we loaded it as a macro. In line 4 look at the 2000 *wait* commands; they stall the program for 2 seconds each time, so that we can clearly see the text displayed on the status line. As the text is changed, we can watch the progression. We are using register Q7 and a *qswitch* macro to get to and from the register.

The macro tells the editor to clear register Q7, to show us that it is clear, then to write a message in it. Next, the editor is instructed to show us the message, then to add some text, and then to show us the complete sentence.

You can reproduce this effect on your system, if you wish, just by copying this macro. Common sense tells us that when it is complete, it should display the message:

```
Mary had a little lamb whose fleece was white as snow
```

But, alas, it displays instead the message:

```
whose fleece was white as snowMary had a little lamb
```

Mary appears in an inverted sentence, the poor thing, because we didn't know a point from a mark. Furthermore, our program didn't even have the courtesy to put a space between the beginning of the first string and the end of the second string. You see how a misplaced point or mark could easily scramble your text.

It could have been slightly worse. If you write and run this composite macro, and if you don't use the *mark* macro, you'll discover that *TestPoints* moves into the Q7 register writes the test string directly to your screen. Your current file seems to have disappeared. You'll see an otherwise empty screen, no ruler, and the inverted sentence in lines 1 and 2. You can get back to your current file by pressing **Ctrl-F9** and selecting it from menu of open files.

The *mark* command, in this example, enables you to keep your place in the current buffer. If you don't use the *mark* command, you are not returned to your work but left in register Q7. Here's our example:

```
mark {7 qswitch

    insert "whose fleece was white as snow"}

message "\nl" Q7
```

We *marked* our spot in our current file so *qswitch* wouldn't send us permanently into Q7, and then we enclosed in braces the commands we wanted executed; in this case, it can be some trailing commands, or all of them. When the editor finished the commands, it returned us to our current file, our current buffer. To repeat again, the *mark* command allowed the editor to go into the Q7 register and do its business, but returned the point to us when the processing was complete. That is only one function of the *mark* macro and the point.

But why did the sentence get inverted? Because the point was at the beginning of Q7. But didn't we just say the point was in our current file? Well . . . yes.

In fact, there are many points. Each buffer has its own point, and there can be as many as 24 buffers. There also can be 24 registers (the Q0 to Q9 and QA to QP memory buffers), and each of them has a point and is sometimes called a buffer. When you move from file to register to glossary to file, you should think of where the point is.

It is always at the last place visited by the editor, or at the top of the file. It is always *between* two characters, while the cursor usually is *upon* a character. If the cursor is upon a period at the end of a sentence, the point is between the period and the next space. When the cursor is on the Letter s in space, the point is between the s and the p.

In our example macro, we said in part

```
Set Q7 "Mary had a little lamb"

message "\n" Q7

2000 wait

mark {7 qswitch

    insert "whose fleece was white as snow"}
```

When we used the *insert* primitive macro, it inserted the string of text at the point in the Q7 register—that is, at the top of the Q7 register. That is why the sentence was inverted; the end of the sentence was inserted at the point at the top of the file. To correct this, we can just edit the code to read:

```
toend insert "whose fleece was white as snow"}
```

We still get poor output because we did not insert a space between the point and the end-of-file. Because we moved the point *toend*, but did not insert a space, the register reads

```
Mary had a little lambwhose fleece was white as snow
```

If you'll bear with us for one little adjustment, we'll add a space to the string so it will format correctly. Now it works:

```
TestPoints :

    Set Q7 " "

    message "\n" Q7

    2000 wait

    Set Q7 "Mary had a little lamb"

    message "\n" Q7

    2000 wait

    mark {7 qswitch

        toend insert "whose fleece was white as snow"}

    message "\n" Q7

Mary had a little lamb whose fleece was white as snow
```

This was an accomplishment. We wrote a string to a register. We used the *mark* macro to safely return to the current buffer. We manipulated a point in a register and added data correctly. We used the status line, the *message* macro, and a *wait* macro to watch the composite macro as it executed. We're practically programming.

MARKS

A few other marks and commands are of interest. The marks are *themark* and *gmark*; and the commands are *aftermark*, *beforemark*, *setmark*, *swapmark*, *tomark*, and *togmark*.

There is a stack of marks. The top mark on the stack, if no other marks are pushed, is called the global mark. This is the mark that is used to indicate selected regions in the editor, when, for example, you highlight a region of text. The top mark is called the current mark. It also is called *themark*. When no marks are in use, the global mark is *themark*.

Every time you use a mark, you add it to the top of the stack. You also assign it to the current point. If you try to highlight a word and press the key **F3** to begin highlighting, you've just set a mark. The mark is at the point, and sometimes they both are at the cursor location.

When you then move the cursor through text to be highlighted, you are moving the point, but the mark remains at a unique location in memory and in text. When you get to the place in the text where you want highlighting to stop, you also stop the point at that place. If you chose to underline the highlighted text, the command would operate between the mark in the file and the point, that is, between the marked location in memory and the current location in memory. In a linear sense, the file is marked from an earlier position to a later one.

But in Q registers, the point can be at the end of file, if we can call it that, and we may select text between the point and the mark. In our example, we were to add the commands:

```
mark (7 qswitch

    r toend set themark 1-> select toend

    draw

message "\n" Q7

2000 wait
```

The macro will select text from the point (at the end of the file, in this case) to the mark (called *themark*, in this case). The macro will highlight the entire string in the register, but by working backwards, as it were, from the point at end-of-file to *themark* at top-of-file.

You might try this macro on your system. The entire macro now looks like this:

```
Testpoints

    Set Q7 ""
```

```
    message "\n" Q7

    2000 wait

    Set Q7 "Mary had a little lamb"

    message "\n" Q7

    2000 wait

    mark {7 qswitch

        toend insert "whose fleece was white as snow"}

    message "\n" Q7

    2000 wait

    mark {7 qswitch

        r toend set themark 1->select toend

            draw

    message "\n" Q7

    2000 wait
```

If you compile and run the *TestPoints* macro, you'll see the *draw* macro redraw the screen and highlight one line of text on a new screen, in the Q7 register which is a buffer with no *fname*.

In the last six lines of code, we set a mark and switched to buffer Q7. From the current point, which happened to be at end-of-file, we reversed the cursor *toend* (the start-of-file), set a mark, selected the text *toend* (now, to the end-of-file), and drew the finished text to highlight it. When the operation was over, the point returned, as you will be able to tell from your screen, to the start-of-file!

The safest way to deal with points and marks is to locate the point, often where the cursor stopped, and set a mark to span a section of the buffer or file.

SWAPMARK

You can find marks through commands that are available on the menus. If you open the Edit menu, you'll see a menu called Place Mark. Open that, and you'll see options to set a mark or to find a mark. If at this very spot in the text we used those menus and set a mark called 9, the editor would process the command:

```
set marknumber 9
```

It would embed the mark, transparently, in text. You also can use the shortcut keys **Alt-M** to set any mark from Zero to 9. If we moved on in text, but wished to return later, we could use the menus to go

```
to marknumber 9
```

Also, we could use the keys **Alt-G** and name the mark we seek, in this case, 9.

Each mark has a unique name. At the beginning of this discussion, we explained mark, global mark, current mark, and themark. The macro primitive *set* can be used with unique mark names, resulting in command lines like these:

```
set themark
```

```
set marknumber 9
```

```
set gmark
```

Macro primitives also can be used with mark names for commands like:

```
before marknumber 9
```

```
after gmark
```

```
swap themark
```

The last command swaps the point and the mark.

Swapping the point and the mark is an important skill for Sprint programmers. In our previous poetry example, we manipulated the point with the command line:

```
toend insert "whose fleece was white as snow"
```

We used the macros **toend** and *insert* to move the point. In an early version of the *FindString* macro developed in Chapter 7, we used another command:

```
mark (found 1 -> select draw 0 wait Unselect swap themark)
```

It swapped the point and the mark—twice. When an expression was located by the program, the point was at the beginning of the expression. We set a mark and issued the **found** command, which moved the point to the end of the expression; then the expression had a mark at one end and a point at the other. Only then could we use the *select* macro to highlight the region between the mark and the point.

After the screen was redrawn with the cursor at the target, we swapped the point and the mark to return the point, as usual, to the beginning of the target expression. In that program, when we used the option Return to Original Location, the cursor returned to the beginning of the first occurrence of the expression, to the point.

It takes a little time to become proficient with points and marks. Load and run some of our macros, and you'll be far ahead of us when we started developing programs.

Appendix E

A Guide to Selected Macros

This is a compilation of only a few of the Sprint macros—about 50 of about 210 macros and macro variables. We focused on macros for navigation, exits, and files because we use them so often. A complete hypertext macro encyclopedia is available on disk from Seyer Associates. See the order card in this book.

When you see the symbol #, it usually refers to a number. The # appears before the macro, such as "# call," and it appears in the description of macros, such as "Returns #".

Frequent reference is made to memory buffers such as Q0. This should be read as buffer Q Zero. We never use buffer QO, although it exists. Buffers are in a hierarchy from Q Zero through QP. Various typefaces and texts can leave readers searching for strings in buffer QO, which is the buffer before QP, when the strings actually exist in buffer Q0, the first of the buffers.

The best way to learn about macro commands is to search the Sp.spm and the Core.spm programs and to copy code fragments. They reveal the operation of the macro in context. There are many more examples than we present here, and in some places in the programs, there are comments as well.

178

abort

Syntax
abort

Function
abort is the macro called when the **Escape** key is pressed. It also is used as a command in composite macros.

Several of Sprint's program macros assign an escape key. When an escape key is pressed or *abort* is used, the editor closes a menu, or the editor halts the macro, or the editor exits to the nearest enclosing *stopped* macro, where the argument carried by *stopped* is changed from False to True.

For example, if the Main menu is opened, then the Insert submenu is opened, then the Variable submenu of the Insert submenu is opened, there are three menus open, with the last menu nested beneath the first two. When **Esc** is pressed, *abort* closes the third menu, aborting to the second menu; if **Esc** is pressed again, the lowest menu is aborted, and the Main menu remains. If **Ctrl-Esc** had been pressed when all three menus were open, all of them would have been closed through the *exitmenus* macro.

abort also can exit to the menu. In that case, the menu is redrawn, and the user tries it again.

abort also is used as a macro command in composite macros to cancel menus, cancel string input, and break infinite loops. If it is nested deeply in the coding, the editor exits only to the macro above *abort*.

Examples

`"Change Directory" NewDirectory abort`

This example from the *DiskDirectory* composite macro in Core.spm executes a *NewDirectory* composite macro to draw a menu, and then exits the *DiskDirectory* composite macro.

```
MarkerJump :

    status "\nGo to marker (0-9): "

    GetKey - 30h -> x

    (x< 10 && x >= 0)? {

    x ismarkset ? (to marknumber x)

    else message "\nMarker not set." } else abort
```

This example from the *sp.spm* macro provides error-handling, by aborting a sequence if a user did not set a marker, and later asked for one anyway.

See Also
abortkey, break, error, exit, exitmenus, exitmessage, menu, stopped

abortkey **(Variable)**
Syntax abortkey
Returns A keyboard value
Function With the *abortkey* variable, you can assign the *abort* macro to any key. If you add assignments or change key assignments with *abortkey*, the new information is written to the overlay file and is read and enabled each time Sprint reloads. By default, *abortkey* is assigned to the **Escape** key. But you can set *abortkey* to any **Control**-key combination, or even to a function key, such as **F9**, which is key 265. More information on key assignments, the overlay file, and key numbering is in Appendix A.

Sprint macros commonly use *abortkey* to assign **Ctrl-U** as a key to Escape all prompts and menus.

Example

```
'^[' -> abortkey
```

This is an assignment statement made when Sprint loads to enable the **Escape** key as an *abortkey*.

See Also | *abort, break, error, exit, exitmenus, exitmessage, menu, stopped*

action

Syntax | action
Returns | True or False
Function | *action* is a flag that is True if there is an enclosing region-action command, such as *delete* or *copy*. It is useful if you want to set the current mark somewhere other than where the command started, but don't want to touch the global mark.

Example

```
Down :

    (if action (tosol setmark) $)

    repeat (toeol c)

    if !action (dcolumn->dcolumn)

        $
```

This macro repeats the down arrow of the cursor as many times as it is pressed by the user. If there is some action, such as selecting an area to be deleted or copied, each stroke of the down arrow covers the region from the start-of-line to the end-of-line; if there is no action, the macro just moves the cursor to the point on the line directly below the current point. So far, this macro has been used only for cursor control. You can read more about marks in other sections of this appendix and in Appendix D.

See Also | *mark*

after | **(mark)**
Syntax | after "mark"
Returns | True or False
Function | Returns True if the point is after (or to the right of) the specified mark; otherwise, returns False. This macro is used in only two composite macros, and only in the Sp.spm code.

Example

```
IndexUnder :
   set QD ""
   message "\nIndex under: "
   set QD    ; text in QD
   mark (    ; build '^[' (0 return)
      if (x CanAssign)
         (
         x keypushback
         if (x > 255) (0 keypushback)
            break
         )
      else
         AssignError
      )
      '^J' return
```

In this example from the *IndexUnder* composite macro, *after* is used to test whether the point is at the end of a word to be indexed. If it is, the point and the mark are swapped so the point can be backed up to a space between words. Then an indexing command can be inserted just before the word to be indexed.

See Also   *mark*

again

Syntax   again

Function   *again* isn't a very popular macro with Sprint programmers, who seem to set up repeat situations rather than *again* commands. One way to explain *again* is that it repeats the last editing command you chose. In other words, it executes again the last macro executed with a *dokey* command. *again* thus executes a macro saved for *again* processing. The argument to this command, and any prefix macros, are preserved with the saved keystroke, so they are done as well. If you type a space, and invoke *again* from the Potpourri menu, another space will appear. *again* is not to be combined with other macros.

Example

```
; Alt-Letter codes

~A : again

~B : Reselect

~C : CustomMenu
```

This example from the key schedule in the Sp.spm code shows that key **Alt-A** has been assigned for *again* processing.

See Also   *dokey, inagain*

append   **(Variable)**
Syntax   # – > append
Function   *append* works through the clipboard to add material, or not add material. If *append* is set to zero, material is not added to the clipboard, and if it is deleted or erased, it is lost. When *append* is set to 1, text will be added to the clipboard without replacing the text already there. If the direction in effect for a *delete* or *copy* command is forward, the text is placed at the beginning of the clipboard; if the direction is reverse, the text is placed at the end.
The *append* variable is reset to zero after each delete or copy.

Example

```
else {

AppendNext->append

0->AppendNext

}
```

This fragment from the *SelectLoop* composite macro in Sp.spm code shows how Sprint programmers use *append.* The functions of *append* are assigned to a variable, *AppendNext.* That can be turned off (zero) and on (one) to append material to the clipboard, or to drop it.

See Also   *copy*

break

Syntax   "commands1" break "commands2"

Returns   Result of command(s) 1

Function   Exits the closest enclosing loop. The macro returns the current argument to the first command after the loop.

Example

```
MenuBind :
   do {
      status "\nShortcut for menu item: " GetKey->x
      if x = '^[' (0 return)
      if (x CanAssign)
         {
          x keypushback
         if (x > 255) (0 keypushback)
            break
         }
      else
         AssignError
      }
   '^J' return
```

This example from the Sp.spm code uses *break* nested in the third level of the macro to break out of an if-then sequence. If a key assigned to a shortcut is legal, it is accepted and the user breaks out of the key assignment routine; otherwise, an error message is given.

See Also   *abort, abortkey, error, exit, exitmenus, exitmessage, menu, stopped*

call

Syntax   # call "string"

Returns   True or False (literally, zero or not zero)

Function   This macro executes a Dos exec-call of a program, which can include the DOS command interpreter itself. The program in effect is a subprogram of Sprint. When the subprogram is complete, the user is returned

to Sprint. DOS returns zero when a program ends normally. That zero is carried as a Sprint argument to the next macro. The #
refers to the argument that determines how the call is done:

1 Prompt the user with "Press any key to continue" after the called subprogram exits.

2 Append the program switches $-p = xxx \ -s = xxx$ to pass the current printer and the current screen to the formatter.

4 Reserved.

8 Run the *restart* macro on reload (only works if bit 16 is on).

16 Overlay the editor with the called program. That frees memory. The editor then reloads by using either its -w switch or its -r switch. Only about 3K of the Sprint program will remain in memory. The 16 argument is especially effecting for running files through large programs and returning to Sprint.

32 Don't do the reset from the screen definition (for example, don't clear the screen under the normal IBM setup). In an IBM-Hercules graphics system, this argument reversed the video. The cursor appears at the DOS prompt, but in the lower-left corner of the screen.

The macro searches the current path, unless a directory is named. The macro will try an .EXE program, or a .COM program if no extension is named. (You cannot call batch file with just *call*; see command /c in the following example.) If the program name is command, the user is given the DOS prompt, and can return to Sprint by typing exit.

When a program and a filename are used in the string, the system will run the program with the filename, if the program has that ability.

Example

```
PArg+8 call "spfmt —l=log.$$$ —p0" cdstrip fname
```

call used here loads the formatter with a printer

description while in Sprint; the PArg + 8 argument restarts the editor.

```
1 call "command/c"
```

This use of the macro loads a DOS command (named elsewhere) that is internal, signified by the /c switch. Also, use command /c when calling a batch file. Here's an example:

```
16 call "command /c MCI.BAT"
```

clear

Syntax   clear

Function   Erases everything in the current buffer. Be careful, you won't be able to recover the buffer. This is much faster but has the same effect as *r toend erasetoend*.

Example

```
ReReadFile :
  if (exist fname) {
    line -> x
    dline -> y
    clear
    $ read fname
    y redraw          ;force back to same line
    0 -> select       ;make sure select is off
    )
  else (error "File not yet saved.")
```

copy

Syntax   commands copy region
             commands copy region Q0–QP
             commands copy region mark

Returns   Result of region

Function   Copies a specified region to the clipboard, to a specified Q register, or to a specified mark.

Description The *copy* command pushes a new local mark, executes the region command (as with all such mark commands, the argument is passed to region). The area between the mark and the point is copied to either the clipboard, or the specified Q register, or the specified mark. In any case, the point stays where it is (it does not move back to the mark), the mark is popped, and the argument is set to the value returned (if any) from region. The *copy region Q0–QP* macro functions the same as the *copy region* macro, except that the copy goes into the specified Q register rather than the clipboard.

The *copy region mark* copies a region and inserts it at the mark (which can be in this or any other buffer). The mark can't be within or immediately after the region. The *copy region* command uses the current setting of the *append* macro variable to decide whether to replace or add to the contents of the clipboard or Q register.

Example

```
CopyRegion :
    if select (
        FixRegionNoMod
        copy togmark
        Unselect
        1 -> AppendNext
        )

KopyWord :
    set Q4 "" set Q7 ""   ; Clear registers,
    r                     ; Reverse direction of cursor movement
    to isgray             ; Move cursor backward to "gray" char.
    setmark               ; Set a mark at the current point,
                          ; which is the gray character to
                          ; the left of a word.
    to isgray             ; Move cursor (forward) past
                          ; end of word to gray character,
                          ; Mark is now on left side of word,
                          ; Point, on right side.
    copy tomark Q4        ; Copy the region between the point
                          ; and the mark to the Q4 register.
```

The first example copies the selected region into the clipboard. The second example copies the word the cursor is on into the into the Q4 register.

See Also   *append*

dokey
Syntax   # dokey
Returns   Result of the macro for the key done
Function   This macro is used in four places in the main Sprint program, to take the place of the compound com-

mand *draw key keyexec. draw* refreshes the screen; *key* fetches a keypress from the Sprint keyboard queue or ROM BIOS; *keyexec* performs the key that was pressed, and, if it is bound to a macro, performs the macro. *dokey*, then, refreshes the screen, fetches the latest keystroke, and does it. If you write the macro *"F1" dokey*, the macro returns F1, because it is echoing a literal character.

Example

```
RepeatCount :
    set QD "Repeat" 1 Arg->RepCount
    key -> RepChar
    if (RepChar >= 32) {
        RepCount repeat (RepChar keypushbackdokey)
        }
    else {
        RepChar keypushback
        RepCount dokey
        }
```

See Also　　*Main*

error

Syntax　　error "message"

Function　　This simple macro just prints an error message and invites the user to press the abortkey, usually Escape. Then it aborts the current macro. You can print the message without aborting the current macro with the composite macro.

```
stopped error "You really screwed up this time, fella"
```

which will allow the macro to continue even after the **Escape** key is pressed.

error also is good for displaying the contents of a buffer. If a macro is being developed and you want to know what was in the buffer that holds filenames when the macro aborted or abnormally ended, you can include in the code

```
stopped error Q1
```

It will halt execution and allow you to peer into a memory buffer before an abnormal end.

Example

```
AssignError :

    stopped error "That key may not be re—assigned."
```

See Also   *abort, abortkey, break, exitmenus, exitmessage, menu, stopped*

exist

Syntax   # exist "filename"
Returns   True or False
Function   This macro is Sprint's command for searching the default disk drive for a filename. The *exist* macro, however, will not search memory buffers, so the file could be on the desktop and the *exist* macro could return False. To search the entire system, the *exist* macro can be combined with the *buffind* macro; if the *buffind* macro returns False, the *exist* macro can check a disk—and if that also returns False, the file is not in the system.

exist also can take some modifiers, some values, that control where Sprint looks for the file:

2   Searches the path for any matching files.
4   Draws a menu with the filename inside, if the filename is found. When wildcard or path symbols are used, Sprint will draw a directory of all related files.
8   Returns the filename with its extension removed.

Example

```
if (buffind Q7)
    (
    message "\nFile already open")
    abort
    )
if (exist Q7)
    (
    open Q7
    StartFile
    )
```

This example searches the memory buffers for the filename in register Q7, and if the file is in memory, goes to the file and tells the user, on the status line, that the file is already open. Note that the *buffind* macro, itself, handles switching into the file that is already open. The *abort* command, here, ensures that the macro ends and doesn't try to open the file on disk.

If the file wasn't in memory, the program then searches the default disk drive and, if it finds the file, opens it and goes to it.

exit

Syntax   exit

Function   This macro is used only once in the Sprint program, to quit the program when the user selects Quit from the main menu, or presses **Alt-Q** or **Alt-X**. The *exit* macro is contained in the *ExitEditor* composite macro. In the example, *ExitEditor* is listed in full because there are so many embedded routines within it.

Before Sprint exits to DOS, *ExitEditor* checks whether a file has been modified, and prompts the user if the new version hasn't been saved to disk. Similarly, if the user alters the overlay file with a macro or a new key assignment, the overlay file is written to disk. A modified screen description also is written to disk.

If the permanent swap file Sp.swp is being used, the editor ignores the *killswap* macro at the end of *ExitEditor* and preserves the swap file so the next time the editor is run, it opens the same files. Otherwise, on *exit*, if *killswap* is True and the backup swap file is only temporary, the swap file is deleted, even if modified files exist.

Example

```
ExitEditor :
  bufnum->x
  do
    {
    if modf=1 {
        draw while keypressed (key draw)
        if length fname {
            message "\nThe file "
            message fname
            }
        else
            message "\nThis Unnamed file"
        if (ask " has not been saved, save it (Y,N,ESC)? ") Save
        }
    else
        if (IsUnnamed && IsOnlyRuler) {
            (if (bufnum==x) (close bufnum->x) else close)
            }
    }
    while (bufswitch && bufnum != x)
    eraseswap || !files -> killswap
    set Q0 "sp.exe" Needdisk
    GlossSave ; save glossary if in use
    exit
```

See Also   *abort, abortkey, break, error, exitmenus, exitmessage, menu, stopped*

exitmessage

Syntax   exitmessage "string"

Function   You can use this macro to display a string when the editor exits to another program. Exiting the editor for another program is discussed extensively in the *call* macro and in Chapter 6. Even if resetting the editor's screen will clear all messages, *exitmessage* will be written to the screen because the message is displayed after a screen reset.

Example   *exitmessage* is used in only one place in Sprint's core program, in the routine that calls a DOS service. After the *exitmessage* command are two escape characters that put the cursor on a new line:

```
SystemCommand :
   message "\nDOS command: " set Q5
   mark (to Q5 delete past isgray)
   set Q0 "sp.exe" NeedDisk
   draw
   if (0 subchar q5)
      (1 call "command /c" Q5)
   else {
      exitmessage "--Type EXIT to return to Sprint--\r\n"
      0 call "command"
      }
```

See Also   *abort, abortkey, break, error, exit, exitmenus, menu, stopped*

exitmenus

Syntax   exitmenus

Function   *exitmenus* is used infrequently in Sprint coding, but it is powerful. It clears all menus from the screen, even if they might otherwise be redrawn so the user could make another selection.

exitmenus is a more powerful version of *abort*. Usually when *abort* is used while a macro is executing, a menu will be redrawn and the user can try again. But *exitmenus* continues to remove menus from the screen, even if they are deeply nested and even if they normally would be redrawn. It is similar to the DOS clear-screen command, CLS.

Example

```
"Open"
   if x (
      OpenFile
      )
   else {
      if !buffind Q0 open Q0
      }
   exitmenus
```

This code fragment taken from Sprint's *DiskDirectory* routine opens a file named in buffer Q0 if a variable x is set to 1 or True and if the file isn't already open.

Once the file is found open, or is opened, the routine erases all menus and prompts from the screen with *exitmenus*.

```
19bhexitmenus '^[',
```

This assignment from the *EditKeys* composite macro in sp.spm assigns the macro *exitmenus* to the key combinations **Ctrl-[** and **Alt-[**;

```
'^U'  exitmenus '^[',
```

This assignment from the *MenuKeys* composite macro in sp.spm adds the **Ctrl-U** key combination to the keys that can call exitmenus.

See Also   *abort, abortkey, break, error, exit, exitmessage, menu, stopped*

false

Syntax   false
Returns   False
Function   Returns False. You can use this to directly set a Boolean variable.

fcopy

Syntax   fcopy "filename1" "filename2"
Returns   True or False
Function   This macro operates on the disk by copying filename1 to filename2. It operates like the DOS *copy* command. If the target file exists, it will be overwritten after the user is prompted, or the user can say no, in which case it will return False, and the entire macro expression will abort. The macro returns True if it succeeds. Like the *fmove* macro, this macro was used only once in the core.spm and sp.spm programs; the single example is from the program core.spm.

Example   `fcopy Q0 Q1`

This operation copies the file in memory buffer Q0 to

buffer Q1. Although the identical file then presumably exists simultaneously in two places in memory, the program can distinguish them by buffer name.

flist

Syntax # flist "string"

Function This macro is used for passing lists of filenames into a memory buffer or among buffers. When the user is seeking or calling a file, the program commonly will force a menu; if a wildcard is in the called file, a list of matching filenames can be passed by *flist* from a secondary buffer to a primary buffer. *flist* can allow a user to enter a filename and then pick a file from a directory list.

flist also operates with the % symbol, the placeholder familiar to C programmers. If the user supplies a name with an embedded % symbol, % turns directly into *fname* and the string passed to *flist* contains *fname*. If the string contains %.xxx, it becomes *fname* with the extension .xxx. If the string contains xxx%, the root of *fname* is tacked onto xxx, which can be a directory path. If the string passed to *flist* contains directory characters such as the backslash, the forward slash, or the colon, the command is handled as it would be with the % placeholder.

Like the *exist* macro, *flist* also can take some arguments, some values, that control where Sprint looks for the file:

2 Searches the path for any matching files. If the user enters the wildcard character *, or if 4 is set, *flist* draws a menu box of all matches found in the directory on the path. When the user picks one, *flist* returns the file name without its directory name.

4 Draws a menu with the filename inside, if the filename is found. When wildcard or path symbols are used, Sprint will draw a directory of all related files. The value 4 is used as an argument if *flist* is used where a string is not expected, so matching filenames can be put into a buffer.

8 Returns the filename with its extension removed.

Examples

```
set Q0 flist Q1
```

A straight assignment of a filelist from memory buffer Q1 to Q0.

```
if stopped {4 set Q0 flist Q1}
```

With the 4 modifier and within an if-then statement, this *flist* shows a directory for the user to choose a file if some operation is stopped.

```
set QD flist "%.MAC"
```

With the % placeholder, this statement attaches the macro extension to all the filenames in memory buffer QD, so the program will recognize the files as macros.

See Also   *fcopy, fmove*

fmove

Syntax   fmove "filename1" "filename2"
Returns   True or False
Function   This macro is used like fcopy to move or to rename a file. The operation ends with filename2, but unlike the *fcopy* macro, only filename2 survives; filename1 disappears. The macro will both copy a file and delete the original (by deleting the filename, filename1). The macro aborts, sometimes transparently to the user, or returns to the program if it is successful. Although apparently well documented in Sprint 1.0, *fmove* was used only once in the core.spm and the sp.spm codes.

Example

```
fmove Q0 Q1
```

This operation moves filename from memory buffer Q0 to memory buffer Q1 and erases the filename from Q0.

F1

Syntax   f1 . . . f12
Function   Names a function key. See the key table in Appendix E for the definition of the keys.

Example

```
F1 : HelpMenu                    ;   F1
```

This example assigns the *HelpMenu* macro to *F1*.

fname

Syntax
fname

Function
fname acts as a string variable for holding the current filename. Whenever a macro requires a filename (including a full pathname) you can use *fname*. For example, if you press **Shift-Alt-X** and enter **fname**, you will see that *fname* returns the name of the file you are currently editing.

You can use the *set* macro to change the contents of *fname*.

Examples

```
; 1.
        if ((modf && ask "File already open, read over it?") ||
            (!modf && (datecheck Q0 > 0))) {
            clear
            read fname
            r toend
            StartFile
            }
; 2.
        set Q0 cdstrip fname
```

In Example 1, *fname* contains the name of a file the user wants to read from the disk. The system has detected that the file is already open and asks the user to confirm the file on disk should be read over the already open file.

In Example 2, the directory path is stripped from the filename and it is copied into memory buffer Q0.

if. . .else

Syntax
if Boolean *statement1* else *statement2*

Function
This macro executes *statement1* if the result of some operation is True, and it executes *statement2* if the operation is not True.

Example

```
OpenFile :

    if (1 checkwild) ; if a default file mask exists

        set Q0 Q1

    else

        set Q0""
```

This expression puts a filename with wildcard characters in the register for filenames, or it clears the register to wait for a filename. It performs the if branch when the expression checkwild returns a 1 (True) and it follows the else branch, and clears the register, if the expression checkwild returns the value 0 (False).

imenu

Syntax   imenu "title" (# "item" commands ...)
Returns   Result of commands
Function   Just like the *menu* macro, except that the text of the item selected is placed into Q0 so that it can be referenced (for example, to be inserted into the buffer).
Note: Item can be one string or several strings. If it's more than one, the strings are concatenated to form the menu text.

Example

```
PickCommandMenu :

    imenu "Choose command" {

        "again",

        "bottomOfFile",

        "bottomOfScreen",

        . . .
```

This example allows the user to choose one of Pot-pourri commands in the default Sprint interface.

See Also   *menu*

inagain   (Variable)
Syntax   inagain
Returns   True or False
Function   The variable is True if a macro invoked by the *again* command is currently being executed. Macros can check this to more accurately reproduce the last action taken. The only place we could find *inagain* in our Sprint code was in the *Core.spm* macro, and there only once.

Example

```
Quote :
  (if !inagain {
     if (!menudelay || !(menudelay wait)) {
        status "\nControl character to insert: "
        }
     GetKey & 9fh ->Quoted
     }
  $)
  if inruler (toeol c)
     repeat
        {
        Quoted case (
           32    '^\' insert,
           '_'   '^^' insert,
           '^['  if ask "Insert [ESC] character? " ('^['insert),
           '^K'  '^K' insert readruler,
           $     Quoted insert
           }
        }
```

See Also   *again, dokey*

InitArg
Syntax   InitArg :
Function   If Sprint is started with a filename on the command line, as in Sp \letters\mike3, *InitArg* will open the file and make that file the first in the queue of open files. If a wildcard character is used, as in sp \letters\mike*.*, Sprint will draw a menu of matches and ask the user to pick among them. In the loading sequence, *InitArg*

is called after *Init* and before *Main*. The code is in the
core.spm macro.

Example

```
InitArg :
    int giveup
    0->giveup
    if (n < 6) (++n->windows)
        0 AllCaps ; convert name to upper case
        if (0 CheckWild) {
            open ""
            draw
            set Q1 Q0
            if stopped {4 set Q0 flist Q1} (1->giveup)
            else if !length Q0 {
                set Q0 Q1
                mark {to Q0 insert "No files match '"
                toend insert "'."}
                error Q0
                }
            close
            }
```

key

Syntax   # key
Returns   A number
Function   This macro waits until a key is pressed or is provided
by the program and then gets that character from the
internal Sprint keyboard queue or from the operating
system. A related macro is *isibm*, which returns True
if the current machine fits Sprint's definition of an
IBM compatible.

If *isibm* is True, and if input is not redirected, input
is read through DOS from the IBM BIOS. Sprint adds
zeros to the value so that the key always returns a full
byte of characters. Although the translated values will
not match the BIOS key codes, the same characters are
returned to the user.

If input has been redirected through DOS, the editor can detect that. It checks for end-of-file in a file
to which input may have been If it finds end-of-file,
it exits and returns the end-of-file character that it
encountered, ^ Z.

The keyboard is explained in Appendix A.

Example

```
draw key -> int x
```

This example draws the screen, executes the next key pressed or send to the macro, and then initializes a variable, x.

keyexec

Syntax # keyexec

Returns The result of the key's macro

Function *keyexec* just executes the key that is named. Usually a macro is bound to the key. *keyexec* usually is used to combine key sequences into a single code. The # is a number between 0 and 511.

In the following example, we checked the *keyexec* macro by giving it the number 257, which is the **F1** key to call the help menu. If a key has been assigned a macro, as has 257, *keyexec* executes the macro.

If # is less than 256, the character is inserted. For example, when we used 38 keycheck, the macro put & in the current file.

If # is greater than 180H (384), it is a meta key and it is translated to be less than 128 (384 is subtracted from #), and if there is a macro bound to the key, it is executed.

If the editor is in a ruler, # is interpreted as a ruler-editing command.

The macro also saves the current macro state for again processing.

Example

```
Check :

    257 keyexec

    '@ : key + 256 keyexec
```

In this example, the function key **Ctrl-@** is pressed and the code is translated from 0, which is not executed, to 0 + 257, becoming key 257, which then is executed; that is interpreted as a space.

keyhelp

Syntax	# keyhelp
Function	This macro is used to explain keys to a user. Some keys, such as **Alt-Z**, use a macro to quickly provide some service—for **Alt-Z**, to turn on screen codes. If a user asks for help with that function key, *keyhelp* does a help parse of the macro assigned to the key, and puts a significant word in buffer Q0. Then the help routine uses the word to provide a help screen explaining the key.
Example	

```
GetKey keyhelp                      ; get macro to Q0
```

This line from a longer macro gets the next keystroke (**w**, say, or **Ctrl-7**), and puts a word describing it into buffer Q0.

```
HelpKeyFunction :
   HelpDisk
   int ktmp
   0-> int quit
   do {
      message "\nPress the key you want help on ("
      -abortkey + 27 message
      "%[Esc%:%27-~+c%] twice to quit): "
      Getkey -> ktmp = abortkey
      ? (1->quit) : (0->quit)
      ktmp Keyhelp 2 help Q0 draw
      } while(!quit)
```

This macro creates a variable, *ktemp*, and puts into Q0 a word describing a key that has been pressed.

keypressed

Syntax	keypressed
Returns	True or False
Function	Sprint uses this macro to learn if there is a keystroke ready in its internal queue or in the hardware. The keyboard is discussed in Appendix A. The internal

keystroke queue sometimes is empty or has been flushed, so Sprint uses this macro to learn if a keystroke is available.

Example

```
{if KeyPressed (1000 delay) else (2000 wait)}
```

When Sprint restarts and displays its herald, this command forces the program to wait a second or two, so the herald can be recognized, before processing a keystroke.

keypushback

Syntax
keypushback
keypushback "string"

Function
This macro places keys into Sprint's internal queue. It uses a three- or four-digit number to represent the key. If the key is a function key above 255, a zero prefix is added. The details of key assignments are discussed in Appendix A. The queue works like a data stack, in that the last character put in is the first character taken out. The # *keypushback* variation of this macro is for a single key.

Example

```
draw key -> int x

if (x = '^M') ('^J'->x)

if (x < ' ' && x!='^J' && x!='^I')

{x keypushback dokey}
```

Function
In its second role, *keypushback* puts a string of characters into the queue, but that string is listed after the macro. It stuffs the characters from last to first, such as t-n-i-r-p-S, so the string is read as Sprint when it is pulled from the queue. The second variation of

keypushback is used mostly to record a string to a Q buffer with the *record* macro; the characters are played back with the of *string* command *keypushback*.

Example
```
if (MacroRepCnt > 0) (keypushback QF)
```

leftedge (Variable)
Syntax leftedge
Function The number of the column that marks the left edge of the screen. This is normally 0, but is nonzero if the user is scrolling horizontally. If you set *leftedge* and, in doing so dcolumn is placed off the screen, the screen will be re-centered the next time a *draw* macro is performed.
Example

```
ScrollRight :


    leftedge + 40 -> leftedge


ScrollLeft :


    if 1 leftedge (1 Bell return)


    if ((leftedge -40)> 0) (leftedge) -40) leftedge


    else 0 -> leftedge
```

These are the macro definitions of *ScrollLeft* and *ScrollRight* in the Potpourri menu.

length
Syntax length
Returns A number
Function Returns the length of the current buffer in characters. It overflows after 65,535.

Example

```
mark {

toend

length message "File contains %d characters."

}
```

length	"string"
Syntax	length "string"
Returns	A number, or True, or False
Function	Returns the number of characters in a string. This macro is used most frequently to test if there are any characters in a memory location.

Example

```
if length Q0
   (set Q1 Q0)
else
   (set Q1 "*.SPR")
set Q0 flist Q1
0 AllCaps
if ! (32 exist Q0) ; if spec'd file mask had no
   (
   matches
   set QD Q1
   if length QD
      (
      mark
         (
         to QD insert "No files match '"
         toend insert "'."
         )
      )
   else set QD "Can't copy unnamed files."
   error QD
   )
set Q1 ""
message "\nCopy "
message Q0
message "to: "
set Q1
if (!length Q1) error "You must specify a name."
```

This long example is offered to show three uses of *length*. In the first instance, the macro tests whether there is anything in memory buffer Q0. If Q0 has a value greater than zero, it also is interpreted as True. If *length* is True, if there is something in buffer Q0, then it is copied to buffer Q1.

In the second example, *length* is used to test whether a wildcard produced the desired file. If the macro returns a nonzero, there is something in the buffer, it is True, and a "no files match" message is sent to the user.

In the final example, the ! (not) operator is used; if the memory buffer Q1 has no length (!length), it is empty, so there must be no name in it, so the user is told, "You must specify a name."

Main
Syntax
Function

Main :

This is a macro that is executed with every key that is pressed. It does housekeeping. It makes sure that files have rulers. It makes sure that any file changes are read into memory. It sets up and checks the queue of open files.

There must be a *Main* macro within every user interface file, or attached to it. *Main* loads when Sprint starts, or if it is restarted, or if there was an *mread* command to load a macro, or an *ovlread* command to read a new overlay. And if the *mread* or *ovlread* commands had negative arguments, the entire program reloads, by executing *mread* or *ovlread*, then executing *Init*, then executing *Main*.

Because the *Main* loop is executed for every key, including letters, it can't be too complicated or it will slow down the user.

Example

```
Main :
    stopped {
    if !files (stopped DefaultRuler)
    else {
        bufnum -> x
        do {
            stopped
            if (!modf && (datecheck fname > 0))
                {
                clear
                read fname
                r toend
                }
            bufswitch
            } while bufnum!=x
        }
    }
    do {
        if stopped dokey
        else {
            AppendNext->append
            0->AppendNext
            }
        }
```

mark

Syntax   mark text

Returns

Function   Used to keep your place a file or a file segment while working temporarily elsewhere. *mark* sets a mark, executes a remote command or string, and returns the user, the pointer, back to the mark.

Example

```
CheckWild : mark (qswitch ('*' csearch || ('?' r csearch)))
```

In this example, the *mark* macro keeps your place in the file while you look for a wildcard symbol in some other filename.

markN

Syntax   markN

Function   There are 16 *mark* variables that store positions (N can be 0 through F in hexadecimal). Some of the commands that work with any of the numbered *marks* are as follows: *atmarkN, before markN, set markN, swap markN,* and *to markN.*

The first time you use a mark after starting the editor, that mark is set to the current position.

Example

```
DeleteRegion :
   if select
      (
      FixRegion
      delete togmark
      curatt -> delatt
      Unselect
      1 -> AppendNext
      set markC        ;   save position of deletion
      )
   else
      DelFwd
```

See Also   *after (mark)*

marknumber

Syntax   marknumber N

Function   Defines a mark as N, where N can be any expression.

Example

```
MarkerJunp:

   status "Go to marker (0-9) :"

   GetKey -30h -> x

   (x<10 && x >0) ? (to marknumber x) else abort
```

See Also   *after* (mark)

menu

Syntax   menu "title" (# "item" commands, ...)

Returns   Result of listed commands

Function   Draws a boxed menu on the screen consisting of the "items". If the user picks an item, the command after it is executed, which usually leads the editor to code that opens another menu or begins some routine.

If "item" is comprised of more than one word, the words appear together as one *menu* option.

A key is bound to a *menu* item if **Ctrl-Enter** is pressed when the item is highlighted. The key and a pointer to the start of the *menu* item are stored.

If the command(s) that follow the *menu* item execute normally, the menu disappears, but if the commands end abnormally, and there is no *exitmenus* macro following, the menu is redrawn, so the user can select an option again. That way, some error-handling is built into the *menu* macro.

The user can choose *menu* items by moving to them with the cursor keys or the spacebar, and by pressing **Enter**, or pressing the first letter of a *menu* item. If there is more than one match to a letter, the first match is highlighted.

The new menu appears to the left of any menu already on the screen.

Menus disappear by pressing the **Escape** key to abort, or by pressing the **Shift-Escape**, the **Ctrl-[**, or the **Ctrl-U** keys to *exitmenus*. That was done by putting the *exitmenus* macro on a key in the *MenuKey* composite macro. You can make menus disappear using different keys if you reassign them through *MenuKey*.

menu items that start with an underline character create division bars that can't be selected by the user. Any text after the underline is centered in the division bar. The code assumes that the bottom item in the menu is not a division bar, and that there are no more division bars than the screen is tall.

Example   This is from the Sp.spm code:

```
; ---------- Main Menu ----------

SprintMenu :
    menu "Sprint" {
    "File"                  FilesMenu,
    "Edit"                  EditMenu,
    " ",
    "Insert"                InsertMenu,
    "Typestyle"             TypeStyleMenu,
    "Style"                 StyleMenu,
    "Layout"                LayoutMenu,
    " ",
    "Print"                 PrintMenu,
    "Window"                WindowsMenu,
    "Utilities"             UtilitiesMenu,
    "Customize"             CustomMenu,
    " ",
    "Quit"                  ExitEditor
    }
```

See Also   *abort, abortkey, break, error, exit, exitmenus, exitmessage, imenu, stopped*

message

Syntax   # message "string"

Function   This macro sends messages to line 25 of the monitor. If there had been a message there, the \n switch clears the previous message. The message string must be enclosed in quotes. An optional argument can be added at # with the % command. The contents of a Q register can be echoed to the screen by naming the Q register.

Example

```
else if (message "\nCreate new file " message Q1   ask "? ")
```

mode

Syntax   MODE "string"

Function   Sets up the string displayed on the second controllable status line.

The second status line is normally not shown but can be turned on or off by setting the appropriate values for statline. Generally, you use the second status line to show a modal instruction, such as "Keyboard recording on; press **ESC** to cancel."

Example

```
KeyRecordGloss :
    mode "Keyboard recording on. Press ESC to cancel."
    MacroCallBegin
    set QF ""
    if record {
        1 Bell message "\nRecording canceled."
        0 -> record
        1 -> statline
        }
    else {
        15 -> record
        2 -> statline,
        }
```

mread

Syntax   mread "filename.SPM"

Function   This macro reads and compiles an .SPM file. Any lines
              in the .SPM file that start with : will be executed
              immediately, but Sprint will not add these lines to the
              current interface. So you can use *mread* with : to execute
              long batch macros that will not be added to your
              current interface.

              Note: The *Init* macro always executes after *mread*.

              Warning: *mread* aborts the current macro so don't try to
              put any commands after *mread*.

Examples

```
MacroLoad : 10 set Q0 flist "*.spm" mread Q0

MacroClear :
    if (2 exist "sp.ovl")
       (-2 ovlread "sp")
    else
       mread "sp"

MacroRunFile :
    set Q0 fname
    if (mark (to Q0 1 search ".spm"))
       {
       if (modf=1 || !exist Q0)
           Save
       mread fname
       }
    else
       if (2 exist "sp.spm") (2 mread "sp")
```

See Also   *Init, ovlread*

ovlread

Syntax
ovlread "overlay"

Function
Reads a compiled overlay file such as BORLAND.UI and executes the *Main* macro within it.

As with many other macros, the *# ovlread* macro overwrites any macros that may be in memory, in the area loaded by the prior overlay file. So those macros and the current macro are destroyed; the current macro aborts. Borland recommends that before you execute *ovlread*, you execute this command:

```
if ovlmodf ovlwrite "%"
```

It means that if the overlay file has been changed in memory, save the changes to disk, using the name of the last overlay file read. That way no work should be lost. The "%" after *ovlwrite* means to use the last overlay file read. Note that *ovlmodf* is a global variable that shows whether changes have been made that should be saved to sp.spm, the overlay file.

Here is a list of the arguments to *ovlread* that take the place of the # sign:

2 Searches the path for any matching files. If the user enters the wildcard character * or if 4 is set, *ovlread* draws a menu box of all matches found in the directory on the path. When the user picks one, *ovlread* returns the file name without its directory name.

4 Draws a menu with the filename inside, if the filename is found. When wildcard or path symbols are used, Sprint will draw a directory of all related files. The value 4 is used as an argument if *ovlrcad* is used where a string is not expected, so matching filenames can be put into a buffer.

8 Returns the filename with its extension removed.

-N A negative number will force the overlay file to be written as *sp.ovl* when the user quits Sprint.

Example

```
if (2 exist "convert.ovl") (ovlread "convert")
```

This example, from a translation macro, looks for the convert overlay file and reads it into memory if it is found.

```
MacroClear :

    if (2 exist "sp.ovl") (-2 ovlread "sp")

    else        mread "sp"
```

This example of *ovlread* runs *Restart* to load Sprint from scratch.

See Also   *flist, ovlmodf, ovlwrite*

ovlwrite

Syntax   ovlwrite "overlayfilename"

Function   When we write and load macros they live but briefly in memory; it is *ovlwrite* that writes them permanently to the overlay file so that they will be available for the next session. If you use % as the overlayfilename the overlay file last read will be the one written to.
If a new macro is to be saved to a special overlay file, the macro *ovlwrite* must be executed with the name of the overlay file. Otherwise, the program defaults and at the end of the session writes any new material to the sp.ovl file.

Example

```
SaveUI : $ ovlwrite "borland.ui" ovlwrite "sp"
```

See Also   *ovlmodf, ovlread*

qswitch

Syntax   # qswitch

Function   The macro can take a value from O to 25. It places a point at the start of a specified Q-register, which can be edited. If there is no value attached to the *qswitch* command, the Q register is specified in an earlier macro. To get back to your previous location, be sure to enclose the *qswitch* macro with the *mark* macro.

Example

```
CheckWild : mark (qswitch ('*' csearch || ('?' r

csearch)))
```

This routine looks for the wildcard characters * and ? in a filename. The *mark* macro is used to return you to your original text. *qswitch* took a value from a previous macro. The routine searches forward in the filename for a *, and then backward for a ?. The ? wildcard character is searched only if no * wildcard character is found.

Restart

Syntax   Restart
Sp –r

Function   The editor calls the formatter by placing *spfmt* in buffer Q6 and by adding 8 to the variable *PArg*. *PArg* is an acronym for printer or paginate argument. The formatter does not output to the screen. To get screen output, as when the user wants to view a file paginated, the program must run the formatter, and then the *Restart* macro, and then read the log file written by the formatter, to insert page breaks and numbers into the text file in the editor.

The *Restart* macro, like the *Init* and *InitArg* macros, actually is a composite macro and not a primitive. It also is one of the automatically called macros.

Example

```
Restart :

    NormalMode

    if (exist "log.$$$") {

        draw pageread "log.$$$"

        fdelete "log.$$$"

        while keypressed key    ; eliminate type-ahead

            {
```

set

Syntax	set "string1" "string2"
Function	Copies the second expression into the first expression. This macro is useful for moving the contents of one buffer into another buffer.
Example	

```
                set Q0 Q1
```

stopped

Syntax	stopped "command"
Returns	True or False
Function	This macro can control use of the **Escape** key and abort sequences. Usually it returns False, a zero value. Normally, when a *do* or a *do-while* loop is executed, the editor checks the keyboard for a press of the **Escape** key. But if a *stopped* is executed inside a loop, the test is disabled. That prevents aborts while critical routines are loading or running. The fact that an error or an Escape or an abort has occurred is carried by the *stopped* macro as an argument of one, a True value, so another macro later can read the value of *stopped* and then abort, or continue.
	That prevents the editor from discarding typeahead keystrokes when it might otherwise flush the keyboard

buffer. It also prevents unexpected exiting from loops. It also allows the programmer to direct aborts and escapes to specific areas in the macro.

Examples

```
if stopped {4 set Q0 flist Q1} (1->giveup)
```

This example is from *InitArg*, one of the macros that loads Sprint. If the user presses the **Esc** key while loading, a variable called *giveup* is assigned a value True; later the macro tests the value of *giveup*, and if it is 1, the loading sequence is aborted.

```
Main :

    stopped {

        if !files (stopped DefaultRuler)
```

This example is from the *Main* macro that must be run when Sprint starts. The first use of stopped is so the user can't abort while the program is checking file dates. The second use of the macro is in a line that executes if there is only one file opened, an empty file. Then *stopped* inserts a ruler before the macro can continue or the user can Escape, so that all files have rulers.

```
do {

    stopped
```

This example appears further in the *Main* macro, nested in the fourth level, a *do* loop. It disables the usual check by the editor of the **Esc** key while Sprint is reading a revised file into memory. File revisions can be saved to disk rather than being lost or discarded when **Esc** is pressed.

See Also   *abort, abortkey, break, error, exit, exitmenus, exitmessage, menu*

Appendix F
Built-in Sprint Variables

Here is a list of Sprint's built-in variables and a brief description of what you can use them for. **Note:** You can peek at the current value of any of these variables by pressing **Shift-Alt-X** and entering

```
VARIABLE-NAME =
```

VARIABLE-NAME is the name of the variable. For example, to see what your current directory is, press **Shift-Alt-X** and then enter

```
CD =
```

Unless a variable is a read only variable, you can move a value into it. To test this, first press **Shift-Alt-X**, then enter

```
VALUE -> VARIABLE-NAME.
```

For example, to set the raw variable to 1 you would give this command:

```
1 -> raw
```

VARIABLE NAME	WHAT THIS VARIABLE CONTAINS
abortkey	Normally set to ASCII 27. This variable specifies which key will abort loops and menus.

append	Returns 1 or zero. If you set *append* to 1, *delete* or *copy* commands will append text to the clipboard.
bufnum	Returns current buffer number (this is a read only variable).
cd	Returns current disk and subdirectory.
cpi	Returns columns per inch specified by current ruler line.
Current	Returns ASCII value of character at cursor location.
curatt	Returns current attribute—a number that shows location of point relative to a typestyle control characters. (See page 219 for more details on curatt.)
Column	Returns column number at cursor location, where first column is zero.
dColumn	Returns cursor location just prior to keystroke.
dline	Returns row number cursor is on in current window.
engine	Returns name of WORD ENGINE that will run when the *runengine* macro is called to do spelling checking.
fontcpi	Return recommended characters per inch for the font last selected by *pickfont* macro.
inagain	Return 1 (True) or 0 (False). It will return 1 if a macro started by *again* is still executing.
indent	Returns value to use for identing from left margin.
ioport	Used to read or write data to an I/O port. (See page 219 for more details.)
justify	Returns number that tells how user wants justification to be done. (See page 220 for more details.)
leftedge	Returns column number that marks left edge of screen.
leftmargin	Returns value for left margin from current ruler line.
line	Returns number of lines in current file.
menudelay	Shows how much of a delay will occur before a menu appears. The higher the number, the longer the delay.
modf	Tells whether user has (or can) modify current file. (See page 220 for more details.)

mouser cursor	Controls where mouse puts cursor on screen.
overwrite	Return to 1 if editor is in overwrite mode and Ovr appears on status line. Set to 0 if editor is in insert mode and Ins is on status line.
ovlmodf	Returns 1 if the Sp.ovl file needs to be overwritten because user has defined some new macros or hotkeys.
previous	Returns ASCII code of character to left of cursor. If point is at the beginning of the file, previous will be zero.
printer	Return contains name of current printer. Don't use this to change the name of current printer. (Use: set printer "printer-name".)
raw	Returns 1 or 0. If set to 1, then editor is in raw mode. In raw mode all, characters are visible.
record	This variable lets you do keyboard recording. (See page 220 for more details.)
rightmargin	Contains value for right margin in current ruler.
rulermod	If set to 1, then ruler has changed and you should do *writeruler* or *insertruler*.
rwtrans	Controls translations that Sprint does when reading files from disk or when writing to disk.
scrollborder	Number of lines cursor stays away from edge of window.
select	If set to 1, then text will be highlighted when user moves cursor. If set to 2, column style highlighting is in effect.
soundur	Specifies duration of tone in milliseconds. (**Note:** The *sound* macro actually creates the sound.)
soundfreq	Specifies frequency of tone in Hertz cycles (HZ). (The *sound* macro actually creates the sound.)
statusline	

If statusline is:	Then:
0	Status line disappears.
1	Status line appears.
2	Status line & mode lines appear.

swapdelay	Time (in milliseconds) to wait before updating swap file. If set to zero, no updating takes place.
tabsize	Space between tabs when no tabs are explicitly set.

windows   Specifies how many windows you want. If you increase the value by 1, the current window will be split into two windows. If direction is forward, the lower window will be the current one. This variable does not reflect a condition where one of the windows is zoomed to fill the entire screen. For example, if you have 5 windows on the screen but one of the windows is zoomed, these windows variable will still contain a 5.

wlines   Number of lines in current window. You can control the size of the current window by changing the value in this variable.

wtop   (a read only variable) Shows where current window starts in relation to the screen top.

zoom   If set to 1, then current window zoomed to fill up entire screen.

Details on Select Variables

curatt   curatt is 0 if the point is not inside a pair of control characters that define a type style (like ^ B ...^ N for bold).

ioport   If you move a value into *ioport*, that value will be sent to the I/O port address that follows ioport

EXAMPLE:

```
255 -> ioport 42H  ;(Send 255 to port at 42H)
```

You can read the value at an I/O port by just giving the address of the desired port after ioport.

EXAMPLE:

```
ioport 42H =  :display value at port 42H

; Note the "=" causes display of the value.
```

justify

If justify is	Then:
0	left ragged
1	left-justified
2	center
3	center-justified
4	right-ragged
5	right-justified

modf

If modf is	Then:
0	File has not been modified since last read or written.
1	File has been changed since last read or written.
2	File is a read only file—user cannot edit the file, only browse through it and read it.

Note: You can change this value and fool Sprint into thinking that the file has been modified when, in fact, it has not, and visa-versa. If you see an asterisk in the middle of the status line, then modf = 1 (the file has been modified).

record   This is a verb as in to record key strokes. To append all key strokes to a Q register, just put a number greater than zero into *record*. To turn off keyboard recording, move a zero into *record*. To play back keystrokes, use the *pushback* macro.

Appendix G

Notes on the Formatter

When you send a Sprint file to the printer, a lot goes on behind the scenes. The Sprint formatter program, Spfmt.exe is sent to memory register Q6. The main Sprint program, Spedit.exe, is assigned to memory register Q0. The filename in the current buffer is taken as an argument to the Spfmt call in register Q6. When the formatter is called, modifiers or parameters such as –p2 and –t=5 can be appended to the Spfmt command to tell the formatter about the printer and the tab stops set in the editor. The formatter then looks to a special format file such as Standard.fmt for style rules. A printer driver is summoned. Errors can be reported by line number and logged to a file.

We don't intend to provide explicit instructions for operating the formatter or invoking formatter macros. We will just be giving you an overview.

HOW THE FORMATTER WORKS

The Sprint formatter is a program within a program. When a file is sent to the formatter, it reads the file once, page by page, for layout items such as footnotes, headers, and tags, and then formats the file, page by page, in a second pass. For more difficult files, the formatter makes more than two passes through the file. You'll notice that when printing, a file requires almost twice as much memory because it is being reproduced in the formatter.

When the formatter sees a command while formatting, it looks ahead at the effect of the command and makes adjustments. That's one reason it makes two or more passes through a file. When the Number of Passes value on the Advanced Options menu of the Print menu is set to Auto, Sprint makes as many passes as it guesses it may need to arrange all layout elements and variables.

Just as the editor calls the formatter to print a file, the formatter calls Standard.fmt to style the file. That is the default style sheet for the Sprint formatter. Just as the editor searches for the file Standard.spg when you ask for a glossary item, the formatter searches for Standard-.fmt when you invoke a formatting command, such as Print, or Screen Preview. If the formatter can't find Standard.fmt, it errors out.

HOW STANDARD.FMT WORKS

A customized formatting file can be named Standard.fmt, and the original file could be renamed, say, Original.fmt, so it can be preserved and reinstalled. The formatter will use the *new* Standard.fmt file by default, but if there is no .fmt file available, printing, even to the screen, will be disabled.

You can open and read the macro text of the Standard.fmt file to discover most of the formatter's habits. For those lucky enough to have a printer that accepts Encapsulated PostScript, a *PostScr.fmt* file could replace the Standard.fmt file. There is even a ReadEPS style sheet command available to verify that a text file is configured for PostScript. The Standard.fmt file begins with the command:

```
@style (comments yes)
```

This simply includes in output even those lines with a ";" character in column 1, which programmers recognize as a symbol indicating that a comment follows. So a simple *@style* command in the formatter file quickly includes or deletes all comment lines *even though they might have been included originally by the editor.* That's one reason we call the formatter a program within a program—you can branch, nest commands, and create filespecs even after leaving the editor.

Notice that the ASCII symbol @ is used, by convention, to indicate that a command string follows. In .fmt files, you enter an @–sign, followed by the name of the command, rather than formatting via Sprint menus.

The Standard.fmt file specifies how headers will print, how much space there will be between lines, how text will be centered, and so on. Here's an example:

```
@ Define(Address, leftindent .5 line, above 2, below 2,fill

n,group,initialize = "@ nohinge")
```

This sets up a template that can use code to redirect text into a specific format. The *Address Formatter* macro (or template) formats a return address, with lines flush left to a left margin indented one-half the distance to the right margin. It uses a keep command called *nohinge* to keep text following the address, so text is not widowed.

CALLING A FORMAT

Definitions for all formats must be in a .fmt file you plan to use, or at the top of the file to be printed, or in the Standard.fmt file that is the default style sheet for Sprint.

You can shift among .fmt files by selecting style sheet from the Document-Wide menu, which is in the Layout menu. When you name a style sheet, which must be a filename with a .fmt extension, Sprint will not use the default Standard.fmt style sheet, but will use the style sheet named. The editor inserts the name of the style sheet above the ruler line. That's because the formatter will ignore any document-wide command that is not at the top of the file, before the ruler line. Only the files with the special style sheet label will be affected by the special style sheet.

Formatting also can be controlled by specific commands at the top of a file to be printed. You can imagine the first pass through the file by the formatter, when the formatter immediately sees a command at the top of the file that includes a recognizable command, such as:

```
@ Style (comments no)
```

You would use this to delete comments, perhaps when printing code, for review before publication.

BUILT-IN FORMAT COMMANDS

Some formatting commands are built into the Sprint program— embedded in Spfmt.exe—and they can't be modified. But most of them can be used from the menus with the Style/Other Format menu command. You also can use them with @-sign commands.

The built-in format commands illustrate the differences between formatter symbols and editor symbols, and the confusion that can result when you are reading formatter code and thinking that it is editor macro code. Peruse Table G.1, and beware.

Built-in commands can be words as well as symbols. In either form, they can be ambiguous for new users. For example, you may recall

Table G.1
Some Built-in Commands

Command	In the Editor	In the Formatter
Hard return	^J	@ *
Ignore whitespace		@ ~
Not	!	
Break a word		@ !
Return zero	$	
Move left margin...		@ $
Delimiter	[	
Set left margin		@ [
Xor	^	
Set tab stop		@ ^

discussion of the editor macro *set*, which can substitute one string for another string, or can set a mark for future reference in memory or a file. In the formatter, as well, there is a built-in formatting command *set*, but it assigns a new value to a numeric variable. The way to tell the *sets* apart, is the ASCII command symbol @ that precedes the formatter's *set* command.

PARENTS AND CHILDREN

If you start a format, by invoking Standard.fmt, and before ending that format, you start another format, say, with instructions at the top of the file being printed, the second format not only has its own set of parameters, but also inherits the remaining parameters of the parent format. Parent formats and parent templates are used extensively in Sprint. Be on the lookout for the parent styling, as well as the custom child styling you may be trying to achieve.

Appendix H
Using Tools from CompuServe

Borland International maintains a computer Forum with CompuServe, a sort of neighborhood, an online club. It's also a valuable resource for free documented macros.

CompuServe offers discussion forums, electronic mail, information gathering, financial services, and downloadable programs. We've used several other commercial services, including The Source, Dow Jones News/Retrieval, and academic networks. We enthusiastically recommend CompuServe. It delivers good programming value for the money.

We can usually get in and out of CompuServe with some valuable macros for $10 to $20. If your programming time is limited, you can maximize your personal output by downloading CompuServe files, modifying them to suit your needs, and using electronic mail to share ideas with other users and macro writers.

SIGNING ON

You can get a CompuServe start-up kit in stores for about the cost of dinner for two at a medium priced restaurant. Through trade shows, subscriptions, or professional organizations, you may be able to get a free subscription packet, which includes a credit for online time.

The communication parameters for your modem need to be full duplex, one stop bit, seven data bits, and even parity.

CompuServe is accessed through networks such as Telenet or Tymnet. Access through the telephone networks should be transparent. Yet there is no computer service we've ever used that didn't require some patience with the telephone network or with the communications port or front end.

We've found that the trick with CompuServe—and every information service has these tricks—is learning the direct address of the area you want. You can spend a lot of time working from the main menu, through submenus, to the Borland Forum. But if you just use the command Go Borland, or, better yet, the Go BorApp command, you'll be plugged into Borland International much faster than you can get there via menus.

Figure H.1 shows the CompuServe main menu, presented as soon as you sign on. At this prompt and at any system prompt, you can get off CompuServe by using the commands Bye, Off, Log, or Logoff; E or Exit only exits a forum, such as the Borland Applications Forum. At the main menu we could logoff, choose a menu option, or go directly to the Borland Forum. Notice that option 11 eventually will lead us to Borland. Instead, at the prompt, "Enter choice number:" we simply issue the command Go Borland.

Figure H.2 reproduces the screen that results. Among the options are Programming Forum A, for Turbo Pascal and Turbo Basic; Programming Forum B, for Prolog, Assembler, and Debugger; and for our area of interest, the Borland Applications Forum, for Sprint and other applications.

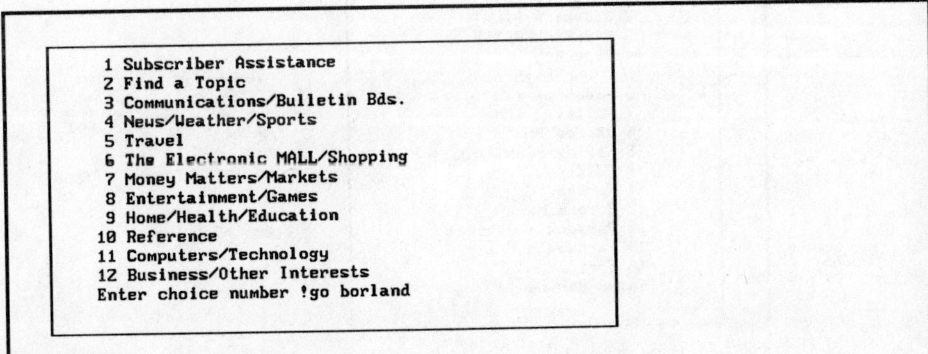

Figure H.1
The CompuServe main menu

```
CompuServe BORLAND

1 What's New
2 Company Information
3 Product Line Information
4 R&D Suggestion Box
5 Product Support
6 Employment Opportunities
7 Borland Programming Forum A (Turbo Pascal & Turbo BASIC)
8 Borland Programming Forum B
  (Turbo Prolog, Turbo C, Turbo Assember & Turbo Debugger)
9 Borland Applications Forum (Quattro, Paradox, SideKick Plus,
  Sprint, SideKick, SuperKey, Turbo Lightning, Eureka)
Enter choice !
CompuServe PCS-10
```

Figure H.2
The top of the Borland Forum.

WELCOME TO THE LIBRARY

If you choose the Libraries option from the main Forum menu, you'll
see the screen reproduced in Figure H.3. To get into the Sprint library,
we choose Option 16.

```
Libraries Available:
 0 General
 1 Turbo Technix
 2 Sidekick Plus
 3 SideKick & TSK
 4 SuperKey
 5 Turbo Lightning
 6 SideKick Mac
 7 Reflex - IBM
 8 SK for PM
 9 Reflex Plus, Mac
10 Quattro
11 Eureka PC
12 Eureka Mac
14 Paradox - General
15 Paradox - PAL
16 Sprint
Enter choice !
```

Figure H.3
Borland libraries.

```
        Borland Application Forum   Library 16

        Sprint

        1 BROWSE thru files
        2 DIRECTORY of files

        3 UPLOAD a new file
        4 DOWNLOAD a file

        5 LIBRARIES

        Enter choice !
```

Figure H.4
The Sprint library menu.

The result is the screen reproduced in Figure H.4. It advises us that we are in Library 16 of the Borland Application Forum. To locate a macro, choose the **Browse** command or the **Directory** command. After choosing the Directory command, you can enter a keyword, like database, or ask for a file by age—the most recent, the oldest, or all of them. The result of a Directory command is reproduced in Figure H.5.

```
[70007,3531]
STAR.SPL                22-Feb-89 6861            Accesses: 7

[73547,3520]
HIDENT/binary           21-Feb-89 1166            Accesses: 13

[73417,2067]
CHAR.SPM                18-Feb-89 2528            Accesses: 20

[76117,3671]
MERGE.ARC/binary        17-Feb-89 1153            Accesses: 9

[73647,1011]
P5200B.SPL/binary       13-Feb-89 10736           Accesses: 4
P5200.SPL/binary        09-Feb-89 6325            Accesses: 5

[72767,1465]
LQ850C.ARC/binary       08-Feb-89 9197            Accesses: 17

[76117,3671]
XEROX.ARC/binary        07-Feb-89 28922           Accesses: 1
PARA.ARC/binary         04-Feb-89 1603            Accesses: 55
```

Figure H.5
The library directory.

The directory listing shows the CompuServe User ID (so you can send a grateful letter to the author, if you like), the name of the file (which you'll need for downloading), the date it was put in the library, a unique file number, and the number of accesses. When we started working in this library, we downloaded the directory and scanned accesses to find the most popular macros. Among those with high access numbers, we downloaded the ones with interesting names, dates, abstracts, and authors.

You can get a brief description (abstract) of a macro, by using the Browse command offered in Figure H.4. The result of a Browse command is reproduced in Figure H.6.

The two macros in that screen are interesting and fairly representative. The first one is for the Sprint formatter, a subject we treat only in passing. We could have found the macro description if we had entered a keyword such as star or printer at the Browse or Directory command. The author joins us in confessing some uncertainty about device drivers controlled under Sprint.

The second macro is for the editor. It is in binary, which means it is archived and requires unpacking after it is downloaded. It exposes control codes usually hidden by the editor. The boldface code, ^ B, for example, should be revealed by the macro. It should reveal the code

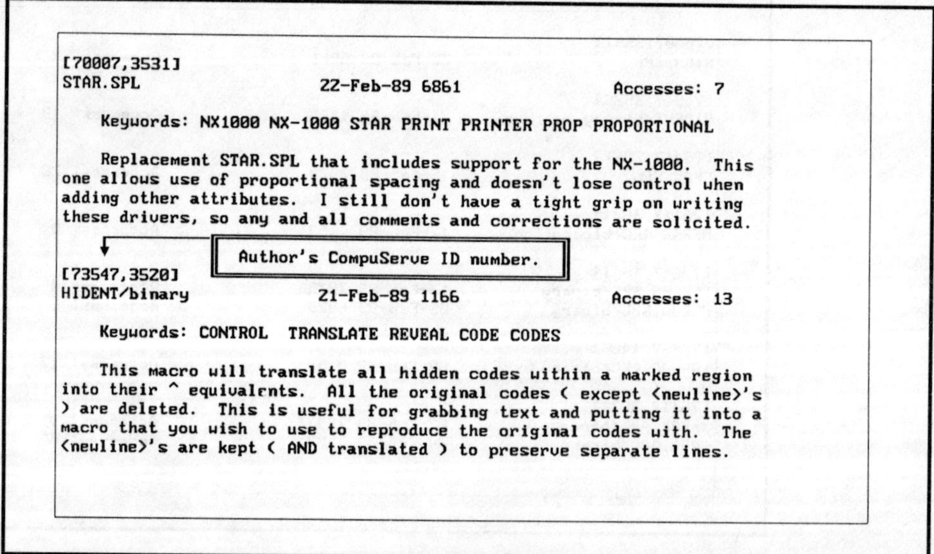

```
[70007,3531]
STAR.SPL                    22-Feb-89 6861                    Accesses: 7

    Keywords: NX1000 NX-1000 STAR PRINT PRINTER PROP PROPORTIONAL

    Replacement STAR.SPL that includes support for the NX-1000.  This
one allows use of proportional spacing and doesn't lose control when
adding other attributes.  I still don't have a tight grip on writing
these drivers, so any and all comments and corrections are solicited.

          ┌────────────────────────────────────────┐
          │      Author's CompuServe ID number.     │
[73547,3520]└────────────────────────────────────────┘
HIDENT/binary               21-Feb-89 1166                    Accesses: 13

    Keywords: CONTROL  TRANSLATE REVEAL CODE CODES

    This macro will translate all hidden codes within a marked region
into their ^ equivalents.  All the original codes ( except <newline>'s
) are deleted.  This is useful for grabbing text and putting it into a
macro that you wish to use to reproduce the original codes with.  The
<newline>'s are kept ( AND translated ) to preserve separate lines.
```

Figure H.6
Macro descriptions from Browse.

after the user highlights a portion of text. Then the text can be cut and pasted into a macro, so that when a macro runs, the original text will be reproduced with the original styling. It is a quick, short utility, the type that's handy to trade over telephone lines.

The final screen that we'd like to show you illustrates the choices available when you try to download a file. Figure H.7 shows the six protocols supported in 1989 by CompuServe. We note with interest the Kermit protocol, a recent addition that we've found very handy with MacIntosh systems. Protocol 4 is the new Hayes Smartcom buffered transfer.

We chose Option 1. You can see the host system initiating XModem and asking the guest system to begin XModem as well. Both sides could use an end-of-file mark to halt transfer when it is complete, but CompuServe simply asks the subscriber to return to the host system and issue a carriage return.

We present this material because we've found consistently interesting macros on CompuServe, and sometimes we've found excellent ones. We give top marks to QU.SPM by Mike Francis, 75410,1772. It provides a queue printing service so multiple documents can be printed sequentially. It alters Borland.UI's Print submenu to provide an option for queuing files to the printer. It even allows you to change the order of printing in a queue. It can load a print spooler so you can get to other Sprint work while printing.

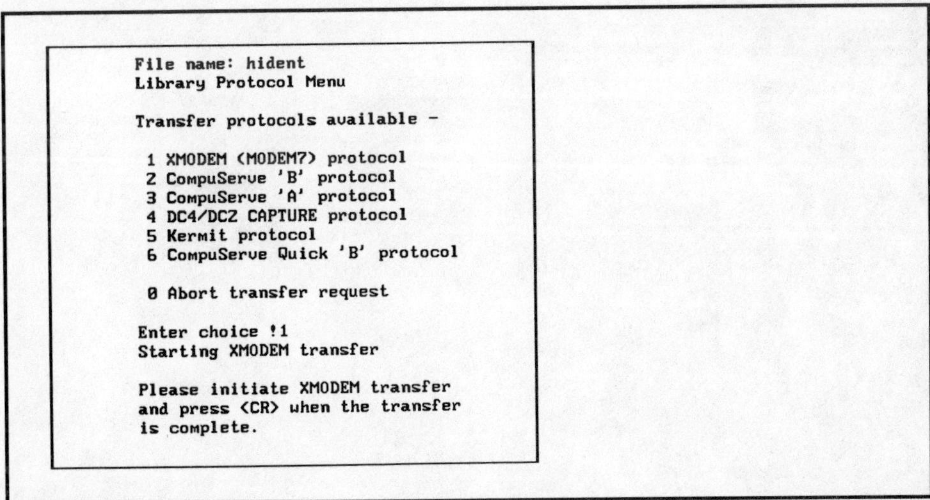

```
File name: hident
Library Protocol Menu

Transfer protocols available -

1 XMODEM (MODEM7) protocol
2 CompuServe 'B' protocol
3 CompuServe 'A' protocol
4 DC4/DCZ CAPTURE protocol
5 Kermit protocol
6 CompuServe Quick 'B' protocol

0 Abort transfer request

Enter choice !1
Starting XMODEM transfer

Please initiate XMODEM transfer
and press <CR> when the transfer
is complete.
```

Figure H.7
The CompuServe downland screen.

We've also found a calculator, a clock, file utilities, an outliner, a table of authorities for lawyers, an index to the main *Sp.spm* program, a C language formatter, an address book, and a database for creating bibliographies. More and more interesting and useful programs will undoubtedly appear on CompuServe.

We share the ethic of other hackers that the authors of public domain software should be acknowledged and thanked, and that a token fee should be paid for public domain programs used regularly. Macros from CompuServe are not available for commercial use without special arrangements. Some copyright protection is available.

Get on the network. Share the wealth of Sprint Macro Programming!

Index